"Amit Goswami has brilliant̶̶̶̶̶̶̶ perceptions of reality once aga̶̶̶̶̶̶ ̶̶̶̶̶̶̶̶̶̶ *Economics*, he has described the reasons for unifying our growing awareness of consciousness with our growing awareness of how badly out-of-date our current economic/political systems are. This most recent offering in a string of books dealing with his unique way of applying quantum physics to modern day society, he engagingly traverses the intellectual landscape from entanglement theory to "the new economics of consciousness." An amazing sweep of perspective, a repeating characteristic of this classically trained physicist, this book both establishes the necessity for a quantum view of economics and then proceeds to describe how it would look.

"No one should think this is a "how to book" in the normal sense. Rather, it is an engaging dialogue that he conducts with the reader in laying out his quantum premises and then applying them to his hoped-for revolution in economic theory. More than just an attack on "scientific materialism," and certainly more than a response to heartless "trickle down" economics, this book opens the door to a radically different way of looking at economics and how it measures human well-being.

"In his highly erudite passages relaying the fundamentals of quantum physics in laymen's terms, and in explaining the benefits of globalization and out-sourcing to what might be a skeptical audience, he never waivers from his fundamental premise: we are capable of an economics of holism. We are capable of understanding the vital energies that our macro reality beings must feed upon. We are capable of creatively interacting with the pure potentiality that the quantum perspective encourages. In a word, we are capable of a new "consciousness-based worldview" that would encompass Quantum Economics."

—Rinaldo S. Brutoco, founding president and CEO,
World Business Academy

"An absolute 'must read' for the enlightened business leader. It provides the justification and quantum underpinnings for conscious capitalism."

—Richard Barrett, author of *The Metrics of Human Consciousness* and *The Values-Driven Organization*

"*Quantum Economics* will overturn how we ordinarily define capitalism, goods and services, and provides the blueprint for creating a sustainable market economy on solid quantum physics principles and practices. As a business coach, I see the book as revolutionizing how we do business, develop human capital, and successfully combine profit motive with social good. Amit Goswami is a visionary who is destined to change the world."

—James Alvino, PhD, founder of New Breed Business Coaching
(For more information, email *info@newbreedbusinesscoaching.com*.)

QUANTUM
ECONOMICS

Unleashing the Power of an
Economics of Consciousness

AMIT GOSWAMI, PhD

RAINBOW RIDGE
BOOKS

Cover and interior design by Frame25 Productions
Cover photographs © Kim D. Lyman and
PaulPaladin c/o Shutterstock.com

Published by:
Rainbow Ridge Books, LLC
140 Rainbow Ridge Road
Faber, Virginia 22938
www.rainbowridgebooks.com
434-361-1723

If you are unable to order this book from your local
bookseller, you may order directly from the distributor.

Square One Publishers, Inc.
115 Herricks Road
Garden City Park, NY 11040
Phone: (516) 535-2010
Fax: (516) 535-2014
Toll-free: 877-900-BOOK

Visit the author at:
www.amitgoswami.org

Library of Congress Cataloging-in-Publication Data applied for.

ISBN 978-1-937907-34-1

10 9 8 7 6 5 4 3 2 1

Printed on acid-free paper in the United States

Preface

In view of the recent meltdown of the economy that gave rise to the great recession, it is pretty obvious that the current economic systems are not working. But economists don't have a clue about which way to go about modifying the existing models. The two political parties of America are bogged down into a locked-horn position between two existing and decidedly ineffective economic modalities: choosing solely from either the demand side or the supply side economics model for government intervention to get us out of recession. Meanwhile, every economist seems to accept that there is only one way to get back into healthy economy: a forever-expanding economy fed by consumer demand.

Adam Smith's capitalism, the basic economic model in most of the world today, was formulated in an age dominated by the philosophy of modernism or Cartesian dualism in which both matter and mind were valued. However, like all scientific theories, Adam Smith's theory of capitalism underwent many modifications. Some of the modifications that occurred were politically motivated, as was the case with the so-called demand-side and the supply-side economics. Along with political pressures another set of modifications took place as well, this time because the scientific worldview gradually was becoming lop-sided, favoring matter while excluding the independence of the mind. Eventually, modernism passed its beacon to post-modern scientific materialism (primacy of matter philosophy), and this led to some serious modifications to Adam Smith's capitalism.

One of these modifications was that economics was recast as a mathematical science. But this is only approximate at best despite the claims of scientific materialists (after all, as we experientially know, human beings are not mechanical machines). So this model, although successful in the short run in making a lot of money for its protagonists, fails in the long view; this is one of the major contributors to the meltdown of 2007-2009.

Another shortcoming resultant of the materialist modification of capitalism has been duly noted; it has left us with the idea of infinitely expanding economy—expansion or bust—entirely fueled by consumer demand. However, in view of our finite planet and the finiteness of its material resources, this theory demands the question: is this sustainable?

Meanwhile, there is a paradigm shift going on in science from a matter-based science to a consciousness-based science, from primacy of matter to primacy of a causally empowered consciousness. My current undertaking—this book—is the result of a developing quantum worldview that is quietly replacing the worldview of materialist physics.

I was at a conference in 1999 with the Dalai Lama as a member of a group of thirty new paradigm scientists when the Dalai Lama challenged us to apply our new science to social problems. This personally inspired me to look into economics. But I was sidetracked by other social problems. It was only when coincidentally several years later I had a call from the president of the World Business Academy, encouraging me to write an article on the impact of the new paradigm on economic thinking, that my attention turned firmly to that subject.

I realized early on that in using the primacy-of-consciousness formulation of science, the power of the subtle (psyche) could be recognized, organized and realized. This relatively recent break-through in our understanding in science states clearly that it is not only our gross material experiences that can be subjected to the scientific process but also our internal subtle experiences (that which we sometimes collectively call the arena of the mind) can be subjected to this testing as well.

Why not expand economics to the subtle arena—to the arena of vital energy that we feel, of mental meaning that we think, and of even archetypal values like love that we intuit? Sounds too preposterous? But didn't the great Abraham Maslow propose a hierarchy of needs? When our material needs are sat-isfied, we yearn for higher needs like love, said Maslow. Adam Smith's capitalism is about matching gifts and needs, which give rise to production and consumption respectively, the two sides of the economic equation of supply and demand. Maslow says that the need for the subtle is already there. My research shows that our science and technology are ready to tackle the gift and production of the subtle. The time has come for an economics of consciousness—quantum economics!

I wrote up my initial ideas in a short paper, which was pub-lished in 2005 by the World Business Academy in one of their publications. I was able to show that, with the inclusion of the subtle into our economics system, we can solve that one perpetual problem of Adam Smith's capitalism that none of its later exten-sions have been able to solve—the problem of alternative boom and bust, formally called the business cycle. My work was later published in an anthology of new paradigm ideas on economics called, *What Comes After Money?* A couple of years later, I was asked to contribute to another anthology, so I expanded my ear-lier notions further in which I found the answer to sustainability and contributed a larger article to this anthology. This article was entitled, "The Economics of Consciousness."

This book is a direct expansion of my earlier papers solving the remaining problems of Adam Smith's capitalism and thereby resolving all the current economic plights. Of course, like the consciousness-based science, this new economics is not going to be immediately embraced. But since it involves the solution to all the pocketbook problems of economics, as well as environmental and sociological problems, obviously its time has arrived.

What is the new economics good for? It is good for resolving all four issues raised above and then some.

1. The new economics takes economics to satisfying the subtle aspects of human needs, in this way discovering new infinite dimensions of economic expansion. Satisfying subtle needs produces a transformed human society in which sustainable economies are quite conceivable. And more. As mentioned above, the new economics gets rid of the business cycle.

2. The quantum worldview is counter to elitism, and in this way, an economics founded on the principles of this worldview will bring down the wealth gap between rich and poor and more. It will eventually solve the poverty problem as far as that can go.

3. Neither the materialist worldview nor the religious worldview before modernism promoted creativity much by their very nature. The materialist worldview is deterministic; not much scope for true creativity is in it. The religious creativity denigrated the world. It could have been creative in the exploration of spirituality, but had lost itself in rituals and traditions. The modernist worldview brought creativity in the world like never before until it dried up under the current materialism. The quantum worldview is the

opposite—it promotes creativity. So with it help, creativity and innovation will come back once again in the arena of economics.

4. The political polarization will not affect economics any more. Democrats like science. The new economics is science based. Republicans side with Christianity, which is implicitly based on spiritual values. The new economics promotes these values by making values into economic commodities to produce and consume. In this way quantum economics should gain support from both camps. And more. The quantum worldview integrates. Eventually, the political polarization itself will stop.

The book is written for both the businessperson and the consumer, in other words, everyone. It touches upon important issues like creativity and ethics in business. It takes you into the already feasible twenty-first century technologies of vital energy. It informs everyone in a developed economy that the time has come to look for jobs that bring meaning and value into their personal lives. It gives quantum hints for new business leadership: a viable science of manifestation, how to vitalize their business arena, how to transform the energy of money.

I thank the Dalai Lama for the initial inspiration and acknowledge a wonderful discussion with Swami Swaroopananda toward that end as well. Thanks are also due to Rinaldo Bruttocko for his invitation to join the World Business Academy. I thank many people for helpful discussions, especially Willis Harman, Paul Ray, Adriano Fromer Piazzi, Maggie Free, and Eva Herr. Last but not least, my heartfelt thanks to Will Hamilton for a complete reading and many helpful suggestions for improvement for which I am truly grateful.

—Amit Goswami

Table of Contents

PART ONE

An Introduction to Quantum Economics

ONE

Introduction: The Need
for a New Economics

"Old order changeth yielding place to new," wrote the great romantic poet Robert Tennyson. This book is about such a sea change—a paradigm shift—in economic thinking. But relax! The quantum economics—you can call it also an economics of consciousness—that you are exploring here is not about a radical revolution in economic theory; instead, it is a natural evolution of capitalism that the great Adam Smith developed in the eighteenth century. The extensions of Adam Smith's ideas that have taken place since the inception of capitalism are either motivated by political agenda and belief, or more recently, by scientific dogma. The extension considered here is based on a dogma-free aborning science founded on the quantum world-view and is demonstrably in right attunement with Smith's original capitalism. With its help we solve all the crisis problems that the current models cannot solve—boom and bust, especially bust, economic ballooning and subsequent meltdown, indefinite economic expansion, creation of meaningful jobs for human labor, keeping the market free, globalization, sustainability, income disparity between classes, and even poverty.

The message of the quantum worldview when applied to economics is simple: There is a new and right direction for our economics and our economy! We don't have to be stuck in vain debates between unworkable alternatives based on faulty, elitist, and outdated worldviews. Consequently, this book should inspire and empower the business leaders, the job seekers, and the consumer, indeed all thinkers and movers and shakers of economics-related fields.

The Search for a Right Direction for a Problem-free Capitalism

The basic idea of any economics is to find economic activities—production and consumption—going smoothly. The success of Adam Smith's capitalism derives from the notion that if producers and consumers alike are left alone to pursue their individual self-interest, the invisible hands of the free market will establish equilibrium between production and consumption, allocate resources between various sectors of the economy, and stabilize prices, etc. Over more than a couple of centuries, we find that although capitalism is workable, there are glitches. We have been searching for a right direction for changing capitalism ever since its shortcomings became clear, the boom and bust or business cycle—alternative periods of inflation and recession— for example. There is also the question of social good. Obviously, when individual good sometimes comes in opposition to social good, what then? Smith implicitly believed that the invisible hands of the free market also guarantees social good.

In truth, even in the 1980s, there has been isolated talk about a paradigm shift in economics in order to extend the concept of the economic person *homo economicus* to a person in community, to generalize the concept of self-interest to include social good (Daly and Cobb, 1994). But there was no science of how to define a person in society. After the economic meltdown of 2007-2009 that gave us the great recession, the talk of a paradigm shift has taken a sense of urgency. Many economists have declared that there is an urgent need for new thinking in economics. But in practice, economists have come up short.

Of course, subsequent to Adam Smith, there have been many macro-economic theories. Some of the ideas were implemented because of political motives—they were based on the notion of government intervention for imposing social good, which could be used to put things right in a hurry in synchrony with the usual four-year election cycle in America. Many of these theories of convenience stand in direct contradiction with Smith's pivotal notion of the free market, although their motivation is in part to solve one of the outstanding problems of Smith's capitalism— the boom and bust or business cycle. These models, called the demand-side model and the supply-side model respectively, use government intervention to jazz up either the demand side of the economic equation or the supply side. The demand-side model creates middle-class jobs through middle-class tax cuts, unemployment benefits, and government funded public works infrastructure. The supply-side economics creates more capital supply by tax cuts to the rich; the idea is that this will stimulate direct business investments, trickling down to the middle class by creating jobs. Currently in America, the two political parties are bogged down in a battle of these two alternatives with various new gimmickries. But when viewed through the lens of pragmatism, all these efforts are simply versions of the same old, same old.

Other modifications of Adam Smith's capitalism came about because of a growing belief in scientific materialism—the dogma that all things are based on matter and material interactions. These models tried to recast economics in the image of the outdated physics of Isaac Newton. In this way, they began using mathematics to describe economic changes. Such distortive extensions of capitalism would have been fine if human beings were determined Newtonian machines—robots, zombies, computers, or whatever you may want to call them under the belief system of scientific materialism. But human beings, even animals really, are not machines; for example, higher animals certainly have feelings that are not computable. So it is no wonder that such materialist extensions, though sometimes successful in making money for the greedy protagonist in the short term, do not work in the long term. Indeed, they produce huge instabilities. The meltdown in 2007-2009 was partly due to such instability unleashed by greed.

Meanwhile, economists of all ilks seem to agree that we have to have indefinite economic expansion in order to deal with periodic but inevitable recession, the bust part of the boom-bust cycle. But how can a finite ecosystem with finite resources provide such indefinite expansion?

Scientific materialists grossly misunderstand the nature of capitalism, forcing it into the straightjacket of a matter-based worldview. Before capitalism came about, we had feudal economics with the straightjacket of the religious belief system, in the West, of Christianity. Capitalism was discovered at a time when the worldview held, as a compromise between religion and the aborning Newtonian science, that both matter and mind are important components of reality—a worldview called Cartesian dualism named after its protagonist, Rene Descartes. Later, this worldview came to be called Modernism and became the philosophical basis of a truce between scientists and the enlightenment-era humanists, dividing up the territory of dominance for each. As Adam Smith understood quite well, capitalism crucially depends first on ethics and morality and second on creativity. Only when the market operates incorporating these features of the mind, does its invisible hands maintain overall social good. To summarize, Adam Smith's capitalism had the following implicit message in bullet points:

1. Producers and consumers, do pursue your self-interest with gusto, but . . .

2. When dealing with competition, do remember ethics;

3. And producers, don't forget to fan the creative power of your team to forever create renewed interest in the consumer for what you produce;

4. And then, the invisible hands of the free market will distribute capital to make room for new innovation, will produce the needed economic expansion, will grow capital, and will maintain equilibrium and stability to bring not only your personal good but the good of everyone—social good.

But neither ethics nor creativity can be included in scientific materialism with any causal potency; as a result, their role in our society is undermined when that worldview gains prominence. Much of the current economic crisis has its origin in this decline of ethics and creativity in our society as a whole and our businesses in particular. Don't doubt that.

Quantum economics is an extension of Adam Smith's capitalism in the right direction because it is based on a scientific worldview that incorporates the matter-mind, religion-science compromise that prevailed in Smith's time and clearly influenced him. The new economics makes room once more for both mind and matter in the economic arena, only this time in an integrated scientific way. Consequently, the new economics makes capitalism ever more appropriate for conscious human beings. It puts not only our gross material side into the economic equation, as Adam Smith had, but also our subtle side—consciousness, feeling, meaning, and intuition—which Smith failed to include explicitly; it was premature in his time.

Although you probably don't consciously think about it, the most striking experience on your subtle side is your experience as the subject of awareness. Awareness has two poles, subject and object. And in every experience, you are the subject experiencing the object(s). Consciousness, in its subject aspect, is obviously important in how we make business decisions, both on the production side and on the consumption side. Can these decisions arise from the interactions of elementary particles of matter, even from the interactions of our genes? It boggles the mind as to how it could, although materialists try to ascribe everything that appears to be causal at the human level as an epiphenomenon of the survival motif of the genes (Dawkins, 1976; Dennett, 1996). In economics, this attitude translates as the supremacy of competition as the operating word for businesses. However, our recent experiences have been clearly showing the importance of cooperation as well (Capra, 1982).

Materialists try to undermine the causal power of our subjective "I" further by pointing out the conditioned nature of this "I", the ego. Who can deny the power of conditioning on the human ego? Who can deny that even many business decisions, both for producers and for consumers, display the effect of conditioning—personal and social. Indeed, commercial conditioning of the social unconscious is very powerful. But is that always the case? Who can deny that creative business decisions and new innovations always move the economy forward? Who can deny that acts of creativity are not examples of conditioned "machine creativity" (Goswami, 2014)? Who can deny that - ethics in human decision-making comes from wisdom—a higher consciousness than the ego?

Adam Smith's capitalism, although prone to the ups and downs of the business cycle, highly valued creativity and innovation, recognizing how they are needed for the economy to come out of the periods of recessions. So the consciousness Smith's capitalism implicitly assumes must extend beyond its conditioned aspect of the ego. It boils down to the question: Does consciousness have causal power, does it extend beyond the ego?

Are materialists right in veering capitalism down the garden path they have? It boils down to the question: Are we machines, or does our consciousness have the causal power that enables us ethics and creativity? Is the causal power of consciousness really important in business decisions?

Economics within Consciousness

What is consciousness? Etymologically, the word *consciousness* originates from two Latin words: *cum* meaning "with," and *scire* meaning "to know." Consciousness is our facility with which we know. Materialists assume that whatever we come to know is from the old conditioned repertoire; there is nothing new under the sun. Obviously, when we are dealing with old knowledge, no causal power is needed; the conditioned ego will do, and that is just brain behavior, according to scientific materialists. In fact, most materialists have put to rest questions of causal power of consciousness by asserting that consciousness is an epiphenomenon (secondary phenomenon) of the brain; that it is an ornamental experience associated with the brain and is an operational concept; it does not really have causal power.

ific materialists, complex material interactions in
explain all the complexity of the multilayer expe-
consciousness. Focusing on details, though, eas-
ily reveals that all the brain can do is to process stimuli via old
knowledge, what is already stored as memory in the brain. However, questions of ethics and creativity raise doubts that known
knowledge cannot resolve; the resolution of these doubts involve
new meanings and new contexts that weren't present before.
So the materialists' arguments don't do anything to resolve the
question:, How does consciousness acquire new knowledge that
it needs to process ethical questions and questions of creativity?

Nor does materialist science address the question: How do
we include our subtle experiences in our science? It is a fact that
apart from the gross material experience of sensing, we have feelings, we think, we even intuit very subtle objects that we value
(Plato called them archetypes—stuff like love, beauty, justice,
goodness, abundance, wholeness, indeed, truth itself) and that
science is supposed to value and pursue. What good are scientific
laws if they are relative truth, not absolute truth? Contrary to
materialist thinking, our experiences of feelings, thinking, and
intuition are not computable or at least not wholly computable,
and therefore, it makes sense to posit that they arise from subtle
nonmaterial worlds. So far so good, but how do we develop a
science of a causally potent nonmaterial consciousness with both
gross and subtle experiences?

Scientific materialists deny the concepts of a nonmaterial
causally potent consciousness and other nonmaterial worlds
within it because of the inherent problem of dualism. They find
themselves stuck by the paradox of interaction: how do these
nonmaterial worlds (of consciousness, mind or whatever dual
world we posit) interact with matter? Since these worlds have
nothing in common with matter, in order to interact they must

need a mediator. In materialist science, such mediation requires signals that carry energy. And here is the crunch! The energy of the material world alone is always a constant; energy neither escapes from nor enters into the material world from outside.

In Adam Smith's time, we had neither the science to resolve the paradox of dualism, nor the technology to explore such subtle stuff in science in general, let alone economics. Now three centuries later, we do. This is thanks due in the main to a paradigm shift in physics from Newtonian physics to quantum physics.

Here is the biggest secret of the quantum worldview that can now be revealed: quantum physics unleashes the creative causal power of the individual human being by embedding it within a universal higher consciousness. It also unleashes the power of the subtle. Let's put the last sentence in another way: Quantum physics provides a theoretical framework for including the subtle in our science: a causally potent consciousness with both material and subtle experiences. Quantum physics allows us to develop a viable science of consciousness that includes all of our experiences, including the subtle (Goswami, 2000, 2004).

Quantum physics is the physics of possibilities; every object is a possibility of consciousness itself to choose from. How does consciousness choose? It is choosing from itself, needing no signals. How do the subtle worlds interact with gross matter? Through signal-less instant communication called quantum nonlocality mediated by nonlocal consciousness.

Don't worry about details at this point (see Chapter 3). Just appreciate that quantum nonlocality, which you have always suspected through personal experiences such as mental telepathy, is now experimental fact thanks to recent experiments replicated many times over (Aspect et al, 1982; Grinberg et al, 1994). Shouldn't such a momentous discovery affect how we do things, how we carry out our personal social affairs?

Concurrently, the biologist Rupert Sheldrake (1981), while exploring the phenomenon of morphogenesis—how biological form is built from a single-celled embryo—has clarified the nonphysical world (call it the vital world) from which our experiences of feelings arise. Feelings are our experiences of vital energy, the movements of the morphogenetic fields of the vital world that act as the blueprints of biological form. Biological form—the organs—are physical representations of the morphogenetic fields. The physicist/mathematician Roger Penrose (1991) has mathematically proven that there is a defining quality of the mind—its ability to process meaning—that computers cannot process, that brain neurons likely cannot do. The neocortex of the brain makes representations of mental meaning. And millennia ago, Plato theorized that our concepts of love, beauty, justice, goodness, truth, abundance and all that really come from a subtler world—the abode of the archetypes. The philosopher Sri Aurobindo (1996) has called the world of these archetypes the *supramental*. Mind and subsequently, the brain, merely make representations (concepts) of these archetypes. In this way, the archetypes are obviously beyond the brain that makes representations of mental meaning (the memories).

Thanks are also due to a shift of biological thinking about our physical body. Since the 1950s, biologists in the main have insisted that the human body is purely biochemical. But now a vast amount of research by biophysicists has shown that, apart from the biochemical interior, we also have a biophysical body at the surface level. This has given us the technologies needed to measure the subtle vital energies associated with our feelings through biophysical measurements.

Similarly, new magnetic resonance imaging (MRI) techniques, when interpreted with the new science, give us a way for objectively measuring the mind—states of mental meaning—by measuring the brain representations of the mind.

Now that both a supportive scientific theory and objective quantification techniques are available for the subtle, a paradigm extension of Adam Smith's capitalism can be built to include the subtle in the economic equation. This is the subject of the next section.

To cut to the chase, a new paradigm of science based on the quantum worldview of the primacy of consciousness has been in the offing for a couple of decades now (Goswami, 1989, 1993, 2008a; Stapp, 1993; Blood, 1993, 2001). Where should this paradigm shift lead us for the society at large, in particular, in the field of economics where the need for change is most urgent?

In 1999, I was part of a conference in Dharamsala, India, at which the Dalai Lama met with thirty scientists and other new-age thinkers with a view to examine this kind of question (you can find some details in a documentary film entitled *Dalai Lama Renaissance*). We didn't go very far in that conference about specifics; but ever since, I have been interested in the impact of the new science paradigm on economics, politics, business, health, education, and religion.

My answer for economics is the subject of this book: a quantum economics within the primacy of consciousness, or in short, the quantum economics of consciousness. It is a quantum extension of Adam Smith's capitalism to include the subtle dimensions of the human experience.

The time for a new paradigm of economics has come, andI will sum up the reasons why. The truth is, capitalism requires indefinitely expanding economies, hardly achievable in a finite material world with finitude of material resources. The signs of shortage of material resources are everywhere. Hardly a day passes when the newspapers are not talking about high oil prices or the possible shortage of water in the future. The materialist answer of extending the arena to the moon and the asteroids is too energy intensive to be serious. Face it! Our current paradigm of indefinite economic expansion is just not sustainable if current trends continue. Then there is the threat of environmental pollution, global warming being the major one, that material technologies invariably produce.

The most obvious sign that a radically new change in economic theory is needed is the fact that the boom-bust cycle, usually of manageable proportion, has now gone haywire twice: the "great depression" of the 1930s and the "great recession" of 2007-09. Another obvious sign is that the gap between recessions is getting smaller and smaller, and recoveries are becoming slower and slower. And it does not take a genius to see that despite all the political rhetoric, it will take a long time to dig out of the ill effects of the recent recession if we fail to bring back ethics and creativity in the economic arena. We need new persuasive ideas, a new case for ethics considering that all the large corporations push unethical economic activities. It took World War II, not economic theories, to get out of the great depression. How can we rest assured that we will not need another similar catastrophe to keep out of future great recessions?

The materialist influence has restricted economics to growth only in the material dimension—the domain of sensing—pretty much leaving out the subtle dimensions of human existence, the domains of consciousness and its experiences of feeling, thinking, and intuiting. The current materialist paradigm of economics is moreover designed to satisfy only our ego needs, if that, but certainly not our emotional, creative, and spiritual needs. Most importantly, it does not work; witness the recent economic meltdown that has led to a complete loss of credibility of economics itself as a serious science. Can the new quantum economics of consciousness, an idealist economics to be sure, save us from such meltdowns? As proclaimed above, in this book, I will show that it can. Additionally, I will show that if we include the subtle in our economics; if we include the causal power of consciousness; if ethics and creativity comes back in a hurry, and we can not only keep out of serious recessions—the meltdowns—but also solve the problem of boom-and-bust cycle, then we can restore the free market enough to achieve social good in addition to personal good. We can also remove income disparity between classes, and we can even achieve a sustainable economy.

I will give you one big example of the potential power of the subtle. Currently health care is a big item of the economy. In America, it constitutes about 16 percent of the economy; that is huge. You also know that health care in America (and elsewhere) is in a crisis, as the costs keep on rising.

It is dubious if health care can be treated as an economic commodity subject to the free market. This is because, especially when we hit old age, health care often becomes a question of life or death; in other words, pretty much compulsory, not optional like our other needs. In the 1960s, under the presidency of Lyndon Johnson, American government recognized this and developed Medicare, a government-supported health care program for the elderly. Over the years, however, Medicare costs have been skyrocketing, and it is estimated that at the rate the cost is increasing, soon Medicare costs will consume the entire budget of the United States government.

What's the remedy? Some politicians suggest changing Medicare by partially privatizing its operation and allowing free market competition to bring the cost down. But what about that old problem: Health care is not a choice for older people. Does free market economics apply?

So we debate the subject incessantly with no remedy in sight. It turns out that for health care only the strictly materialist system of medicine—allopathy—is costly. There are old and new medicinal systems which are quite cheap and yet demonstratively effective. These systems are labeled as alternative medicine, of which a prime example is acupuncture. But practitioners of materialist medicine—allopathy—cannot explain the success of acupuncture or other alternative forms of medicine such as homeopathy because of its adherence to scientific materialism, and hence they generally oppose this type of medicine. Now suppose they open their minds towards the power of the subtle. Some time ago, I wrote a book called *The Quantum Doctor* (Goswami, 2004) in which I pointed out that alternative medicine is quite scientific if we recognize the power of the subtle via the new quantum science within consciousness. I also demonstrated that with quantum physics to guide us, we can develop an integrative medicine in which both alternative medicine—now seen as subtle body medicine—and conventional allopathic or gross body medicine can be integrated. They serve complementary roles: allopathy is important as emergency medicine, while for chronic disease alternative medicine is much more effective, preventive, and certainly in most situations, adequate.

Why is this relevant for saving Medicare? Care of chronic disease amounts to some 75-80 percent of all medical costs of the elderly. So if we extend government support only to satisfy emergency needs with allopathy and leave most of the care of chronic disease to alternative medicine, the cost of Medicare can immediately come down. Of course, alternative medicine in its preventive aspect requires cooperation of the consumer. For non-cooperative consumers and others who desire availability of additional health care, allopathic medicine would be a choice and could be subject to free market capitalism. This would apply to costly pharmaceutical drugs, and market competition is sure to bring their price down, too.

Needs and Gifts: An Outline of the New Paradigm

Adam Smith's idea of capitalism is fundamentally based on how our needs and gifts come together; people's gifts lead to business production, people's needs lead to consumption (Eisenstein, 2011). Smith suggested that if the market is free, its "invisible" hands will establish equilibrium between production and consumption, prices will be stabilized, and resources will be allocated properly among the different sectors of the economy. In the eighteenth century, Smith saw people looking to satisfy only their material needs, and the developing science of matter was ripe for people with the gift of production of material technology. In the twentieth century, the psychologist Abraham Maslow proposed that human beings, aside from material needs, have a whole hierarchy of needs. The new science within the primacy of consciousness helps us to further elaborate and redefine Maslow's hierarchy of needs.

In quantum physics, objects are waves of possibilities for consciousness to choose from before they manifest into actuality when an observer looks (Goswami, 1993; Stapp, 1993). In the old science, only material objects exist. To allow for all our experiences—sensing, feeling, thinking, and intuiting—consciousness is recognized as the ground of being in which there are four worlds of quantum possibilities from which arise these experiences: the physical for sensing, the vital for feeling, the mental for thinking, and the supramental (archetypal) for intuiting. When consciousness chooses actuality from quantum possibilities as we look, the four worlds of our experience manifest: physical that we sense, vital that we feel, mental that we think, and the supramental that we intuit. Out of these manifest worlds, only the physical appears to be external and public and, therefore, called gross. The other manifest worlds are experienced as internal and private and, therefore, called subtle. It is useful to think of even the whole ground of being—the whole enchilada, consciousness itself—as a world that includes all worlds in potentiality; call it the world of happiness because of its inclusive wholeness. The world of happiness is also called the causal world because herein resides our power of downward causation.

We have "bodies" in each of the "worlds": the physical body, the vital body, the mental body, the supramental body, and the happiness body (for which there is no direct manifestation; it is unconscious in us). Maslow's hierarchy of needs beyond the gross material needs must be redefined as the needs of our subtle bodies: vital energy needs that we have in order to feel alive; mental needs that we have to explore meaning of our lives and our world; supramental needs we have for archetypal values which we explore to gain love, clarity, and satisfaction; and the happiness needs we have for rest, holistic healing, and rejuvenation.

The economic and business leaders of the twenty-first century need to understand and engage the power of the subtle needs to drive economic development. They do nibble at it; in commercial advertisements, we often find that the arousal of sexual feelings (libido) is used to attract consumer attention. But can we go further? Can we look at the feelings themselves as marketable objects of consumption? You say, sexuality, and yes, substances (aphrodisiacs) that make us ever more horny have been around, but nobody would consider buying anger even if we package it nicely. But how about love?

You think this is absurd? How can we talk about extracting a feeling like love and packaging it? In the new science, the source of a feeling is vital energy of movement of morphogenetic fields—the blueprint of biological form. Thus, every living being has vital energy, and you are familiar with some of the feelings they can arouse in you. For example, in traditional societies, flowers are always a part of romance. They look pretty, of course, and smell good, but could it be that all traditional cultures have recognized that romance is enhanced in the presence of roses?

Suppose I tell you that we already have the know-how to extract all the romantic vital energy in a roomful of roses into a small vial of perfume. Can we not then think of subtle products such as this as an additional arena for the production of goods for consumers to help them satisfy their subtle need of romantic love? Can we use the subtle arena as the vehicle for economic expansion in the twenty-first century?

We already do this to some extent for satisfying our mental needs. I explore meaning of quantum physics; I write about it in a book that is then a physical representation of my mental meaning, which you then consume when you read and enjoy my book. In economic jargon, I have produced "cultural" capital. In the same vein, if you come to a workshop that I teach and allow yourself to be amused, then I serve you meaning directly and you pay for it.

As I said, we do nibble at developing subtle products for consumption. This is similar to the situation before the industrial revolution, when we similarly nibbled at producing consumer products with early material technology. My point in this book is that the technology of the subtle is ready to make a quantum leap, because we now a have a science of the subtle—both in theory and quantification—which is enough for such a revolutionary change.

It is not a coincidence that at the same time we are conceiving that there may be a demand for subtle goods in a new economic arena for economic and business expansion, we are also discovering that there are people who are gifted to produce subtle goods. Today, people complain about the lack of innovation in business. The truth is that the material well for new business production ideas is running dry. Recently, a newspaper columnist wrote that there has hardly been any innovation that has led to new innovative technology since the 1950s. All of today's great ideas of business innovation—computers and robotics, communication satellites and cell phones, bioengineering, nuclear power, solar energy, aviation, nanotechnology—all are products of creative ideas of earlier times, with only a lot of fine tuning still going on.

In contrast to the material world, the subtle worlds are infinite worlds for new creative exploration for the production of subtle goods that will satisfy the consumer needs for the subtle for all the future to come, until all times are done.

A fallout of the success of materialist science in its exploration of matter and machines is that today we have the capacity to mechanize most of the routine jobs that human beings have been performing since the beginning of the agricultural and industrial ages. We have robots already, and they will only get better in replacing humans. Futurologists worry, but really, this problem already showed up during the recovery from the 2007-2009 great recession; many old jobs did not come back to humans in that recovery because they were mechanized.

In the coming era of subtle technology, the deployment of the subtle energies will involve not only the non-living, but also the living, including people. Thus, people never have to worry about being out of work because machines might replace them, not in the subtle arena.

In the rest of the book, we will explore these ideas in detail: how quantum physics leads to a new worldview and a new view of consciousness that include all our experiences; the details of how production and consumption take place in the subtle sectors; how an economics that includes the subtle and the causal solves the problem of business cycles, and even sustainability and economic inequality between classes.

And more. Adam Smith never clarified what he meant by the "invisible hands" of the free market. Today, we tamper with the free market all the time. There is government intervention for creating public service jobs; there are tax cuts for the rich to have more money to invest; monetary economics to control the money supply and interest rates, and all that. So much intervention goes on today that the whole idea of a free market has become a myth. And we are blindly curbing the freedom of the market because we don't really know where the freedom of the market comes from or what keeps the free market free. We will see that with a quantum economics of consciousness, we are able to understand the nature of the movements that lead to the freedom of the market. We can choose to align with these movements.

The new economics gives us insights about other subjects as well; for example, globalization—outsourcing of routine manufacturing and other jobs from advanced economies to as yet underdeveloped but growing economies. Some economists and politicians are against globalization; some are for it. The new economics throws new light on the subject and resolves the controversy in a satisfying way with a timely contextualization of the priorities of the labor force. The fact is that these priorities are not the same for the labor in advanced economies vis-à-vis the labor in developing economies.

As I said, even the question of sustainability can be addressed and solved in the new economics. Today, there is a lot of talk about sustainability. All serious thinking people understand that without sustainability, not only will we run out of energy, but long before that, the environment also will be affected so detrimentally that life as we know it may be endangered. Unfortunately, under the worldview of scientific materialism, our values have been denigrated that include truth itself. So in America, there is Fox News and Rush Limbaugh, continuing to defy the truth of global climate change due to global warming and influencing a lot of people with angry emotions—those who would like to return to an older time because in those times, in their perception, "values reigned." Of course, you can question that, too. The truth is, because of the worldview polarization today—scientific materialism versus the religious "dualism"—there is much confusion on the subject.

Fortunately, there is also a lot of awareness. I was in a hotel in London a few years back, and I noticed a sign saying that there is a new set of three R's for the twenty-first century: reduce, reuse, and recycle. The old 3 R's as you know are: reading, (w)riting, and (a)rithmatic. Out of the new three R's, reuse and recycle are already widespread, although not as much as needed. But reduce? How?

Can we actually go backward and reduce our lifestyle dependence on energy guzzling and environmentally wasteful big technologies? Some time ago, Gandhi used to suggest such things, and the economist E. F. Schumacher wrote a book, *Small is Beautiful*, that seriously brought Gandhi's idea into economics. "There are two different paths to being rich," said Gandhi. "One is the way of multiplying material wealth beyond bounds . . . the other is to simply reduce our all too human needs to the domain of plausibility, civility, and grace."

"It was not workable!" was the verdict of mainstream economists. Also reducing the standard of living will never be politically correct. "It smacks of sacrifice," they declared.

Behold! With the opening up of subtle arenas for economic expansion, we make room for consumers to be conducive to transformational changes so that they may want to explore noble emotions, because they enjoy consuming such emotions that would bring them an extended sense of the self that includes the environment. The new worldview emphasizes not only ecology in the usual sense of "shallow" ecology—taking care of the external eco-system—but also recognizes the importance of deep ecology—transformation of our interior ecosystem, even our unconscious. The truth is, only when Gandhi's "other" "way becomes the "American way of life," nay, the world's way of life under the aegis of quantum economics, then there will be sustainability.

Income disparity between classes and poverty still plague many parts of the world. The rapidly developing economies like the BRICS countries—Brazil, Russia, India, China, and South Africa—are among them, and in truth, even the developed economies are not exempt. As the economy becomes a sustainable economy, with both gross and subtle sectors, we will see that economic prosperity will no longer be gauged by GDP (gross domestic product) alone. Additionally, an index of well-being will be called for. This and the overall quantum society, with the quantum worldview and quantum lifestyle demands, will lead to the much-needed redefinition of our concepts of wealth and poverty and eventually will help eradicate wealth disparity between classes and even poverty.

In summary, what can the economics of consciousness do for us? Let me count the ways in which the new economics promises to solve the big-time economic items that plague us today and give us frequent crisis conditions.. What is the new economics good for?

1. For the remedies of business cycles and for preventing economic meltdowns

2. For creating new arenas of economic activities that will bring meaningful jobs for humans

3. For creating new capital in the form of human capital

4. For solving the problem of government interventions and how to keep the free market as free as possible

5. For dealing with globalization and its discontents

6. For achieving an economy of sustainability

7. For eliminating wealth disparity between classes, poverty and hunger

With all these crisis issues successfully addressed, my exuberant optimism about the new economics is that with its help, we will never again have economic problems that require more than a little tinkering for their solutions; we will never have meltdowns like the great depression and the recent great recession.

Let me make one comment in passing. There is one aspect of the power of the subtle that is always available for us to use to heal economic malaise, and we have used it before. It works by injecting hope. Ronald Reagan did it in the US in the 1980s, and Barack Obama did it to get us out of the tail end of the great recession.

A Change in How We Think about Money

One of the most important fallouts of the new economics is that it is forcing us to think of money in a new way. How do you think of money? You may be surprised. Do an experiment. Think of something that makes you feel good and expansive. You can easily feel this expansion in the region of your heart, the heart chakra in the new psychological parlance. In the new science, we say that your vital energy has risen from your navel chakra (the seat of your body ego) to the heart chakra (the doorway to an expanded consciousness). After you are comfortably situated in the warmth of your heart chakra, think of money, say how much more money that your friend Stella makes than you.

Instantly, the vital energy will drain from your heart chakra back to where it was—the navel.

The truth is, for many of us, even today, the perceived energy of money is distinctly negative. "Why?" you ask. Because many of us today still alive and thriving have grown up in a worldview where the material world (the domain of science) and spirituality (the domain of religion) are seen as oppositional. Money is widely perceived as worldly, and people who are inclined toward personal growth feel it as grubby and negative.

We constantly perpetuate this myth about money—that it has inherent worldly energy—by such adages as, "money cannot buy love," or "money cannot buy happiness." The truth is, we don't allow money to buy love, and we don't allow money to buy happiness from somebody else who seems to have it aplenty. We never try because we are confused about what it means to embody love or happiness in this materialist age.

Some economists who are looking for an alternative to materialist models of economics, take the negative perception of money in our society so seriously that they see in the recent great recession an opportunity to change altogether the role money plays in our economy (Pinchbeck and Jordan, 2011). Some would even go back to a barter system of the olden days before money became fashionable.

Suppose you and I both have certain material products of value to sell, and we also have our needs. In the barter system, we would have to find each other in search of a match between gift and need, and that is not always convenient. Thus, money is a neutral way to create an exchange currency, an intermediary between production and consumption. It is a representation of what we value, traditionally only material value.

Think about it this way and see that money has no inherent energy except for what we emotionally attribute to it through our confused upbringing in a worldview split between materiality and spirituality.

In the new economics, there is economic value for not only material goods but also subtle goods, even happiness; therefore, money will represent both material and subtle values that include the spiritual. Can money buy happiness? You bet.

Several years ago, my wife and I were walking by the Ganges in a place called Rishikesh in India. Suddenly a door opened, a man came out and asked, "Laughing Baba is giving a discourse. Would you like to join us?"

It sounded good, so we went in and were seated. The Baba (a Hindi word meaning father; highly spiritually advanced teachers are often called Baba) was giving a discourse on the *Bhagavad Gita*, a famous Hindu treatise that I had read. But the lecture was in Hindi, which I do not follow very well. My mind wandered. I started looking around and soon found something quite strange. Everybody seemed to have a smile on their face. And this was no faked smile. Their eyes were smiling like they were feeling happy. I examined myself; yes, I was doing the same thing and feeling happy. Suddenly, I understood. This is why this man is called Laughing Baba. In his presence people feel so happy that quite automatically, they break out in happy laughter.

Now suppose some entrepreneur picks up on this phenomenon, reads my book on *Quantum Creativity*, and realizes that such people can be grown using the creative process (Goswami, 2014). He sets up such a person in an office with a sign on the door: "Happiness for sale, $200 an hour." Wouldn't you be tempted?

This is not as far-fetched as it may seem at first. We really have the science, the know-how for the production of subtle quantities, even happiness, even of such exalted kind in a demonstrable way.

If money is allowed to buy happiness, what happens to the energy of money? It changes. What happens is that money then becomes consecrated. There is a saying in Islam, "If Mohammad does not come to the mountain, the mountain will come to Mohammad."

The Financial Sector of the Economy

The concept of money as the symbolic intermediary of the exchange or barter of gift and need is simple, but then the story of money gets more complicated. Suppose somebody has a potential, a gift to produce, but it takes capital to produce it, and he or she does not have it. On the other hand, other people are sitting with capital but no gift to contribute. Wouldn't it be nice if these two parties could get together? But when you take account of human nature, you realize that there has to be an added motivation for the matching of these two mindsets. Thus, banks that sit on capital lend money, charging interest to people who will create a future product (and of course, if only such people offer an equity or at least have a good credit rating).

If you think of value only as material value, obviously money is more abstract than the concrete value it represents. Hence, you can think of money also as an abstraction. The idea of interest—making money on money—generates the possibility of creating further abstractions. This creates progressively more abstract financial instruments that you hear about today— stocks, bonds, futures, derivatives, and all that. I will give details later, but suffice it to say here that these abstractions give playful investors much bigger capital fields in which to invest. Thus is created the financial sector of the economy that today is a much bigger economic volume than the production-consumption traditional sector.

The financial sector played a huge role in precipitating the great recession of 2007. Can we remedy this by creating the subtle sector of the economy, by allowing money not only to represent concrete value, but also subtle values, so we can indefinitely create real capital, not risky capital like the abstractions of money? The answer given in this book is yes.

How? The basic idea is this. The problem with the financial sector of abstractions is it tends to grow much faster than its concrete values would allow; even with regulations, this is hard to control. When does it go out of control? As the economist John Greer (2011) says, "… it is when the world's supply of abstract representations of wealth is so much vaster than its supply of concrete wealth that something has to give sooner or later." With a subtle economy, with regular satisfaction of subtle needs, life becomes more present centered, and the need for gambling in a vast amount of largely imaginary future wealth lessens.

How Do We Get There? The Question of Implementation of the New Economics

After being exposed to the concept of subtle economics, after you see the problem-solving potency of the new economics, your next big question is the million-dollar question: How do we implement this new economics? This is intimately connected with the question: How do we change our worldview from the two poles of religious and materialist worldview prevalent today to the integrative worldview of science within consciousness?

The religious worldview gave us the dark ages of feudal economy (that Adam Smith called mercantile economy). Capitalism of materialist vintage is threatening us with a "glacial" age precipitated by global warming. All the progress of civilization in the modern era has come from the three centuries—eighteenth to twentieth—when modernism still ruled and both matter and mind were valued. Can we integrate matter and mind once again and go back to the glory days of civilization?

Quantum physics was discovered in 1925-1926, and in its first fifteen years, it made great promises of relaxing the stranglehold of the Newtonian machine worldview, thus advancing the cause of the Cartesian truce. But then World War II intervened. After the war, our attention shifted from worldview problems to practical problems. Soon a postmodern pessimism set in, and scientific materialism began to challenge the prevalent dualistic worldview of modernism of the West that had a truce with religions—mainly Christianity—in a major way. Now scientific materialism has become so entrenched in America and elsewhere among scientists and academics, and something like 30-40 percent of the world's population has become so convinced of it, that it is difficult for a consciousness-based worldview to make inroads even though it incorporates the old materialist worldview within it. And in truth, although the new worldview makes spirituality scientific, religions are not particularly willing either to give up their monopolies. That is another 30-40 percent of the population in America.

So we have the current crisis of polarization of politics in America as well as many other countries of the world. To get out of the polarized thinking, which has given us only crisis problems, and embrace the solution space of the new paradigm, what can we do?

If you go back three hundred years, the Christian/religious worldview pretty much dominated the Western world until the eighteenth century; although taking advantage of the modernist truce, modern science was able to develop in the academia quite rapidly since the sixteenth century. But peoples' perception of modern science as a viable force in society began in earnest only in the eighteenth century, partly due to political activism that gave us the American and French Revolution, and that eventually led to democracy all over the world. The change came partly because of liberal education—education dedicated to liberate people from religious bigotry, nay, all dogma. Most importantly, the change took place because of Adam Smith's capitalism and the industrial revolution.

I think today we need a similar three-prong approach—political, educational, and economic activism. You can also think of this book as a manifesto for quantum activism in the arena of economics, and business, and politics, and education that today are inexorably connected.

Quantum activism is the idea of transforming ourselves and our society, using the principles of quantum physics, toward right worldview that integrates science and the subtle, toward a way of life that balances conditioning and creativity, and toward livelihoods for people that leave room to explore feelings, meanings, and values. The discussion above is a preview of your vehicle for right thinking about economics and business. We have to supplement this with the politics of integration. We have to supplement this also by freeing up liberal education from the materialist dogma.

The new economics of consciousness, by emphasizing the consumption of feeling, meaning, values, and happiness as business commodities, leads to a more creative and emotionally positive consumer society. Businesses will follow the same trend as the society at large. This book will help businesspeople (the producers) who will need to explore the special aspects of creativity in business— seen now as the creative exploration of the archetype of abundance—in their own lives. This is right living for you if you are in business: using quantum creativity to reshape not only your business but also your life.

Today businesses are learning about ecological awareness, and even corporations are talking about sustainability. The signs are everywhere—the three new R's of the twenty-first century mentioned earlier: reduce, reuse, and recycle. But how to reduce, and how to actualize the crucial factor for sustainability in your life as well as in your business? This book will show you how.

As part of creative living, as business leaders, you will also learn about the vital energy associated with money. You will learn how to get over your childhood conditioning, and you will learn how to consecrate money. You will learn what is wrong with the financial investment sector today as well as how the new economics gives us clues for how to right the wrong.

As quantum business leaders, you will learn the science of manifestation and the art of intention. Both are added gifts of quantum physics for a business leader. You will also learn to use the three I's: Intuition, Imagination, and creative Insight for your exploration of leadership. You will explore creativity not blindly, but as quantum connoisseurs, and encourage others to do the same.

The Subtle Sector: It Can Be the Growth Engines of the Twenty-first Century

Today, the material sector of the economy is plagued by the finiteness of material resources. The subtle sectors, as I mentioned above, are infinite by contrast. I will show how the subtle economy will provide us the growth engine for businesses in the twenty-first century and beyond.

In particular, I submit that vital energy technology will be the business frontier of the twenty-first century. In the book, we will explore some ideas for business ventures in vital energy. The big breakthrough has already taken place: vital energy is theoretically validated and is objectively measureable and quantifiable.

Our big question is how to take this auspicious beginning to a full-fledged technology?

How to grow the economy in the subtle sectors of meaning and values, how to produce happiness as a business commodity, and how to unleash the power of capitalism in these sectors? These are our additional big questions.

What is not normally realized is that the sector of meaning is largely taken over by institutions of higher education that are government-supported monopolies. The government support comes from two sources: indirectly through tax benefits and directly through research grants to big science. Meanwhile, these institutions of higher education have become the bastions of scientific materialism. Rather than teach liberal education—how to liberate oneself from dogmas—they propound another dogma—scientific materialism. In this way, they even contribute to the value-polarization in our society and politics.

These much-misdirected monopolies have pushed the cost of higher education higher and higher much like the health care costs. Could it be that it does not fit the elitist agenda of the movers and shakers of higher education to have a well-informed and educated middle class? But unlike health care, higher education (unlike secondary school education) is a consumer need of choice that can easily be subjected to the market forces of capitalism, and they will be better for it. The truth is, big science is a thing of the past. Government intervention is no longer necessary to support most scientific research. One can safely go back to the pre-1950s situation. As costs of higher education return to earth, students will no longer be burdened with huge student loans, nor will the government be loaded down with costly student loan interest subsidy.

And religions, especially in the West, have a monopoly on values and value education. These institutions also currently contribute to the political polarization. They, too, are optional needs for people to choose from and do not require protection from the free-market economy.

In short, the twenty-first century will see great advancements in both meaning education and value education as we abolish these monopolies and allow the market forces to take over.

What's in the Rest of the Book

I begin with a history of Adam Smith's capitalism including the worldview in which it saw daylight. The rise and fall of scientific materialism and how it has influenced economics comes next. This is the total content of Chapter 2.

In Chapter 3 I will discuss quantum physics and its world-view—how from the get-go it was speaking volumes against taking the simplistic ideas of scientific materialism seriously, how these early warnings were suppressed, how we got back on track, and how the quantum worldview helps us develop a science of the whole human experience. I also explore how new research in biology and neurophysiology, medicine and mathematics, and psychology has all contributed crucial ideas to the new science. I discuss worldview polarization and how to remedy that, all in Part 1.

In Part 2, I then lay out the basics of the quantum economics of consciousness as an economics that serves all our needs— gross and subtle and happiness (Chapter 4).

In Chapter 5 I examine all the important ramifications of the new economics: how it solves the problem of the business cycle, how it explains the mystery of the free market, and how it can avert all future economic meltdown.

Chapter 6 discusses sustainability, globalization, income distribution, and poverty. There is also the question of politics. Materialism has converted the modernist politics of meaning into a politics of power resulting in a do-nothing stalemate of polarized politics.

Part 2 concludes with Chapter 7, in which I review how the new economics helps to define the proper role of politics and the government.

Implementation via economic quantum activism is the subject of Part 3. We begin Chapter 8 with mindset change and quickly delve into how the change affects consumers and businesses, both the consumption and production aspects of the economy. We then discuss business leadership in Chapter 9 to bring balance and integration instead of separateness, a balance of creativity and conditioning, and a balance of self-interest and greater good .

In Chapter 10, I explore how to expand the economy in the subtle arena including a thorough discussion of the revitalization technology whose time has come. Chapter 11, the final chapter of the book, speculates about seven steps to reach the promised land, a conscious economy.

If the book empowers you the reader in all your roles—the business leader, a struggling innovator or small business person seeking satisfaction while earning a livelihood, a conscientious consumer, an open-minded economist or politician or educationist looking for new answers—my efforts will have been rewarded. Bon Voyage!

TWO

Adam Smith's Capitalism, and Its Modifications as the Worldview Changed

As already mentioned, when Adam Smith (1994) developed his far-reaching economic ideas in the eighteenth century, the philosophy of modernism, based on Cartesian dualism of mind and matter, defined the worldview. Since matter, science, and technology were developing in Adam Smith's time, it is not surprising that Smith defined wealth (capital), production, and consumption, all in material terms, as his capitalism was designed around satisfying the material needs of people. Economic wealth or capital requires raw material of natural resources to be converted with the help of innovators, and eventually labor, to the goods and services that people want to satisfy their needs. The main idea was that if the merchants of production, and the consumers likewise, intend only on their own self-interest to do their respective job, and the market is free to allow them to do so, then the invisible hands of the market would lead to an equilibrium of production and consumption, supply and demand, of all the various goods and services. The hope was that the invisible hands of the market would allocate the resources and capital not only to maintain equilibrium but also to work for the overall social good.

Although its main thrust was intended for the material world, Adam Smith's capitalism recognized mind in one important respect. Mind is spiritual territory, and God is still in the equation. In the eyes of God, everyone is created with equal potential, and everyone should be given equal opportunity to fulfill that potential. The more capital is distributed, then greater is the opportunity for investment in a gifted person's innovative idea to start a new line of business production. Smith recognized this implicitly as a driving force of capitalism. The avowed goal of Smith's capitalism is to make capital available to increasing numbers of people. The more people have a piece of the economic pie, the harder they work and productively, too. Thus, production increases, increased consumption follows, and standard of living increases, along with it affluence of the entire society. Crucial to the picture is the creation of a middle class consisting of innovators and entrepreneurs and, in general, explorers of meaning. Freed from the burden of physical work, these people of the middle class engage the mind and explore meaning with creativity. And what a crucially important role they perform!

And indeed, from the beginning of the industrial revolution until the advent of the third decade of the twentieth century, capitalism worked to not only create a viable middle class, but also it was the new middle class that rescued us from the dark ages. Before capitalism, there were only the rich and the poor, barons and serfs. Rich had the opportunity, but little or no prerogative for meaning processing. Poor had no time to do it, and no education, and only untested ability. There was one exception to this situation consisting of the people of the religious oligarchy with a lot of spare time. These people explored meaning and created a few meaningful enterprises, even in the middle ages, if they were not caught by such great intrigues as how many angels can dance on the head of a pin. As you can guess, Copernicus and Galileo were such people.

With capitalism and the creation of the middle class, however, the middle class kept growing and gave us all the fruits of the exploration of meaning—science, the arts, the humanities— that we are justly proud of today. Indeed, as Adam Smith implicitly assumed, some social good did come about when capitalism was practiced under the aegis of modernism.

But there has been one major glitch among others that required a major modification of Smith's basic idea. You already know what that is. In the history of capitalism, there has always been ups and downs, booms and busts, periodic recession and eventual recovery, followed by an up-cycle dominated by inflation. In the 1930s, the recession became so huge that it was called the great depression.

Naturally, Adam Smith's economics needed modification. The first such modification that made the mark was proposed by the economist John Maynard Keynes (1936) consisting of government intervention to maintain demand even in the face of recession. When recession comes, the government invests to create public service jobs; even partial employment creates enough demand to keep the economy going. The money for the government investment comes from increased taxes on the rich. (Nowadays, the money mostly comes from deficit financing. A combination of lawyers, lobbyists, and politicians has made this and other countries' tax laws complicated enough to allow massive tax evasion.) Eventually, the businesses regroup, and recovery and subsequent growth takes place. Since Smith's capitalism is supposed to be a capitalism of equilibrium, is growth compatible with it even though it is designed to grow the economy out of a recession? The answer is yes, so long as growth is brought about through new innovations and, I submit, involves the processing of new meaning.

Economists still debate if President Roosevelt's deployment of Keynesian economics brought America out of the depression or World War II. What is there to debate? In the decade before the depression, during the roaring twenties, ethics and idealism, and creativity with it, had declined in America. Idealism was playing second fiddle to the advent of scientific materialism. Only with the outbreak of the war did a whole bunch of innovative technology come into play. And idealism came back, meaning came back, and ethics came back—saving the American, nay the entire Western culture.

President Roosevelt also enacted the idea of social safety nets. In America, there are now several safety net features: social security, unemployment insurance, Medicare, and Medicaid. In Europe, the idea of social safety net has gone even further to create universal health insurance. Recently, with Obamacare, even America is following suit.

The idea of social safety net is sometimes denigrated by labeling it socialism, but it is quite consistent with Adam Smith's capitalism since among its main contributions is to protect the middle class and produce social good. And don't forget that the latter reduces times of desperation by the dispossessed, thus providing additional contribution to raising demand.

In the subsequent decades until the 1980s government intervention a la Keynesian economics was always used to soften the effect of recession whenever it occurred. I will call the combination of Adam Smith's capitalism plus Keynesian economics as classical economics. Whereas the idea of social good was implicit in Smith's capitalism, it is explicit in Keynesian economics. Business profit must be shared with social good financed by taxing the profits—this idea of "great compromise" became one of the stabilizers of the fluctuations of Smith's version of capitalism (Byrnes, 2008). In contrast, the new economics proposed in this book is called quantum economics; in this approach, social good is built into the fabric of the economics itself.

Keynes also had the idea of maintaining an "aggregate demand" that would stabilize the "aggregate production" (supply). But how to maintain such an aggregate demand! And here in the post World War-II period, American economy (and indeed economy of the entire Western world) was lucky: cold war. Loosely speaking, the cold war created the military-industrial complex that maintained the aggregate demand (Reich, 2007).

Interestingly, the cold war also produced a great surge in scientific and technological creativity. Academics could ask for grant support either from the military-industrial complex itself or from other branches of the government. Perception is everything! The perception was created that all scientific research contributes indirectly to weapons research. In this way, academic scientists could pursue explorations of meaning that had nothing to do with weapons, but everything to do with developing a civilization that is worth saving with the weapons. And meaning continued to be an aspect of production and consumption for a few decades.

But this did not last. First, in the late 1970s, oil prices began to increase in a spiral, eventually producing deflation of the economy. (What is deflation? Deflation is a broad decline of both wages and prices.) Second, the cold war was not forever; it ended in the early 1990s. And then, maintaining aggregate demand became a fresh challenge. Can we maintain the great compromise if we cannot maintain aggregate demand? With a differently structured economy, we surely can, as I will demonstrate in this book.

Finally, as the academic worldview changed from modernism into a post modern one based on scientific materialism, in which matter is recognized as the reductionist basis of everything, including mind, meaning, and values, Adam Smith's ideas were majorly modified by academic economists to fit economics into the straightjacket of this new worldview. The materialist influence began pretty early, even in the 1920s. By the 1980s, these influences had quite solidified.

The Rise of Materialist Influence on Economics

The Newtonian worldview—that the world is made of matter moving in space-time, is determined by physical laws through the workings of local interactions [interactions that always operated via the exchange of signals with finite speed limited by the speed of light], and is objective—gained a very important milestone with Darwin's theory of evolution. Before Darwin, inanimate matter, and even animals, were regarded as part of the mechanical world with tacit approval of the Church, but humans were treated to be exceptions because they had "free-willing" minds. Darwin proved with his theory, backed by fossil data, that humans originated from animals, and now one could argue that if animals are machines, humans must be machines, too. Another important milestone in the 1950s cinched the case of a mechanical Newtonian universe that included both living and nonliving: the discovery of the molecular structure of the biological hereditary molecule—the DNA. With this, most scientists were convinced that there isn't any fundamental difference between the living and the nonliving—all is mechanical.

Ever since, the worldview of scientific materialism has been gaining ground among not only academics, but also the media, in replacing modernism with a post-modern deconstructionist philosophy that denigrates all idealist reference to mind and, in the process, implicitly elevating scientific materialism as the replacement of Cartesian dualism.

Materialist science's crown jewel is modern physics whose success has largely come from reductionism (the idea that upward causation from the microcosm determines the macrocosm) and the "predict and control" power of mathematics. Naturally, the notion of making economics similarly bottom-up and mathematical became important in economics and became the preoccupation of academic economists. Although the bridge between microeconomics and the macroeconomics of the real world has never been built, the influence of mathematical economics has been huge (Samuelson and Nordhaus, 1998).

Initially, the mathematical economists were using ideas like utility that recognized the role of individual need; but very soon the need of mathematics took over, and they ended up with only some basic statistical rules for ordering peoples' choice of goods, which became the backbone of a theory of average mainstream consumer behavior. The mathematics became tractable as a result, but the price paid was huge: the feelings and meanings and values a consumer derives from goods are no longer considered as a part of the economic transaction. In fact, economic transactions were no longer regarded as need-based because needs can be created and manipulated by manipulating behavior.

Soon economists were suggesting (and businesses were following) the idea that consumer economics could be based on simply promoting behavior through marketing. In other words, the idea grew that even meaningless products, with no inherent feelings attached, could be sold by the power of marketing.

The marketing would generate feeling and meaning, and even "spiritual" value for the consumer. This led to the meaningless proliferation of consumer goods such as the rows and rows of breakfast cereals, all pretty much of the same utility in terms of nutrition (not much, too much sugar for one thing) that you see in supermarkets today. I still remember one cereal ad from the 1960s. If you eat this cereal, the ad declared to gullible children who were watching during the commercial breaks of their favorite cartoon shows like *Popeye*, you will gain so much strength that you will be able to fight off bullies. But of course, even a child can figure out that the bullies can also get hold of the cereal and gain even more strength; thus, the cereal ad declared, this cereal will not be sold to bullies.

In materialism-influenced economics, even the idea that it takes innovative technology to bring the economy out of recession, was replaced by the idea that consumerism—if you continue creating products to consume, and sell them as a field of dreams, "American dream" consumers will come—alone can do it. And it was assumed that consumerism alone could maintain an aggregate demand, thus creating the expansion of the marketing industry and its exponentially increasing salaries.

Money became the be-all and end-all of economic activities—the new God of economics. How you make money does not matter nor does it matter what you do with your money. The goal of life is to become a member of the billionaire club and to have every kind of consumer product available to engage in.

Hand in hand with this came the information technology, a digital technology that deemphasized meaning. Futurologists hailed this as an advent of the information age—information is money and power. Not knowledge with its implicit emphasis on consciousness, not meaning with its implicit acknowledgement of the mind, but cold objective information that matter alone can process without help from mind or consciousness. (Of course, information per se is not good or bad. Like money, information can be of positive or negative use.)

One important aspect of the consumer orientation of economics is a new hierarchical class system—producers (upper class) and consumers (lower class), and what is worse, a "star" system among the producers. It started with the entertainment industry first with Hollywood movie stars, then with rock stars; then it spread to sports heroes. These "stars" at the top of their profession were given exorbitant compensations. As materialism sank its teeth into the society, the star system spread to other professions as well. One of the newer entries is the business leader, corporate CEO and management in general. In the 1960s, a CEO's salary was a mere thirty times greater than that of the ordinary laborer. Now it is more than two hundred times.

Religious worldviews produced an elite in the feudal tradition. The nouveau riche became new additions to the same tradition—conservative to the core.

Modernism gave us democracy, capitalism, and liberal education—powerful weapons against the elite system. Unfortunately, with scientific materialism the previous liberals became elitists once again; in addition to the previously mentioned meritocrats, the members of the new liberal elite consist of some of the nonreligious rich and famous, and the "government knows best" bureaucrats and lobbyists.

Eventually, the result of a mixture of the old religious elitism of the conservatives and the new elitism of the liberals has been a huge wealth gap between the elite rich—old and nouveau— and the rest of us. Now only one percent of Americans own most of its wealth and earn most of the income. The income disparity is hugely on the increase.

Believe it. The economist Thomas Piketty (2014) has in a recent book done a historical study of tax records for the last few centuries in countries like USA, UK, Germany, France, and Japan; it became a best seller. How does a serious book on economics touch a popular nerve in this way? Because Piketty empirically proved what many of us have suspected hithertofore: in spite of capitalism, the gap between the rich and the poor in the USA today is almost as bad as it was in France before the French Revolution!

What do the one percent elite do with their money? They make more money. Some economists assume that their money trickles down to the 99 percent through investment in production-consumption economy. But that happens only if the return on the capital is better than what the capital would earn in the financial sector of the economy. And the last is a rare occurrence.

Anyway, the bottom line is: Money is power; information to make money is power. Power is to have any and all forms of consumptions available and people to provide them. Power is the ability to influence and orchestrate change, or the lack thereof, amidst strong dissent from the majority of population.

To summarize the materialist influence on capitalism in bullet points:

1. Scientific materialism veered economics towards the use of mathematics for which more and more behavioral and mechanical assumptions were made about human beings to make mathematics applicable. Real behavior of human beings is full of non-rational emotions and intuitions which were ignored.

2. The belief grew (originated and perpetuated by the elitists) that consumerism alone can restore an economy from recession, it alone can maintain aggregate demand, and creative innovations are really not

necessary. Machine creativity—creativity limited to permutations and combinations of past learning—is not much good anyway for producing innovative technology. But machine creativity may be adequate for the new information technology.

3. The idea of eternal archetypal values was denigrated. This undermined science itself so that scientifically discovered truths could also be debated as relative truth and science got mired in controversy.

4. The employment of ethics in business behavior became ambiguous. People of politics made some attempts to replace ethics by regulatory laws with very limited success. Clever lawyers and accountants helped to neutralize the effect of regulations.

5. Elitism came back in a new form but is in truth much the same as old-fashioned feudalism; in fact, worse. In feudal times, at least a few of the elite invested in meaning and values, and there were changes that eventually broke free the human spirit of creativity. Today, the elite mostly process information and serve the wisdom that that is where the money is.

6. Money became the new God of economics. However, this God is very different from the old God of religions. The old God favored spiritual values—ethics and love, meaning, creativity, and the like. The new God favors only material values or ego values, if you will, centered around pleasure. Helped by the media, younger generations all over the world are lapping up these pleasure-centered ego-values.

The materialist ideas do not work, of course; for example, consumerism fluctuates too much to create a stable aggregate demand. Manipulation by sophisticated marketing techniques notwithstanding, our tastes and desires fluctuate unpredictably. Without new meaningful innovation, new consumer demand cannot be created, and the economy loses dynamism. How many generations of cell phones can you sell as new and kindle the public's interest? And don't forget. The emphasis on information processing shrinks peoples' attention span! I think the dependence on consumerism to maintain aggregate demand is the major reason why recessions are more frequent today than ever.

Take another materialist idea: denigrating and abandoning ethics in business practices in favor of government regulations. Ethics is a way to balance the negative tendencies built into our brain such as competiveness and greed. We glorified greed in the 1920s and again in the early twenty-first century; the fall-out in both cases was economic meltdown.

There are other fall-outs, too. Daniel Pinchbeck (2011) talks about one:

> Modern [materialist] capitalism makes sociopathic behavior humdrum and routine. What else can we make of a corporation like Wal-Mart, which takes out insurance policies on its harassed and humiliated employees utilizing statistical "quaint" analysis to cash in on their aggravated death rates? ... [Or] complacent CEO's like Tony Howard of BP, happy to attend yachting races while his company's activities terminated entire ecosystems?

An unknown author contributed a poem toward the same theme:

> *We have bigger houses but smaller families;*
> *more conveniences, but less time.*

We have more degrees but less sense;
More knowledge, but less judgment;
more experts, but more problems;
more medicines, but less healthiness.
We've been all the way to the Moon and back,
But have trouble crossing the street to meet our new neighbor.
We have more computers to hold more copies than ever,
But have less real communication.
We have become long on quantity, but short in quality.
These are times of fast foods and slow digestion;
Tall men but short characters;
Steep profits but shallow relationships.
It's a time when there is much in the window
but nothing in the room.

(Quoted in, Eisenstein, 2011)

Supply-Side Economics

We accept elitism in America. Elitism is a common feature of the two competing worldviews we have today in America, namely, Christianity and scientific materialism. This is the way it is in many countries. (One notable exception may be Australia where each individual is considered to have equivalent worth.) Naturally elites raise the question: Why should they have the burden to pay for social good in the form of higher taxes? In the eighties, this kind of question opened room for another suggestion for a possible solution to the problem of recession that came about during the presidency of Ronald Reagan. It is called the supply-side economics because its premise is to improve the supply side rather the demand side to create economic movement and jobs. It also works, like its demand-side cousin, through government intervention. But instead of middle-class tax breaks, unemployment benefits and public service jobs, the supply-side economics gives the rich huge tax breaks as an influx of capital (new money supply). The idea is that the rich will invest the capital in business ventures thereby stimulating new production and creating jobs. Again the tax breaks will come from deficit financing.

The critics call this "trickle-down" economics, too slow to revive consumer demand to make a difference. In practice, the money does not even seem to trickle down. Instead, actual history shows that it creates a huge wealth gap between the rich and the poor, antithetical to the spirit of Adam Smith's capitalism.

The fact is that the wealthy already have enough money to invest in demand creation if they were sure of making money that way. Thus, the strategy of stimulating the economy by giving the rich more money via tax breaks plays directly into the hands of the wealthy elite to increase the wealth gap further by investing the extra capital in the financial sector and making even more money. The net effect of supply-side economics was summarized best by the songwriter Peter Garrett: "The rich get richer and the poor get the picture."

The recent 2008 economic meltdown should have led to the extinction of many businesses, especially financial institutions, if we followed the dictums of classical economics. Instead, the government bailed out the financial institutions "too big to fail" to maintain the supply side of the economic equation. (A cynic would say, "too politically influential" to fail.) Eventually, that too, has further enlarged the gap between rich and poor. And worse. If these bailouts of "too big to fail" business institutions become the going practice of economics, then the rich can make speculative investments for which they keep the profit, but government (that is, people) picks up the losses. George H. W. Bush characterized the supply-side economics famously as "voodoo economics." That can be debated since there is some evidence that suggests that it rescued the economy from the

Carter/Reagan era deflation, but there is no doubt that supply-side economics is not in tune with Adam Smith capitalism; it is more of an elitist economics.

Many economists today believe that in order for Adam Smith's capitalism to function at all, the idea of a completely free market cannot be maintained. So today, most economists favor government intervention either through the Keynesian approach (tax the rich and increase government programs to increase jobs and economic movements; give tax incentives to small businesses) or through the supply-side economics (cut the taxes of the rich and wait for the wealth to trickle down and enrich everybody). Notice, however, that both remedies work only if strong economic expansion returns in a hurry. In reality, under scientific materialism, the creativity of our society has become so anemic that business investment just does not quickly return to robust levels. Businesses prefer a wait-and-see attitude.

Many economists, correctly I think, also point out that the effect of both Keynesian and supply-side intervention in lifting the economy out of recession is mostly psychological. In both kinds of intervention, there is a considerable time lag as to when real jobs are actually re-created. In truth, usually the economy recovers before then, and the real usefulness of the interference in either of these forms is a little suspicious. In the quantum economics of consciousness, we use government intervention on the demand side in direct service to social good by increasing demand in the subtle sector of the economy; we also boost up the supply side by giving tax breaks to people who are "rich," not only materially but also spiritually because they invest in the subtle and the spiritual. And these people don't wait for a better business climate before they invest but get down to business immediately (see Chapter 5).

Currently, economists also favor quasi-government inter-vention by a central agency of every nation to control its money supply by changing interest rates as needed or creating new money (see below).

The net effect of Keynesian, supply side and monetary eco-nomics of the kind just mentioned, is the same: if we implement them, free market is not free anymore. Is this good or bad? In the absence of any understanding of the mechanism behind the "invisible hands" of the free market, it is impossible to evaluate. And this problem, too, finds solution in the quantum economics of consciousness (see Chapter 5).

Monetary Economics, the Fed, and the Rise of the Financial Sector

So what happens to the money given to the rich via tax cuts according to the supply-side economics if they do not invest it in new business ventures? Do the rich just keep the money in bank accounts earning interest?

There was a time when interest rates were quite high in this country, but a new invention has taken us away from those days. This is called monetary economics.

Money is a complex subject, and the history of its growth in complexity is fascinating (see below). Suffice it to say here that there is now a central apolitical agency called the Federal Reserve, or simply the Fed, which keeps track of the amount of money circulating in the economy (the money supply) which it has the power to control by adjusting the interest rate and printing new money. The Fed can also adjust the exchange rate between currencies that affects trade between countries.

The theory goes that by adjusting the money supply and interest rates, the Fed can control, at least by a fair amount, the fluctuations giving rise to boom and bust (Friedman, 1962).

History shows that the Fed can certainly control inflation by raising the interest rates and diminishing the money supply, but the opposite is not true. During 2010-2013, the interest rates were kept very low, and the Fed was injecting new money into the system all the time, but this did little to grow the economy to visible robustness until the middle of 2014. Thus, the Fed has little control in preventing great recessions or helping to get out of a great recession.

So here is another form of quasi-government control of the market, via the Fed and its various machinations. Today, the interest rates are destined to be quite low by design, and all people have to figure out new ways to earn money on money (if you have plenty of it) especially if you don't see the business environment profitable enough (for example, due to a dearth of innovative business ideas to perk consumer interest) to start new ventures of business production.

Above, I mentioned speculative investments by the rich. What kind of speculative investments do the rich engage in these days? This brings us to the subject of the financial sector of the economy. Something very ironic has happened in our materialist economy. As the worldview more and more has devalued our subtle experiences, relegating them to mere ornamental fixtures good for survival alone or at best for entertainment, money itself that represents material value has given rise to more and more abstraction, much like the subtle. To put it another way, we have not seen the subtle as potential capital because of our myopic conceptual lens. Instead, we have created the pseudo-subtle abstractions of money in our search for greater and greater capital. Never mind that sustainability of economic expansion is antithetical to expansion in this kind of abstraction.

Anyway, these abstractions of money are here to stay, or so it seems. In 2006, all the world's capital in stocks was valued at about

51 trillion dollars; in the same year, the derivatives—one of these high-flying abstractions—had a capital value of $400 trillion.

Dealing with these abstractions of money is tricky, and mathematical economists have not been entirely successful in figuring out ways to predict their dynamics. Thus, there is always an amount of speculation, much like gambling, that is involved in investing in this financial sector of the economy.

But we are going ahead of ourselves. Most of us are quite unfamiliar with these abstractions of money. Moreover, the financial sector is almost 9 percent of the economy now; no politician dares to eliminate it entirely or lower its share of the economy, gambling or not. If we cannot get rid of it, the least we can do is to know the beast.

The Inverse Pyramid of Money and its Abstractions

I have already said money itself is an abstraction. Economic activity in human societies began millennia ago with the direct exchange of things of value (real wealth). It is interesting that this exchange evolved to paper money also through an abstraction similar to the one we are discussing. First, one or more prized commodities (gold, silver, and the like) became the standard measure of all other kinds of real concrete wealth; at the next stage, receipts exchangeable for a fixed sum of the prized commodity became the unit of exchange. Finally, paper money, a promise to pay a designated amount of these receipts, replaced the receipts themselves.

Suppose you need money, but you don't have it; but if you do have illiquid property to act as collateral, or you have a trustworthy record as a producer of capital goods (good credit rating), then you can go to an intermediary to get cash. These intermediaries are, of course, the banks. The banks lend you money at an interest rate; that's their profit motive. The bank is making money on money and so can you. If you have a surplus, you can deposit your money in the bank, and the bank will pay you an interest but at a rate way below the borrowing rates.

How do businesses raise money? They could borrow from the bank. But today, much more likely, a business corporation would sell off a portion of its value to the public by getting the public to own its shares or stocks. The stocks do have a face value, but usually they would sell at a premium (maybe ten or twenty times their face value) depending on what the market decides what the value is.

So now if you have excess money and you want to make money on it, you not only have the choice of intermediation—the bank—but also disintermediation—invest in the stock market directly.

Stocks are another form of abstraction, subtler than money itself no doubt. Because of the inherent risk involved and because of the unpredictability of the market, before the 1980s ordinary people seldom invested in stocks. But then came mutual funds where experts created a portfolio of stocks for you, the novice, thus reducing your risk.

So nowadays if you have a long-term investment to make, you really have the relatively risk-free choice to invest in the stock market via mutual funds. There are many funds now: bonds, hedge funds with different kinds of functions and so forth.

Are mutual funds really safe? Please notice the words "relatively safe," as the following cartoon episode from Dilbert will testify.

Dogbert is talking to the pointy-headed manager. "Studies have shown that monkeys can choose stocks better than most professionals. That's why the Dogbert Mutual Fund employs only monkeys." Then he goes on elaborating, "Yes, our fees are high, but I don't apologize for hiring the best."

These capital markets create much more capital value than other business ventures. In the long term, indeed, the value of the stock market as a whole has increased manifold. You get a feel for this in America by keeping track of the Dow Jones Industrial average, for example.

The latest abstraction is the already mentioned derivative, an instrument that gains its value from a stock or some other financial instrument of concrete value. For example, a simple derivative is a future, in which the trading of the stock will take place at some future date. Additional risk? Yes. But derivatives easily can sell at ten times the value of a stock today. By introducing another level of abstraction at more risk, the financial wizards of today's economy have created ten times more capital value.

Banks that are supposed to lend you money have discovered another choice—to make money by creating relevant paperwork to produce different forms of marketable securities that they can then leverage many times and make much more money than by directly lending it to you. This is one of the reasons that money remains tight for lenders even with adequate money supply. The latest in this class of abstraction is a derivative called CDO—collateralized debt obligation. These played a major role in creating the financial meltdown of 2007-2009 (see Chapter 5 for more on this).

There is an ongoing political debate: should we serve the interest of the consumer and eliminate financial speculation in our economy through government regulation, or should we depend on the good sense of the rich, the "job-creators," not to take the economy down the garden path again? After the great depression, we created regulations that kept the speculative aspect of the financial sector to a minimum. But in 1999, the genie was let out of the bottle once again, and within a decade, economic disaster struck. Once again, there is debate. More recently, some control in the form of regulation on maintaining transparency is back under the leadership of President Obama. Not enough to eliminate investment in the new abstractions of money, but hopefully enough to prevent speculations to run amuck.

The Current Logjam of Econo-political Thinking about the Role of the Government: Is There a Way Out?

So there you have it in simple terms the history of capitalism as it has been practiced in this country and how and why it came to the recent great recession (more details in Chapter 5). There is one more element of complication that leads to endless debate: the question of the national debt.

Both the demand-side and the supply-side government intervention, in practice, depend on deficit financing once we succumb to materialist economy: economic expansion based on consumer demand for material goods and services. The deficit financing increases the national debt.

In the 1970s, the gold standard became impractical, and money had to switch to the "dollar standard." I will give details later, but this made debt easily available to both American people and the nation as a whole (meaning the federal government). But we do have to pay interest on the national debt, and even at low rates, it comes to a substantial amount that takes away from the future flexibility of the government to handle the economy. Hence the debate about how to cut down the national debt to a manageable amount goes on and on.

In this country, a lot of government spending involves the social safety net—social security and Medicare for the elderly and Medicaid for the poor. The critics of social good object: should we increase our national debt to pay for the dignity of the elderly or to maintain social good? But proponents of social good can equally argue that we can easily and effectively reduce the national debt by eliminating tax loopholes for the rich!

The politics of polarization between the Republicans and Democrats has made it a standstill in the department of government intervention in our economy. Increasingly, it is seen as a left versus right debate, and the pejorative name of leftist ideas is socialism. The word *socialism* reminds people of Marxism, communism, and all those vile things that produced the cold war. And one criticism of socialism is undoubtedly true; it does tend to produce bureaucratic nightmares. But of course, unregulated free market also produces nightmares, leftists correctly point out! According to them, religious ethics that kept businesspeople ethical in a bygone era is not scientific, and it is never going to come back. The left still tries to make the debate between "we are in this together" tied by humanistic philosophy (humanism) versus "you are on your own" individualist elitist conservative philosophy. They don't remember that both philosophies are important for a healthy functioning of a capitalist economy; and that under the increasing influence of scientific materialism, the left, too, are increasingly favoring the "numero uno," the ego values. I believe that if we ignore any important segment of society from the economic solution proposed, we will be creating a time bomb that will come back to haunt us. It is, therefore, important to develop an inclusive economic structure engaging all sections of society with adequate choice to work hard and achieve economic success.

The problem here, of course, is the same one that other great thinkers of the past have struggled with— Marx, Veblen, and Keynes. It is about how to combine compassion with capitalism and how to achieve the great compromise. Didn't even President George W. Bush talk about compassionate conservatism? But socialistic bureaucracy throwing borrowed money toward achieving social good may not be the right answer. The experience in Europe—the resulting economic chaos in Greece, Spain, Ireland, Italy—has amply shown us that.

I don't think you, the reader, appreciate that the political polarization that we see today all over the world is really due to a worldview clash between scientific materialism (the liberals or Democrats in this country) and the religious/Christian worldview (the conservatives or Republicans). But each of these two worldviews gives us paradox: the former, the quantum measurement paradox of the observer effect, and the latter, the paradox of dualism (see Chapter 3). The logical paradoxes show the incompleteness of both worldviews. There are also plenty of empirical anomalies that neither worldview can explain. Resolution of the paradoxes and the empirical "facts" demand the integrative worldview of quantum physics that gives us a new science within consciousness (Goswami, 2008a).

Conservatives approve of the subtle domain of the human experiences, at least the value and the spiritual dimension. But the conservatives do not like creativity, the way to explore these dimensions. In the view of the scientific materialists, also, creativity is at best mechanical creativity based mostly on information processing, determined creativity, if that makes any sense; it is a pale facsimile for the real thing. On top, materialists denigrate the subtle because they cannot include it in their philosophy.

Says the philosopher *Raja*ni Kanth (1992):

Markets [under the aegis of scientific materialism] produce the continuously recycled illusion that our [material] needs are limitless, our cravings infinite; that we are pathologically obsessive consumers before we are anything else, friends, relatives, citizens, social beings, producers, creators and artists—and the market will satisfy these urgings … from here to eternity. *But living is not consuming alone, and life is not a craven tale of boundless lust of privatized, personal, self-indulgent, material satiation, like a pig in a big trough wallowing all by itself,* we are, incurably *social beings* that must not be trapped by its own artifacts, ensnared by the designs of Capital, enmeshed in the schemes of profiteers, or caught in the plans of those who seek to amass profits, expand commodities, and reduce our lives, destroying the very fount of our well-being, proportionately.

We will see in these pages that if we change the worldview to the quantum integrative one, there will be a brake in the further advent of the influence of scientific materialism; the religions will relax and move to a post-secular era that will bring back ethics and creativity not as religious dogma but as scientific values, and the politics of polarization once again will give way to working together to bring about the new quantum economics of consciousness with a recognition to both material needs and subtle and spiritual well-being.

In the quantum economics of consciousness, we solve the problem of large fluctuations of the economy via creativity and via investments in the subtle domain without increasing the wealth gap between rich and poor and without squeezing the middle class. The new approach gives us a steady state economics and incorporates a solution to the finite resources and finite environment problems that worry all economists and businesspeople.

When the world's net oil production curve turns downwards instead of going upwards and upwards, that is the signal that this "free ride on cheap oil" of the materialist expansion economy cannot go on forever and that we must turn to sustainable technology. Some say world's crude oil production has paused since 2004, oil from oil shale through fracking technology (which is short term anyway) notwithstanding (Geisel, 2014). The usual materialist argument is that as a resource becomes depleted, its cost increases; the increase in cost then enables technological alternatives to become cost competitive, ad infinitum. The implicit assumption, of course, is that an infinite amount of alternative sources of energy exist and that suitable technology can always be found to deploy it if the cost is met. This was perhaps justified assumption in Bacon's time, but now we know most everything about physical energy. The prognosis is definitively bleak unless you believe the glib misdirected talk about "free energy," and to their credit, most materialists don't.

There is no doubt about it. We have to have sustainability, but how? The proposal in this book is that we realize that science needs a paradigm shift from scientific materialism to the primacy of consciousness and build an economics of consciousness. In conscious economics, we bring about sustainability which is also the answer to how to reduce consumption and how to reduce the national debt.

Some new-age thinkers are not ready to commit on the need for a worldview change; they do agree that we need to change how we think of money. Their thinking is that the way we use money now is the evil, and we try to look for serious alternatives to the prevalent usage of money. I agree in part and suggest in this book that we consecrate money by using it as currency of exchange not only in the material arena but also in the subtle arena so that if money is the economic God, at least It looks after all human needs and interests—material and subtle and spiritual.

Another group of serious thinkers believes in a mass awakening to an ecological awareness that will enable people to embrace the sacrifice needed for an ecologically sustainable economy where "small is beautiful." I believe in "small is beautiful" except that embracing it should not be much of a sacrifice. By and large, we should be pragmatic enough to recognize flatly that fairness demands that no sacrifice is demanded from anyone. The saving grace of the quantum economics of consciousness is that it works to change consumers' attitudes and contexts of thinking and feeling. If the government imposes a tax on meat consumption because meat is highly energy intensive, for meat-eaters the tax would be regarded as a sacrifice. But to a vegetarian, especially one who sees the health and environmental benefit of such taxation, the tax would be welcome news.

Politics and Economics: It's the Worldview, Stupid!

I mentioned above that right now, here in America and in many places elsewhere, there is a polarization between two major political parties. What is the root cause of this polarization? In order to think beyond polarization, we need to discover the root cause and eliminate it.

I will repeat. In America, there are the Republicans—the old guard, the conservatives—and then there are the Democrats—the liberals. The Republicans support the supply-side economics that includes tax cuts favoring the rich; in general, they favor less government and fewer regulations, especially fewer regulations on how to carry out businesses that provide jobs. They maintain that corporations are humans and must be extended the right to influence politics as they see fit. In other words, Republicans are traditional elitists: fathers know best, the traditionally rich know best, and corporations know best. No evolution of ideas as circumstances change and no creativity.

Republicans also enjoy huge support from the Christians—the once-declared moral majority of the country. As such, they support not only Christian values to live by but also share the disdain for science that many Christians still maintain. So I think it is fair to say that Republicans uphold the worldview of religious elitism.

The Democrats are the party of the labor movement. They are also the party of the liberals, people with the traditional agenda to rebel against all kinds of orthodoxy—the religious orthodoxy to be sure, but also the orthodoxy of the rich and powerful. Power to the people, said the Democrats of tradition, opposing the orthodoxy of the powerful rich.

But something happened in the way to today. Democrats also support science—supposedly the vehicle that liberates us from religious and other dogmas, science that judges what is the case by careful experimentation of facts and nothing else. But the liberal spirit of science gave way to the dogma of scientific materialism so unobtrusively that hardly anybody noticed it. There was huge two-way trade between the academe and the government in the form of big science and the cold war. Big science brought scientific materialism to the academe, and the initial resistance of the "liberal arts" was swept away through the ideological purge by the deconstructionists (not unlike what happened in Soviet Russia and communist China). In its turn, the "liberals" (now translated as the upholders of scientific materialism) began to exert huge influence on the non-religious half of our political parties, the Democrats. Many Democrats still hold on to values, but they have to carefully dress it with the philosophy of humanism—values are human values, and therein is their importance.

In summary, the reality now is this: the Republicans are religious elitists, the Democrats are scientific materialists—also elitists albeit of a different sort, see the discussion earlier—and the American people are torn between, polarized if you will, two elitist exclusive dogmas. The Cartesian truce of modernism that gave us a respite from elitism is almost completely forgotten.

With this background it is easy to understand why Republicans favor supply-side economics. True elitists do not like anything like modern democratic government where people get a voice, because how can we trust "ignorant" ordinary people who have to be told by the elite what is good for them? This is the position of the ultra-conservative Tea Party. Pragmatism, however, demands that we accept that democratic government is here to stay. In that case, at least make sure that the elite/ordinary divide is maintained. Supply-side economics does that by giving tax benefits to the rich. Also the rich, being religious, know how to bring social good; we need not worry, say the supply siders. Governments stay away; private charity to the worthy poor will take care of social good, they add.

Democrats support demand-side economics, partly because of tradition (Franklin Roosevelt, the most notable Democrat in the twentieth century started it), partly because in spite of the influence of scientific materialism, many of them hold on to traditional values (because they are human values). Unfortunately, they buy into the elitism created by scientific materialism—the "meritocracy"— the elitism of people who "really know better." (And these people can be rich and famous, too!) Naturally, Democrats want to bring social good through the bureaucratic elite, through regulation.

Are Democrats socialists? Democrats in America avoid that term to no end. But this idea that social good can be injected in a materialist society through regulation is the same idea that Marx suggested, and that failed.

Furthermore, do Democrats' policies remove income disparity? Only if these policies consist of taxing the rich, not if they involve deficit financing. But the political polarization makes it impossible to tax the rich; it is not a politically correct option.

Is the elitism of the Republican kind any better? No, history has already proven that. Supply-side economics combined with Christian oligarchy is a step backward towards the feudal era.

The problem is that neither the traditional elite, nor the bureaucratic elite, or the rich and famous elite can bring "good" to the society because human beings have negative emotional brain circuits (the source of "corruption") built into them whereas, at this stage of our evolution, the "good" in human beings is only potentiality and only occasionally available as actuality to those who are sensitive to their intuitions. The good needs to be cultivated. The intuitions need to be followed up with creativity in order not only to be able to balance the negative but also to carry us to the positive.

How do we cultivate the good? How do we create interest in creativity in the picture? Traditionally, we try to do it through education, which tends to produce the elite, of course, religious or materialist, take your pick. Capitalism suggests another way. Cultivate the good by making it part of the economic equation of production and consumption.

Can human nature be influenced by technology and consumption? Of course. How did we become such materialists as we are today? The worldview polarization is more about how we think than about how we live. The material technologies of computers and cell phones have influenced everyone so much that the nature of human relationships itself is rapidly changing. Children today walk side by side while exchanging text messages, not spoken words. They have already discovered that keeping feelings out of communication is more efficient! They already have been taught that they must learn to process information, not get lost in the search for meaning. Information is where the money is., Isn't this the information age?

But isn't delving into emotions more fun and more conducive to aliveness, and isn't exploring meaning more satisfying than making money, the reason humans have interacted the way of meaning and feeling ever since they have existed until now? You have not noticed, but today's societies and cultures are nutritionally deprived not only in terms of materially healthy balanced diets but also (and even more so) in the departments of the subtle and the spiritual—vital energy, mental meaning, and archetypal values, and spiritual wholeness.

We think we live in our external environment, but truly this is only partially true. We live in our internal environment —the psyche—much more. When the psyche is impoverished because of a lack of nourishment, we lose enthusiasm, and we feel generally depressed. We vainly try to fill up our lives with technological escapes, but the lack of the subtle shows up in our relationships, or rather in the lack of it.

Suppose we bring explicit vital energy technology to produce goods for vital energy consumption. Children consuming such goods will be vitalized with energy that they will then want to dissipate through interaction with other humans. This is our way back to relationships.

We don't realize how scientific materialism has robbed us of vitality because of its claim that all is matter and biology is chemistry. Take the case of everyday food grains. Biologists claim that organically-grown food and bioengineered food bring the same nutrition because the chemical composition of the food is the same. The new science says otherwise. The vital energy content of the bioengineered food is likely to be different, and it matters.

The proof is in the pudding. Taste organically-grown rice and genetically-engineered Monsanto rice. You will be able to feel the energetic difference, more vitality, in the organic rice. And it is not just food grains. Today, if we live in cities, we get water only after much chemical treatment that may very well rob us of the precious vital energy that we should get from our water. Is there any doubt in your mind that natural spring water without any chemical treatment tastes more refreshing?

Agreed, we cannot grow all our food organically or have all our drinking water needs satisfied from natural spring water any time soon. In the long term, we may hope that by using our available soil effectively and developing other sustainable technologies, we may be able to farm all our land organically. In the meantime, we should recognize that we already have the technology to revitalize regular grains, even grown with chemical fertilizers, so long as they are not genetically modified. And the same thing is true of chemically-treated water

These are just two huge examples of vital energy economics. "Chemistry gives us good life" philosophy has given us many chemically-treated products that have no correlated vital energy left in them. Revitalization of any and all of these products will not only give us more health and wholeness but will also revitalize the economy and, to boot, change the direction of the entire culture back to re-humanization.

The same goes for mental meaning. Scientific materialism denigrates meaning. The pundits of today's science flatly declare stuff like, "the more we look at the universe, the more it seems pointless." Of course, it does, if the lens through which you are looking is tainted with scientific materialism.

A Sufi story. Mulla Nasruddin is seen struggling with water, shaking it, beating it, doing all kinds of shenanigans. A friend asks, "Mulla, what are you trying to do with your water?"

The mulla says, "I trying to make yogurt."

The friend is shocked. "Mulla! You cannot make yogurt out of water."

"But suppose I can," says the mulla and goes on with his task.

The truth is you cannot make meaning out of matter without your mind. But if you think your mind itself is matter, brain, then you are stuck. As Abraham Maslow said, "If you have a hammer in your hand, you see the world as nails." If your worldview only acknowledges matter that cannot process meaning, you see the world as meaningless; you see the world as information.

With conviction in ultimate meaninglessness, you can satisfy your human thirst for meaning only with pretend meaning, as the existentialists teach us, or become information junkies. You can convince yourself that your occasional thirst for meaning must satisfy some survival necessity; otherwise, why would Darwinian evolution bring it about in matter somehow? But all this does is to help you rationalize living in the gutter of conditioned pleasure/pain-oriented life at the service of your instinctual emotions.

Not so long ago, a character of one of Bernard Shaw's plays (*Heartbreak House*), had this conversation:

Ellie: A soul is a very expensive thing to keep: much more so than a motor car.

Shotover: Is it? How much does your soul eat?

Ellie: Oh, a lot. It eats music and pictures and books and mountains and lakes and beautiful things to wear and nice people to be with. In this country you can't have them without lots of money: that is why our souls are so horribly starved.

Today we live in a computer culture where peoples' souls are starved because they can't find meanings to eat and nourish their souls. Today, music is mostly negative, and most pictures and books don't inspire. Mountains and lakes are there, but who has time to look at them? As the philosopher Russell Means puts it, " ...philosophers have despiritualized reality so there is no satisfaction (for them) to be gained by looking at a mountain or a lake or a people in *being*. Satisfaction is measured in terms of gaining material—so the mountain becomes gravel and the lake becomes coolant for a factory. "

Likewise, beautiful things to wear are still there, but are there nice people to be with? Under scientific materialism nice guys finish last, remember? You have to be narcissistic to wear beautiful clothes and converse with your friends on the cell phone. And isn't that the truth today, that narcissism prevails among our youth?

And, of course, where is love? Where are people in the service of beauty? We are confused: Do these archetypes even exist as timeless guides to our search of meaning and purpose? Torn between two worldviews—religious elitism and scientific materialism—we are thoroughly clueless. Especially about archetypal values. We use our confusion opportunistically to sacrifice social good for personal good in any and which ambiguous situation—Republicans and Democrats alike. In other words, we are hypocrites of the worst kind, hypocrites who rationalize their hypocrisy.

Advent of civilization is about making better and better representations of the timeless archetypes (see Chapter 3). In view of the above, our civilization is in danger. So our cultural polarization not only affects our politics and economics but also the progress of civilization itself.

Democrats and Republicans cannot agree as to their values, but I am convinced both groups believe in capitalism and would be enthusiastic about applying capitalistic notions to our explorations of the subtle. You have to remember: above all,

Americans are pragmatic. A devout Hindu will rather starve than eat beef; a Moslem would go hungry rather than consume a pig; a religious Jew likewise will not eat if he/she cannot find kosher food, but an American will always choose to eat rather than starve (Kanth, 1992). Materialist changes in capitalism have given us powerful techniques of marketing. Today we use these techniques for subtle deception, but they are as easily used for subtle education. Democrats like giveaways directly to the needy to create demand, but Republicans only like giveaways to the rich. Both giveaways take away incentive to engage in capitalism. Perhaps both parties could agree on giveaways with an earmark: giveaways must be used for education in the subtle domain so that people—poor and rich—become capable and interested in consuming subtle energies. Agreed, this form of giveaway will require a lot of skillful and targeted salesmanship to become broadly accepted. But once subtle energy production and consumption become the going thing in our society, the cultural polarization will also beat the dust.

The lesson from our past is clear. It is technology that changes economics, and economics necessitates changes in politics. Then the culture can follow the needed integration and adapt the integrative worldview of quantum physics. This integrative worldview is the subject of the next chapter.

THREE

Human Experiences, the Quantum Worldview and the Scientific Basis for Quantum Economics

All knowledge systems should help us with all three of our existential challenges: how to think, how to live, and how to make a livelihood. Four hundred years ago, and through much of a couple of millennia before then, we lived under the aegis of religions that, despite periods of success, failed most of us on all three scores much of the time. In many parts of the world, as a result, we had the dark ages when most people lived in material misery. Modern science grew out of the human creative urge to end the misery, to find a knowledge system that works universally toward that end.

Things began to change in the sixteenth century, with the advent of modern science. For the next four hundred years, so much knowledge about matter was gained by science, that this knowledge system seemed to be able to control and predict most things in our external inanimate environment, and even began to make a stab at understanding the living including the human being. Unfortunately, an old philosophy that everything is made of matter, and everything is caused by material interactions, was reinvented. Called scientific materialism, this philosophy precluded the development of a science of human experiences.

In this philosophy, all movement, including social and economic movements, are objective, local, and determined, determined by scientific laws and evolution driven by blind chance and survival necessity. And there is only one level of reality: matter moving in space and time. Mind in this view is wholly computable, and creativity is computer creativity, novel rehash of the past. Values are epiphenomena of our survival need. Obviously, who can blame anyone for a dose of skepticism in such a science? So religions have maintained some credibility, and the worldview split, and polarization is the result.

Religions could not understand how the external material world works; thus, they denigrated it, inviting misery in our material level of living. Materialists cannot explain our internal subtle experiences, so they denigrate feeling, meaning, values, and consciousness that matter cannot compute. As noted already, this is also inviting disaster.

How do we know we are not simply brain-driven computers? We know because we have those internal experiences, don't we? We have the experience of the subject/self; we build civilization assuming that this subject/self is causally potent and must take responsibility for its actions. We have feelings; in part, they are predictable brain phenomena no doubt. But sometimes they come with surprise, they seem unpredictable, not brain related but more visceral. And in truth, we think not only computable content but also incomputable meaning. We intuit those archetypal values that Aurobindo (1996) called supramental! And we know now, again from research experience thanks to creativity researchers, that we have creativity to engage and transform our feelings, to explore new meaning, and to embody values. But experiences are subjective, private and subtle. How do we include them in our science, which is objective, public, and gross material? The poet T. S. Eliot lamented:

> *"Where is the life we have lost in living?*
> *Where is the wisdom we have lost in knowledge?*
> *Where is the knowledge we have lost in information?"*

Is lamenting what has been lost under the advent of material science all that we can do? No, we can do better. The know-how came from quantum physics, the most recent paradigm of the physics of matter.

Quantum Physics and its Worldview

In quantum physics, originally conceived for material objects, objects are depicted as objects of possibility—waves of possibility. If you place an electron at rest in the middle of a room, the electron will not stay put according to Newtonian physics; instead, it will expand all over the room in a matter of moments. But if you set up a three-dimensional grid of electron detectors all over the room, not all the detectors will tick at once either. In one experiment, only one detector ticks. Only when you do many identical experiments, do you find that the electron does not appear in any one given place all the time like a force-free Newtonian particle; instead it appears all over the room with various probabilities forming a bell curve (fig. 1). Naturally, we interpret this to mean that the electron spreads but only in possibility, as a wave of possibility outside space and time. When we measure, the wave of possibility becomes the particle of actuality; the many possible facets of the wave collapses to one facet.

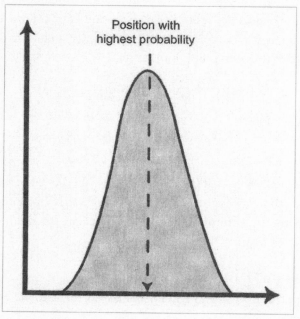

Figure 1

So there are not one but two domains of reality—one for potentiality and one for actualities. The domain of actualities is space-time, of course; then the other domain must somehow be "outside" space and time. This idea is not entirely new. Mystics, especially Eastern mystics are talking like this for millennia; for them the two realms are called transcendent and immanent. Psychologists, in the form of what is now called depth psychology, have the concept of the unconscious, which smacks of two domains of reality—unconscious and conscious. It seems that for the third time in human history, we have discovered this essential truth and this time with the complete certainty of experimental data behind us.

Opposition still tried. How do we know that the domain of potentiality is nothing but mathematical artifice? The big breakthrough came when a group of physicists headed by Alain Aspect (1982) discovered that there is an experimental way to distinguish the two domains. In the domain of actualities or manifestations, as everybody knows, we need signals carrying energy to communicate. But you know what? In the domain of potentiality, no signal is needed, this according to Aspect et al. The signal-less instantaneous communication via the domain of potentiality is called nonlocal.

So through this nonlocal domain, all things are interconnected. The separateness we experience arises only because we ordinarily communicate via local signals. But once in a while, everyone has experiences of instantaneous communication like mental telepathy.

If there is nonlocal communication, there must be a causal field involved with it. The researcher Ervin Lazlo (2004) called this field *akashic* field, acknowledging the esoteric origin of the concept (*akasha* in Sanskrit means outside space and time). But how to get from this concept to consciousness?

Now here is the worldview changing paradox. If the electron is a wave of possibility, how does the wave become an actuality, an actual particle at a detector, every time we observe it? There is a mathematical inviolable theorem in quantum physics: no material interaction can ever transform a quantum wave of possibility into actuality (von Neumann, 1955).

The implication of this theorem is no less than forcing a change of our scientific worldview. It is important for you, the reader, to clearly appreciate this before you take the worldview changing aspect of quantum physics seriously. Look! Both theory and experimental data have convinced physicists that the material macroworld is built out of the microworld of elementary particles like electrons and quarks in a ladder-like way

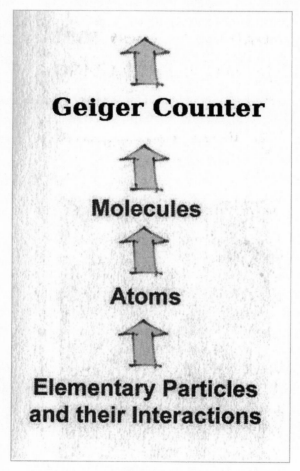

Figure 2

through what is called upward causation—cause rising upward from the micro level of elementary particles to the macro level of the detector (fig. 2). So, in truth, since electrons and quarks are possibility objects, so is an electron detector. And material possibility coupled to material possibility cannot give us actual-

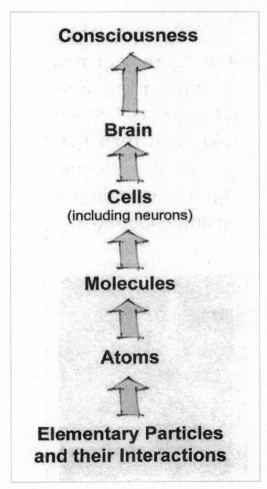

Figure 3

ity. So an electron detector cannot really actualize the electron and detect it. True, it becomes a very complex wave of possibility distributed over many, many facets, so that it is very hard to detect its quantum nature. But still, the theorem above holds; the detector is a quantum wave of possibility.

How about the observer's brain? Biologists have assumed since the 1950s, that biological beings are built according to the same kind of ladder as other material objects, all the way to the observer's brain (Fig. 3). But here is something called the observer effect that we cannot debate: in the presence of an observer the wave does collapse, which is the physicist's favorite word for the transformation of a possibility wave into an actual particle.

What enables a human observer to collapse an electron's wave of possibility? What happens in the event of collapse as the electron's wave changes into a particle? Simultaneously with collapse, as Werner Heisenberg, a co-discoverer of quantum physics, pointed out, our knowledge about the electron changes. Our facility of knowledge processing—consciousness—is involved in a quantum measurement.

The physicist John von Neumann was the first to propose that consciousness collapses the electron's possibility wave by choosing one facet out of the many-faceted wave-object; collapse requires downward causation via choice by consciousness. But he was assuming dualism—nonmaterial consciousness as a separate world from the material world. That assumption suffers from the paradox of dualism as you already know—how does a nonmaterial consciousness interact with matter without violating the law of conservation of energy?

You have to think of consciousness in a radically new way: consciousness is not separate from matter; neither is it made of matter, the brain neurons. Consciousness is the ground of being in which matter exists as waves of possibility. Don't get bogged down puzzling how gross matter can be made of consciousness—the subtlest of the subtle. Behold! According to quantum physics, matter, too, exists as subtle possibility before the choice/

interaction by consciousness make it gross (Blood, 2002). Realize that reality has two domains: first, consciousness and its possibilities. This constitutes the unmanifest (which psychologists call the unconscious and religious esoteric traditions call the transcendent). Second, the manifest (psychologists call this conscious and religions immanent) where there are manifest collapsed objects and a subject—the manifest observer—experiencing them. The event of collapse caused by the "downward causation" of choice by nonlocal consciousness manifests subject-object split awareness.

The most important lesson for practical pragmatic people is this: the world is made from both upward and downward causation, the power of the gross material and the power of nonlocal consciousness; we will see below that the latter is to be accessed through the subtle. The first gives us possibilities, the second, choice and manifestation. Neither can be ignored nor should be ignored. Both material and spiritual are important. Businesses and consumers alike realize: we are both; we need both. Further realize that while material interactions are entirely causal, a choice can be purposive. Activities like business activities are purposive. Isn't it good to know that quantum physics is giving (finally!) a scientific way that purpose gets into the world?

Science of Experience Including the Subtle: Quantum Psycho-Physical Parallelism

Once we realize that the material world consists of quantum possibilities of consciousness, and that the material experience of sensing arises from the collapse of these possibilities, we can easily see how to expand this notion to build a science of all our experiences. Suppose consciousness contains not just the one world of matter but a multiple of worlds, each world consisting of quantum possibilities, the collapse of which is responsible for each of our experiences (fig. 4).

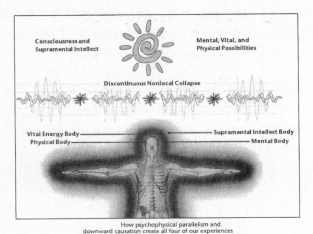

How psychophysical parallelism and
downward causation create all four of our experiences

Figure 4

Long ago, the philosopher/physicist Gottfried Leibniz enunciated a philosophy called psycho-physical parallelism to avoid the paradox of interaction dualism. The psyche, said he, coexists parallelly with the physical. No interaction is needed, no paradox of dualism. Not quite, said critics. Pray tell, who maintains the parallelism? For this, Leibniz had no answer, but we do. In quantum psycho-physical parallelism, consciousness maintains the parallelism. In every event, along with the physical, one or more of the other worlds of possibility collapse and manifest as experience due to conscious choice. In the process the physical makes a representation of the subtle mental and vital.

Appreciate the wisdom of making the physical world in the micro-makes-up-macro reductionistic way. According to quantum mathematics, the macro-world objects of matter, having large mass, lose most of their capacity of quantum movement becoming approximately Newtonian. This is a powerful camouflage no doubt for us to penetrate, as it is difficult to think that the skyscrapers of Wall Street become a possibility when no one is looking! Yet this confusing approximate Newtonian fixity is important: it enables macro-matter to make representations of the subtle for you to refer to. If matter was quantum all the way and were capable of running away while you are making a representation (imagine yourself writing down a thought with pen and ink about an important business matter), your representations would not be very useful, would they? But without representation, how would we ever retrieve the subtle?

Notice one more important thing about all this. Because macro-matter loses most of its quantum potency, chairs, tables, and buildings always appear when we collapse them in seemingly fixed positions, and different observers can compare notes forming a consensus reality about them that all agree must be external of them. In contrast, subtle objects retain their quantum nature always; there is no micro making up macro there. So it is always pretty unlikely that we can collapse the same thought or feeling or intuition together with somebody else; naturally, we perceive thoughts, feelings, and intuitions as private and internal. In this way, internal/external is not a fundamental dichotomy; it is a consequence of the way the external matter is made vis-à-vis the internal psyche. Hence my appeal to businesses: some of you already value the external ecosystem. This is good. Can you make it even better and consistent with the science of experience and put value also on the internal environment, the subtle environment of our psyche? The philosopher Arne Ness called this deep ecology. Along with shallow eco-friendliness, you need to cultivate deep eco-friendliness.

Life, Purposiveness, Form-making, and Vital Energy

What is life? How do you know that you are alive? Almost any layperson would tend to say that I know I am alive because I feel vitality—a kind of energy—moving in me. But biologists

as a class have bought into the philosophy of scientific materialism—everything is matter, and therefore there is no distinction
between living and nonliving. Biology is really biochemistry.

I once asked a biologist colleague about what characterizes
life as opposed to nonlife. He immediately said, it is evolution.
Fine, but can evolution be understood in terms of a purely materialist theory? What about Darwinism? you may say. Darwinism
has two prongs: chance variation in a hereditary component, the
genes (portions of the DNA molecule), and natural selection
from these variations on the basis of survival necessity. Usually,
this passes as a materialist theory, but there is one rather evoca-
tive word in the theory that suggests otherwise—the word "*survival.*" In general, material objects don't have the characteristic
of survival. Specific molecules of viral RNA have been shown
in the laboratory to be better capable of replicating themselves
than other such molecules; but this molecular replicability, an
entirely physical phenomenon, cannot be shown, and has not
been shown, to translate into reproducibility of even a single-cell
organism that is crucial to survival.

Characteristics such as survival have "purpose" written all
over it. This is the crucial point. Biological objects such as organs
perform a purposive function, which I call a program-like behavior to contrast it from the "law-like" behavior of physical and
chemical objects. So whereas physical objects are purely law-like,
biological beings are both law-like and program-like. Program-
like behavior refers to behavior that follows logical step-by-step
instructions having a purpose (Goswami, 2008b).

Think of biological beings then in analogy with computers. In a computer, it is possible to think in two complementary ways: a hardware point of view in which electrons act on
electrons, and a software point of view in which symbols act on
symbols via programs. Similarly in biological organisms, at the

law-like physical level (hardware), molecules act on molecules. And on the program-like software level, programmed forms act on programmed forms carrying out purposive functions.

And of course, nobody should claim that the software program-like behavior should follow from hardware law-like behavior! So there goes naïve reductionism down the drain. We can never understand the software program-like behavior of living form from the law-like behavior of the hardware nonliving substrata, from physics and chemistry!

For the computer, we know that we, the programmer, use the physical hardware (through downward causation of choice by nonlocal consciousness) to perform software functions that are purposive and meaningful. The purpose and meaning of the programs running the symbols come from us. Similarly in biology, can there be purposive traits without a purposive consciousness? The conventional biologists get bogged down fearing the intrusion of a personified Christian God in their territory, and try to deny the role of consciousness calling it an "intelligent designer" of religious connotation in disguise, but the details of the consciousness-based theory clearly indicate that the purposive actions of consciousness are entirely objective.

Biologists assert that selective advantage, Darwinian adaptation, programs the genes to produce seemingly purposive traits. But there is a logical circularity, a paradox, in the argument.

The point is this. Darwinism is a two-prong theory, chance variation and natural selection on the basis of survival necessity. Variation occurs in the microlevel of the genes, but natural selection takes place at the macrolevel of form. Unfortunately, there is no straightforward relationship between micro and macro. So biologists introduce the ad-hoc idea of genetic determinism: genes and genetic programs determine form.

Do you now see the circularity of logic? The idea that genes determine form makes Darwinism work. Where do genetic programs come from? Darwinian evolution.

So face it! Objective consciousness, a natural programmer using downward causation, is needed to produce programmed biological form. In religious parlance there is a wise saying, that God makes man in His own image. So to figure out if consciousness uses any other organizing principle besides itself in producing living forms, we can study our own behavior when we write a program on a computer. Well? We use our mental imaginations, patterns of meaning really, to map them as software into the computer hardware. In other words, we use a blueprint, the meanings of our minds.

The program-like behavior is built into biological form-making that starts with a one-celled embryo. Technically, the form-making process is called morphogenesis: *morph* means form and *genesis*, of course, means creation. The blueprints of biological form making are called morphogenetic fields, the fields that are used as blueprints to help program biological form.

How does the liver cell function so differently from the brain cell although they both were made through cell division from the original one-celled embryo? The answer is that the liver cell is differentiated from the brain cell by programs that enable different sets of genes to make different sets of functioning proteins in these two organs. The morphogenetic fields provide consciousness with the tools for choice from the material quantum possibilities involved in cell differentiation programs.

But where do these fields reside? It is gradually being accepted that they are epigenetic, but how far down the rabbit hole are biologists willing to go? The truth is, in biological morphogenesis, for example, in cellular regeneration with the stem cells (undifferentiated cells), the question is unavoidable: How does the cell know where it is in the body? How the cell "knows" when it is extracted from bone marrow and is introduced in the brain to program itself as a neuron cannot be understood in terms of local transfer of information alone. The morphogenetic fields have to be nonlocal somehow. But all material things interact via local signals! See the predicament. In science within consciousness, the morphogenetic blueprints are the substance of the vital world of possibilities within consciousness. They are nonlocal and nonphysical, an idea first proposed by a maverick biologist named Rupert Sheldrake (1981).

To every biological form or organ, there is an associated, correlated morphogenetic field that acts as its blueprint. Consciousness mediates the interaction of these blueprints with matter as it makes form in accordance with the blueprint. Let's call the conglomerate of these morphogenetic fields correlated with biological forms of an organism its vital body.

A healthy organ not only means that the physical organ, the representation is healthy, but also that the correlated morphogenetic field is healthy, too. The feeling of health or wellness, vitality or vital energy, comes from the movements of the correlated vital body, the morphogenetic fields. Wellness speaks of the state of balance and harmony of these movements—vital energies.

How do we verify all this with empirical data? The Eastern spiritual traditions discovered long ago that there are points in the body, roughly located along the spine where our most intense feelings occur, called the chakra points (fig. 5). Indeed, the neurophysiologist Candace Pert has noted an abundance of movement of molecular correlates of emotions along the spine (Pert, 2008). Many researchers have noted that the chakra points are close to the important organs of the body. Now realize that when we collapse a physical organ, we are also collapsing its correlated morphogenetic vital fields. The change (from possibility to actuality) of the correlated morphogenetic field is the movement that we experience as a feeling. If this is correct, then the feeling at each chakra will correspond to the function of the correlated organ(s) at that chakra. And this bears out our scrutiny (see figure 5).

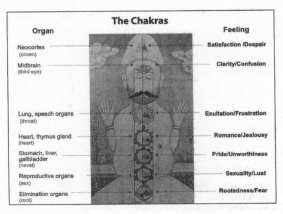

Figure 5

You can see why this paradigm shift in biological thinking is important for economics. Fully 16 percent of our economy is health related. Moreover, food and all other organic products that we consume have correlated vital bodies. The quality of these products depends not only on their physical make-up but on their vital make-up as well. Under the aegis of scientific materialism, we have been oblivious to the vital dimension of much stuff that we consume. Imagine the economic opportunity that can open up here. Biology without vital energy is like Newtonian physics without electromagnetism!

As an example, take the case of dietary supplements that Americans routinely use when they go on a diet. You can make sure that these supplements, which are extracts from their organic original, provide adequate quantities of material nutrition such as protein, but the extraction process is sure to get rid of most of the correlated vital energy of the original food. In this way, these supplements lack vitality, and taking them would be nutritionally inadequate in untold ways. Perhaps this is the reason that people on a diet lose weight but gain it back soon after they go off their diet! Their lack of vitality produces the helpless tendency to eat. Wouldn't it be nice if somebody figured out a way to put the missing vital energy back in and sold the revitalized diet supplement?

Evolution has given us humans instinctual brain circuits of negative emotions—circuits of feeling in the limbic brain correlated with circuits of meaning in the neocortex; together, feeling plus the thought of their meaning are responsible for what we experience as emotions. These brain circuits mask the functioning of the low chakras as precursor of these experiences.

One good thing that comes from renewed acquaintance with the chakras is that we begin to experience not only the low chakras but the higher chakras as well, chakras whose functions are not taken over by instinctual brain circuits. Initially, the higher chakras are activated through intuitions, but we don't pay much attention to them when we are adults; however, as we learn to act on them, as we engage creatively with them, we can make new brain circuits that convey positive emotions that can balance our negativity. As already mentioned, such rewired "transformed people" can be the human capital of future quantum societies. The power of the subtle in action!

The Mind: More Organizing Principles for Our Biological Make-up

I have been emphasizing the importance of the inclusion of our subtle internal objects in our economics. The psychologist Carl Jung (1971) gave us an empirical classification of four personality traits, based on the four-fold nature of our experiences—sensing, feeling, thinking, and intuiting. Sensing is the experience of the physical, this much we know. We now have identified the experience of feeling with the experience of the movement of the vital body morphogenetic fields. If our experience of feeling is due to a new entity—the morphogenetic field—we can then ask if there are two other entities—principles of biological organizations that correspond to our conscious experiences of thinking and intuition respectively.

Let's consider thinking first—the realm of the mind. A related question is, if mind is not brain, then what is the proper role of the brain in relation to the mind?

Biologists believe in the main that mind is an epiphenomenon of the brain arising from neuronal interactions. But recently, mind has been rediscovered in science as an independent entity; its purpose is to process meaning (Searle, 1994; Penrose, 1991). Then the proper role of the brain vis-à-vis the mind suggests itself—it is to make representations of mental meaning. And the brain does it with the neocortex.

Check it out. What do you think ordinarily? You think old meanings already charted in your brain memories creating the confusion that mind is brain! But once in awhile, you think of a new thought that you never had before, one that surprises you. Where does a creative thought come from? There must be a mind behind your brain.

The great Canadian neurosurgeon Wilder Penfield discovered why the mind has to be different from the brain while poking his (epileptic) patient's brain with an electrode. Suddenly, the activation of a little spot in the brain evokes in the patient the vivid recall of an entire Beethoven symphony. Clearly, Penfield realized the memory is in the mind, poking the brain in the right spot just activates it. The neuronal substrata are just movements of physical stuff, like the electronic movement on a TV screen. There is no meaning there. We give meaning to the electronic movement of the TV screen and make a story line out of it (fig. 6). Similarly, with the quantum language, we say the brain neuronal memory records are triggers for the recall of correlated mental experiences whose meanings come from the mind.

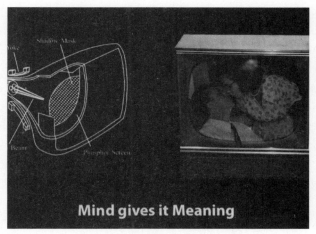

Figure 6

Intuition and the Supramental

There is more. Can the law-like behavior of the electronic hardware of a computer tell us anything about the laws by which the symbols operate on one another, the logic of the computer programs? Can the law-like behavior of the electronic hardware tell us anything about the programmer? The answers are again, No.

So it is a little more complicated. Biology needs the morphogenetic fields of the vital body that are the blueprints of the vital functions that have to be represented in the physical form that carry out these functions, but then it also needs more. First, it needs the programmer, this we know and have already introduced—consciousness and its agency of downward causation. In addition, biology needs one additional organizing principle, the reservoir of the contexts of the logic by which the biological programs operate, or the functions that the morphogenetic fields are blueprints of.

This is related to the question: Where do physical laws reside? This is a question that has long been discussed by many physicists and philosophers, and the most sensible answer is still the one given long ago by Plato. Physical laws are not written in the physical hardware, nor are they derivable from the random motion of the material substratum. Instead, as Plato says, physical laws are from the domain of archetypes, the most esoteric domain of the possibilities of consciousness from where our experience of intuition comes. The laws of movement of the morphogenetic fields come from the same place (fig. 7).

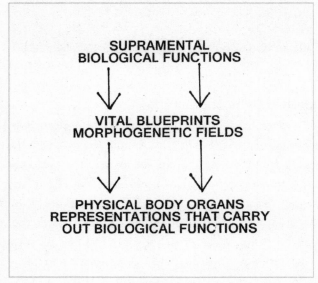

Figure 7

Obviously the domain of archetypes is beyond the mind as well. In fact, it must set the contexts of mental thinking also. Since this domain is beyond the mind, the word *supramental* used to denote it is justified.

Finally , what is your own experience? Do you intuit? Intuition is a very subtle experience, and many scientific materialists try to convince us that it does not exist, and that it is just thinking. Introspect hard and realize that intuitive thought is qualitatively different from ordinary thought. They always hint at something of value but abstract—notions like love, beauty, justice, truth, goodness, abundance. These abstract notions are the Platonic archetypes of thinking. The intuitive thoughts you have are mental representations of these archetypes, the instant mental meaning you give to them.

Biological matter has not evolved yet to make direct representations of the archetypes in the physical body. So, we make representations of our intuitions with the help of the mind and the vital body, in the form of intuitive thoughts and positive high-chakra feelings respectively.

Experiences and Needs

As humans evolved, our first needs to be emphasized were physical needs. Our minds gave meaning to the physical world and we developed the physical mind. We were hunters (men) and gatherers (women) in those early days. Women were second fiddle those days; the men brought home the bacon—big food. With the evolution of small-scale agricultural machinery like the hoe, men and women worked together in the garden. Their ongoing interactions aroused feelings, and mind began giving meaning to feeling—the age of the vital mind. Our feeling needs dominated us then.

With the evolution of large-scale agricultural instruments like the plough, the scenario changed again. Only men could work these heavy instruments. So women were relegated to child bearing and rearing once more, and men became the "head honcho" again and were the only ones allowed to process the meaning of the mind—abstract thinking. Even among men, hierarchy was created. Only a few men—the landowners and their cronies—had the leisure time to really process abstract thinking, but the motivation was low. So the exploration of meaning processing was slow in those days.

The industrial revolution brought democracy and especially capitalism to redistribute capital enough to create a middle class who had the leisure time and the motivation (for moving up the social ladder if nothing else—recognize the power of the American dream here as the American dream is the dream of all humans). Thus, meaning processing took off. With the development of birth control technology, women eventually broke free and joined the meaning processing adventure.

So until recently, our meaning needs have been on the increase second only to our physical survival needs. The long habit of suppressing their vital mind has made men somewhat impervious to their feeling needs. With women, however, who still value vital needs and gaining equal social status, our feeling needs are now coming to prominence also all across our societies.

Roughly about three thousand years ago, some great human beings in different parts of the world independently discovered the importance of what we intuit in a cogent and coherent way, coherent enough to create our first books of ethics—moral codes to live by. Soon their teachings gave us the world's major spiritual traditions whose popular versions were the major religions. Unfortunately, because of incomplete knowledge, spiritual traditions and especially the religions always emphasized the transcendent over the immanent. Turn your attention upward toward the heaven, they admonished, not to the needs of the earth. The lack of attention to the earthly needs gave us the dark middle ages until modern science came along.

In the eighteenth century, along with democracy and capitalism, liberal education evolved whose purpose was to emancipate us from the shackles of the limiting religious dogmas. But it took only two centuries for science to become corrupted to the limiting dogma of scientific materialism. Neglect all other needs except the physical, which can be studied with quantitative science. There is no real meaning in the universe; our feelings are lazy diversions of which only survival, pleasure and pain need to be acknowledged. The first takes care of itself. So delve into the second and avoid the third; in fact, better yet, replace it with a devotion to information processing. Eat, drink, and be merry again if you are in pain or at least process information to shove pain under the rug. Go to the information superhighway just to meaninglessly cruise along, misusing the creative potential of the Internet.

In economic terms, this philosophy says: Veer the economy toward limitless expansion of consumer material needs including pleasure and information processing. Never mind that we live in a finite planet with a finite environment! If that expansion is not enough, expand more in the arena of finances, with abstractions of money. Never mind the risks to the regular economy this may create. And beyond it there is the world of information which is vaster yet! We have almost found that which is limitless. Never mind that our children are rapidly becoming information junkies suffering from attention deficit hyperactive disorder (ADHD) now with a 20 percent frequency!

Although scientific materialists have monopolized the institutions of higher education, they have not been able to convert the rest of the society, not before another large movement of consciousness has begun to bring a genuine integration this time between matter and mind, science and spirituality.

At about the same time, technology has given us the Internet (it's not all bad!) that has made it possible to break the monopoly of the higher educational establishment. At the same time, an influx of Eastern religions and new forces of psychology are helping to break open the monopoly of Christianity over spiritual values.

If you wear the straightjacket of dogma, your creativity dries up because you are limiting the possibilities open for you to explore. Your domain of exploration of the subtle is now restricted to the known. The infinite looks very finite because of your faulty lens be it the lens of materialist science, or be it the lens of popular Christianity.

With the integrative worldview that quantum physics demands, with the quantum science of experience, the subtle domains can become infinite domains of exploration and economic expansion. All we have to do is to expand capitalism to include the subtle needs, explore the vital domain and develop vital energy technology, and free up the domains of meaning and value from dogmas while beginning new explorations. Tall order, but very doable, especially when we have an urgency of a crisis to push us extra hard toward creativity, which is now once more allowed under the umbrella of the new paradigm. And more. With quantum physics to guide us, we have discovered how creativity works; we no longer need to delve in it blindly (Goswami, 2014; see also Chapter 9).

The Science of Manifestation: The Three Quantum Principles

Businesses are often big time manifestations of creative ideas. If you are a businessperson, wouldn't you like to know if there is a science behind our ability to manifest? Wouldn't you like to empower yourself using this science?

Ever since von Neumann suggested that consciousness collapses quantum possibility into actuality, there has been a buzz about our ability to manifest. The physicist Fred Alan Wolf gave us the catchy phrase, we create our own reality. With a sense of quantum omnipotence, people in America tried for a while to manifest a Cadillac, a popular car in the 1970s. And when success did not come in that enterprise, they concentrated on manifesting parking spaces for their old cars in busy downtown areas. And when even that did not work, people wrote books on how to manifest. The books sold well, but alas! They all missed some subtleties of quantum measurement.

We know those subtleties now. Consciousness is not a dual partner of matter as von Neumann conceived, nor is it an epiphenomenon of everyone's individual brain. Instead, it is the ground of being in which matter and psyche (with its three worlds) exist as quantum possibilities. When consciousness collapses a quantum possibility wave by choosing from its many facets, it is choosing from its own without exchanging signals—nonlocal communication.

This nonlocality is the first quantum principle of manifestation. In order to manifest, you have to access nonlocal consciousness. Your perfect freedom to choose, create, and manifest depends entirely on your ability to access your nonlocal consciousness where you and everybody else are one. The reason you don't regularly experience this consciousness, the reason we all lose easy access to it, is that we become conditioned. As we grow up, more or less the same stimuli bombard us; if our response is suitable, it is reinforced. The mechanism we have—the brain—makes memory with this reinforcement capacity. We identify with these memories of psychosocial learning; this identity is our individual ego/character (Mitchell and Goswami, 1992).

We are also capable of being conscious by replaying brain memory, reconstructing it to suit the situation, to please ourselves and others. This gives us the other component of the ego—ego/persona. With personality development, we become individual selves, sometimes so self-absorbed that we are downright narcissistic. This is a Bette Midler story:

> A woman meets a friend after a long time. "Let's catch up with each other." She invites the friend to a coffee house and begins to give her friend all her news. She talks and talks about herself for about half an hour, finally becomes a little aware, and apologizes.
> "Oh, I have been talking about myself all this time. Let's talk about you. What do you think of me?"

The second principle of manifestation is discontinuity. All events of collapse are instantaneous. Naturally, since no time is wasted exchanging signals, collapses are sudden, discontinuous. When electrons jump from one atomic orbit to another, they never go through the intervening space; this is called a quantum jump.

All events of collapse are quantum jumps in principle. However, in our stream of consciousness experience, because of conditioning, our responses to familiar stimuli are all quite predictable. And so the discontinuity gives way to an apparent continuity similar to the apparent loss of quantum movement for material macro-objects.

Creative choices from quantum possibilities that give us the creative experiences retain the discontinuity, however. Hence an aha! surprise always accompanies a creative experience; we sometimes call them "an aha! experience" for this reason.

The third quantum principle of manifestation is called tangled hierarchy. As said previously, in the event of collapse, consciousness, undivided from its possibilities, appears to become divided into a subject and objects. If you think about it, in every event of quantum measurement, the observer's brain is involved. Initially, it must also consist of possibility; only with collapse does it become actualized, but we never see it. Instead, we identify with it. The brain has somehow captured consciousness enough for consciousness to identify with it. It's a self-identity, identity with a particular brain. But how is the brain made so that it could enable consciousness to identify with it?

The answer is: tangled hierarchy. Tangled hierarchy means circular two-way causality instead of the one-way causal relationship that is called a simple hierarchy you are used to (see figure 4 for an example of simple hierarchy).

To see how circular causality gives self-identity, examine a tangled hierarchical sentence: I am a liar. See the circularity. If I am lying, then I am telling the truth and so forth ad infinitum. Once you get caught into this circularity, you can stay in it indefinitely. You can identify with it; you can look at the rest of the world of sentences separate from you. In other words, you have a self-identity, separate from everything else.

Now recognize that for the self-identifying sentence, the situation is a little artificial. After all, it is only because you are sophisticated in your knowledge of English grammar that enabled you to interpret the meaning of the sentence in the manner needed to appreciate the logical circularity of the sentence. You consciously live in a world transcending the world of the sentence in a level where the sentence can never go. In other words, you live in an inviolate level for the sentence. So you can move in and out of the world of the sentence; for you, getting caught is only an option.

Finally, realize that the situation with the brain is quite different. If the brain captures consciousness the same way the liar's sentence caught you, the transcendent consciousness in its wholeness is still at the inviolate level. Can you go there? Yes, but only in the state of unconscious. So because of the unconscious/conscious two-level reality, once consciousness identifies with the brain, the apparent identity becomes compulsory and seems real.

Does the brain have a tangled hierarchy in it? At the macro-level, brain has a built-in apparatus of perception that is fully quantum. It also has a memory apparatus which is near-Newtonian like usual macro-objects. Now recognize that perception requires memory and memory requires perception. If we tried to conceive how to build such a tangled hierarchy starting with the micro going toward macro, we would need an infinite number of back and forth between the two levels to succeed, an infinite number of oscillations between levels (fig. 8).

This is what we call a tangled hierarchy (Hofstadter, 1980). Obviously, we cannot build such a tangled hierarchical dual system from scratch. It takes creativity of downward causation by nonlocal consciousness to evolve a brain with tangled hierarchy (Goswami, 2008b). The self-identity arising with the association with the tangled hierarchy of the brain is what we call the quantum self in contrast to our conditioned ego.

Somebody once wrote, "If the brain were so simple that we could understand it [via reductionism], we would be so simple that we couldn't." Well said! And, in passing, we must recognize that there is a tangled hierarchy also in the making of a single living cell. Biologists have long known that it takes DNA genetic code to make proteins, but it takes proteins to make DNA—circular causality. In this way, self-referential quantum measurement takes place even in a single living cell, which is how we distinguish living from nonliving.

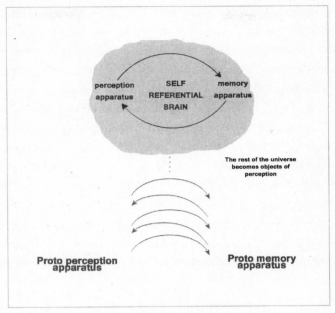

Figure 8

Any of these three quantum principles can be used to access quantum consciousness, the seat of downward causation. We cultivate the path of nonlocality through cooperation with others with like-minded intentions with whom we meditate and contemplate, even make business decisions. We cultivate the path of discontinuity via creativity, including creativity in business innovations. We engage in the practice of tangled hierarchy in intimate relationships including business bosses and their personal assistants, collaborators in research, and in some special cases, even producers and consumers.

There is very good scientific evidence today that our intentions are important. The neurophysiologist Jacobo Grinberg, in 1993 at the University of Mexico, was able to demonstrate quantum nonlocal communication between two brains. To this end, he first correlated them: the two subjects of his experiment meditated together with the intention of direct (signal-less, nonlocal) communication. After twenty minutes, they were separated (while still continuing their unifying intention), placed in individual Faraday cages (electromagnetically impervious chambers), and each brain was wired up to an electroencephalogram (EEG) machine. One subject was shown a series of light flashes, producing in his or her brain an electrical activity that was recorded in the EEG machine from which an "evoked potential" was extracted with the help of a computer upon subtracting the brain noise. The evoked potential was somehow found to be transferred to the other subject's brain as indicated by the EEG of this subject that gave (upon subtraction of noise) a transferred potential (similar to the evoked potential in phase and strength). This is shown in fig. 9.

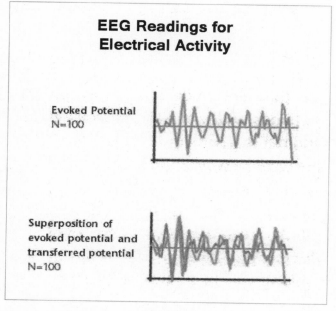

Figure 9

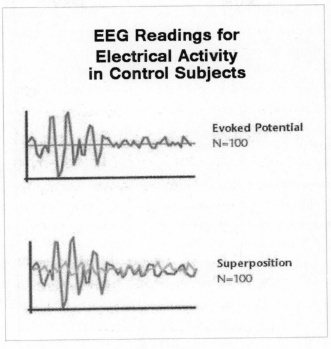

Figure 10

Control subjects (those who do not meditate together or are unable to hold the intention for signal-less communication during the duration of the experiment) do not show any transferred potential (fig. 10).

The experiment demonstrates the nonlocality of brain responses to be sure, and something even more important—nonlocality of quantum consciousness. How else to explain how the forced choice of the evoked response in one subject's brain can lead to the free choice of an (almost) identical response in the correlated partner's brain? As stated above, the experiment since then has been replicated maybe as much as two dozen times. As an example, read the research by the Bastyr university researcher Leana Standish and her collaborators (Standish et al, 2004).

I hope you did not miss one of the most important aspects of the experiment of Grinberg—the power of our intention. Grinberg's subjects intended that their potential nonlocal connection would manifest in demonstrable actuality. Control subjects who could not hold the intention never manifested a transferred potential.

The Power of Intention

The parapsychologist Dean Radin (1999, 2006) has done some more experiments demonstrating the power of intention.

One of his experiments took advantage of the O. J. Simpson trial a few years back. At the time, lots of people were watching TV, and Radin correctly hypothesized that peoples' intention (generated in connection with the TV watching of the trial) would fluctuate widely depending on whether the courtroom drama was intense or ho-hum. So, on the one hand, he let a bunch of psychologists make a plot of the intensity of the courtroom drama (and hence the intensity of peoples' intentions) as a function of real time. On the other hand, in the laboratory he measured the deviation from randomness of what are called random number generators (which translate random quantum events of radioactivity into random sequences of zeroes and ones). He found that the random number generators deviated from randomness maximally precisely at those times when the courtroom drama was high. What does this mean? The philosopher Gregory Bateson told us the meaning, "the opposite of randomness is choice." So the correlation proves the creative power of intention.

In another series of experiments, Radin found that random number generators deviate from randomness in meditation halls when people meditate together (showing high intention of synchrony), but not at a corporate board meeting where egos collide.

Our intentions are important, but even more important is to align our intentions to that of the whole because that's where causal power is. Business leaders, take heed.

The Intention of the Cosmos

How can we know the intention of the cosmos, the whole, quantum consciousness itself in the unmanifest, the unconscious? We look at evolution (Goswami, 2008b).

Evolutionism is not Darwinism. The Christian belief in Creationism is a dogma that clearly does not go anywhere against the vast fossil data proving evolution. But almost as seriously, the fossil data display two major and many minor characteristics that do not support the dogmatic belief of biologists in Darwinism in its entirety either.

To recap, Darwin gave us a two step—chance variations and natural selection driven by the necessity for survival—theory of evolution. In this theory, evolution is continuous, gradual, and very slow. It takes a long time to accumulate the large number of genetic variations to cause macroevolution—large-scale evolution, where say an entirely new organ develops as the species changes to a new one. Since natural selection acts individually on each variation, and since usually the variations are harmful to survival, it is hard to see how the thousands upon thousands of variations needed to develop even a primitive organ from scratch can ever accumulate.

The fossil data suggest two tempos of evolution giving us a hint of a solution. There is a slow tempo, and Darwinism seems to hold for this. This does not lead to major organ development. But there are also very fast epochs during which no fossils are found between one macro-species and another (Eldrege and Gould, 1972). This is where we need to look. In science within consciousness (Goswami, 2008b), the fossil gaps are explained as creative evolution; the fast tempo is the signature of the discontinuous quantum leap of creativity. In quantum creativity, part of the processing is unconscious, and during this phase many little variations can accumulate as quantum possibility. When consciousness sees the gestalt of possibilities producing a new organ, it chooses, the possibility-gestalt collapses, and the organ is expressed.

The fossil data also suggests a one-way-ness in the fossil record: the fossils seem to become more and more complex with time. This is called the biological arrow of time. By looking at the fossil data from the primitive times to now, even a child can deduce that much time has gone by. Neither of the Darwinian mechanisms has any directionality in time. Either step can take us to simplification or to complexification. When we include consciousness and creativity in the equation of evolution, we can invoke purposiveness. What is the purposive intention of the cosmos that drives evolution? The answer is the same as the general purpose of manifestation itself: to make the unmanifest manifest, to make the unconscious conscious, as Carl Jung used to say. Through manifestation, the subtle is represented in matter.

Our capacity for making physical representation of the subtle evolves. First, the capacity for making representations of the vital evolved through the evolution of life via more and more sophisticated organs to represent the living functions such as self-maintenance, self-reproduction, self-other distinction, self-expression, etc. Next, the capacity of making more and more sophisticated representations of the mental evolved. This is the stage of evolution we are in right now.

The mind went through two stages of its evolution already: the physical mind (in which mind gives meaning to the physical sensory world) and the vital mind (in which mind gives meaning to the vital world of feeling). We are now in the evolutionary stage where the mind explores the meaning of meaning itself; in other words, this is the stage of the rational mind.

Our capacity to directly represent the supramental in the physical has not evolved yet. However, there is evolutionary pressure on us in this direction, the primary reason some of us are attracted to creativity and spirituality. Right now this evolutionary pressure is trying to take us to a new stage of mental evolution in which we will collectively engage the mind in exploring our intuitive capacity to make representations of the supramental first in the mind and only then in the brain. The vital body will have to be engaged in that process also in a major way, the whole process leading to positive emotional brain circuits. (See Goswami, 2008b, for further details.)

The entrance requirement for the next stage of evolution of the mind is that we complete the current stage of the rational mind. This is why it is so important that we make meaning processing available for all the members of our species as quickly as possible. I see the paradigm shift from the current materialist economics to the economics of consciousness of utmost urgency from this evolutionary point of view. I really think that the recent economic meltdown is a reminder from consciousness (and others like this will follow if we don't heed the message).

So right now, evolution of the vital and the mental is almost over, and wide open is the evolution of the representations of the supramental which we can presently do only through the intermediary of the mind and the vital. To take this evolution further, we need to learn to hear the whispering of the supramental archetypes and explore them in all our endeavors.

To summarize, the answer to the question, what is the one objective cosmic intention to which we must align for best results at the current state of our evolution? Nonlocal consciousness chooses with always this one thing in mind: this choice must be conducive to better and better representation of the subtle in matter. This explains why evolution takes us from simple species to complex species: the biological arrow of time is not a mystery anymore!

How does a businessperson align himself or herself with the evolutionary movement of consciousness? By creatively exploring the archetype of abundance in business, making new representations such as those being explored in this book. The subtle economy is a veritable goldmine to explore if you understand what I mean.

By exploring abundance and not material wealth alone, you include the good of the world as your motivation for business as well as your personal good. As Wendell Berry says:

> We have lived our lives by the assumption that what is good for us would be good for the world. We have been wrong. We must change our lives so that it will be possible to live by the contrary assumption, that what is good for the world will be good for us.
>
> (Quoted in Eisenstein, p. 379)

You can think romantically. Aligning with the evolutionary movement of consciousness is like putting yourself under a "quantum shield" of protection (Petersen, 2011). Protected, you fearlessly wait for success; because you know that in the long run, you cannot fail.

On Wealth

I have already said that the creative exploration of businesspeople from a consciousness point of view is directed toward making new representations of the archetype of abundance. In its most general form, wealth is representation of the archetype of abundance in the physical world arrived at, as usual, through the intermediaries of the vital and the mental worlds.

Now recall, in the time of Adam Smith, our worldview was shaped by modernism, which in its Cartesian form only recognizes matter and mind, no mention of the vital. We have been generalizing "mind" to include all three subtle worlds, but in truth, Descartes and the modernists of the eighteenth century probably meant only the meaning-giving mind. It was still a very male chauvinist culture; feelings were female occupation, therefore denigrated.

With this in the background, it is not surprising that what we call wealth today is the mental concept of wealth, a representation of the archetype of abundance constructed with the intermediary of the meaning giving mind. So we consider material stuff like real estate and gold and jewels as wealth throughout history. Later the concept of money and its derivatives evolved; with the gold standard gone, these also became wealth. Sometime in between, we started putting value in the representations of meaning in matter: a book, a piece of art, a musical composition recorded in more and more sophisticated ways. These were called cultural capital. For businesses, there are problems here that governments negotiate about, the patent rights of cultural capital.

Nowhere here will you find any reference to the representation of the archetype of abundance through the intermediary of the vital feelings. Now that we are moving away from male chauvinism, shall we look at this from a vital point of view? Vital is represented in the living world as biological forms. The representation of abundance in the vital is the feeling of abundant vitality, the feeling of well-being or vital health, which is a necessary condition of physical and mental health as well.

So we are back to the old adage, health is wealth. Our well-being at all levels—personal, national, and planetary—all are important in counting the wealth of humanity.

So consideration of the archetype of abundance is giving us a huge lesson: we must add "health is wealth" when we think of wealth and capital. This has huge repercussions for developing the new economics (see Chapter 4).

It is useful to generalize a little and talk about our subtle wealth in contrast to gross wealth.

Material wealth today, it is said, is unprecedented in its total quantity in the entire human history. Maybe so. But material wealth has a couple of shortcomings.

There is a great Sufi story. A Sufi master arrives at a king's court. Naturally the king tries his best to impress him with the grandeur of his palace and the kingly ways he and his courtesans live. Then he asks, "Mulla, you like what you see?"

The mulla says, "It is a great hotel."

The king is surprised. "Hotel? It is my palace. I live here."

"But you will die. What happens then?"

The king realized his mistake. This is the problem with palaces and material wealth: you cannot take it with you. Sure, you leave them to your children or relatives. But there is no guarantee that this will benefit the movement of capital after your demise. It is not true that children always acquire their parents' creativity to explore abundance.

Second, today's wealth is unstable. Except at the time of economic stability, the value of the wealth can fluctuate wildly depending on the nature of your acquisitions. In the 1990s, quite a few high-tech millionaires lost their millions, never to gain it back; the same thing happened to many speculators of the housing market during the great recession.

Subtle wealth has a little of the last shortcoming in common with material wealth. The monetary value of cultural capital fluctuates with the worldview underpinnings of the society. For example, if the worldview becomes exclusively materialistic, the value of much cultural capital may disappear altogether, as is the case with books and recorded music today.

On the other hand, however, subtle wealth does have some big advantages over material wealth: for example, it has intrinsic value that enables you to put your internal ecosystems in order and brings you happiness and positivity. And another great advantage of subtle wealth is that you can induce it to others. When subtle wealth is acquired in the form of brain circuits resulting in peaceful behavior on your part, others can imitate your behavior through their "mirror neurons," a great neurological discovery (Ramachandran, 2010). Even more importantly, the brain circuits are correlated with modifications of the associated morphogenetic blueprints, and these modifications are stored nonlocally. In this way, they travel with us when we die and reincarnate (Goswami, 2001). In other words, you can take it with you when you die. Are you intrigued? This is the subject of the next section.

And if we are capable of acquiring the subtle wealth working in a group of manifest tangled hierarchical relationships, the subtle wealth inheritance can become a part of evolving humanity itself through the Lamarckian/Sheldrakian biology of instincts (Sheldrake, 2009, Goswami, 2008b).

So here's an interesting point. With evolution, material wealth has become more and more subtle (money, stocks and bonds, derivatives and on and on it goes); but the subtle wealth has become more tangible.

Quantum Nonlocal Memory and Reincarnation

Is reincarnation possible? Can a part of you beyond your physical body survive your death and even reincarnate in a new physical body, a new you in the future? The new science says yes (Goswami, 2001). The straightforward affirmation comes from the idea of quantum memory. Quantum memory is nonlocal memory; it does not reside in space-time locality, in our brain. Instead, it resides "outside" space-time, the potentiality-realm of quantum nonlocality. Clearly, such memory does not die with the death of the brain. So if a future brain uses the nonlocal memory that you produced in this incarnation, does it not make sense to say that the person with that brain is your reincarnation?

In the ground of consciousness both the physical and the subtle worlds (consisting of a vital energy world of feeling, a mental world of meaning, and a supramental world of archetypal themes) exist as quantum possibilities for consciousness to choose from (Goswami, 1993, 2000). As discussed before, the brain is able to establish an identity for consciousness—the quantum self—by virtue of having a tangled hierarchical system of measurement within it—a perception apparatus and a memory apparatus in circular causality—not reducible to the micro. The physicist Mark Michel and I did some mathematics that suggests that if a quantum stimulus (such as a photon from an object we are looking at) interacts with such a system with repeated reflection in the mirror of memory, and the response of the system is always reinforced, then eventually, in the limit of infinite repetition, the quantum response of the system gives way to a Newtonian "conditioned" response. This is then how loaded with a conditioned brain with a correlated conditioned subtle body, consciousness loses its freedom of choice and appears to be the behaviorally-conditioned ego (Mitchell and Goswami, 1992). In contrast, in events of intuition on creative insights, where we experience the supramental for which we do not have the capacity of making physical memory (representation), the self we experience is always spontaneous, is cosmic. It is the quantum self.

In this way, the ego-character of your habit and learning patterns—*karma* in Sanskrit—constitute nonlocal memory and is stored in the modified nonlinear mathematical equations that guide your conditioned behavior. The meta-mathematical laws behind these equations belong to the supramental domain of reality outside of space and time, and a new baby born in the future beginning his/her life using the same set of meta-mathematical laws as you is your reincarnation.

The full theory of reincarnation asserts that the newborn will add to the conditioned set as it grows up and, in due course, die and take rebirth again and again (Goswami, 2001).

Direct Experimental Verification of Nonlocal Memory

There is direct evidence that suggests that the memory of a learned propensity is nonlocal. In the 1950s, the neurophysiologist Karl Lashley (1950) did an experiment in which he was trying to study the location of the learning of a propensity in the brain. So he trained rats to find cheese in a Y-maze and then systematically began to chop off parts of the rat's brain and test if the propensity remains. Strangely, he found that even with fifty percent of its brain removed, a trained rat finds its way to the cheese. The only viable conclusion is that learned memory of a propensity is nonlocal for which the ancient term is *akashic*, a Sanskrit word meaning outside of space and time. (Another conclusion that the brain is holographic was popular for a while but is no longer considered viable.)

Why is Reincarnation Important for Economics?

East Indians recognized long ago that people behave with three kinds of propensity. Conditioning dominates most people. This propensity is called *tamas* in Sanskrit. A substantial number of people, however, can respond to a situation with creative behavior of which there are two kinds. Some people attack a problem creatively, but they do not go beyond known archetypal contexts of thinking. The solutions they find fit the situation, and their creativity is called situational creativity (*raja* in Sanskrit). A few people, when they see a problem, see it in more than the known archetypal contexts, and the solution they seek and find is a discovery of a new meaning in a new archetypal context. This kind of creativity I call fundamental creativity. The propensity for it is called *sattva* in Sanskrit. In recent parlance, *sattva* is "out of the box" thinking even in the dimension of the archetypes.

The explanation of the three *gunas* lies in the phenomenon of reincarnation, which is fully supported by the quantum model that part of our memory—patterns of habit—is nonlocal. Initially, new souls are all *tamasic*. Over a few reincarnations, *raja* develops. Eventually, after many a reincarnation, for "old" souls, *raja* gives way to *sattva*. The process involves a cleaning up of the unconscious which is important for creative processing. Of course, now that we understand the theory of all this, the process of cleaning up can be expedited.

The classification of people into *sattvic*, *rajaic*, and *tamasic* is highly relevant to economics and business. In general, the movers and shakers of our society, and this includes business people, are people of predominant *raja*. You may recognize the Sanskrit word *raja* (which means king) that is the root word for *raja*. People of *raja* have the same empire-building tendency as the kings of the olden days. In terms of creativity, when these people make a discovery in a new context, they will use the discovery in many new situations either solo or combining several old contexts. This is obviously akin to empire building. Sometimes this is called "horizontal" creativity whereas fundamental creativity is "vertical" creativity. The words of the economist Joseph Schumpeter explain their difference perfectly, "Add successfully as many mail coaches as you please, you never get a railway thereby."

In contrast, the traditional labor force of routine jobs consists generally of *tamasic* people who, without fundamental creativity and without the drive of kingly expansion, simply succumb to the drudgery of conditioned living.

There is one more useful concept in connection with reincarnation. The Eastern literature on reincarnation contains one more concept related to karma (habit pattern)—ambient karma (*prarabdha* in Sanskrit), karma that we bring to bear in this life. The idea somehow is that we don't bring all of our accumulated karma via all of our past lives to the current life we are living. Instead, we bring a select number of them.

Surprise of surprise that this idea has been verified by empirical data through the research of a past-life therapist named David Cliness. Cliness has studied numerous subjects who have recalled many past lives. Curiously, he found that people don't bring all their previously learned contexts and propensities from their past lives to the present one. He used the language of the card game poker to describe the situation. It is as if one plays poker with their learned contexts and propensities and chooses five out of the deck of the available fifty-two.

We can theorize following the Eastern psychology. Why do we bring a specific choice of ambient karma? Because we want to concentrate on a particular learning agenda for this life. This learning agenda carries the name of another Sanskrit word *dharma* (spelled with a lower case "d" to distinguish from the word *Dharma* with a capital "D" which denotes the Whole, Tao).

This idea of your life consisting of fulfilling a learning agenda may remind you of the wonderful film *Groundhog Day* in which the hero reincarnates (sort of) from one life to another with a single learning agenda which is a biggie—love.

One more thing I can say about dharma from the Eastern literature. When we fulfill our learning agenda that we bring to the current life, life becomes full of bliss. To the contrary, if we find bliss in our life, we can conclude that we must be following our dharma. The mythologist Joseph Campbell used to say, "Follow your bliss." He knew.

So if you are in business and it makes you happy, good. You are following your agenda. I think one of the problems today is that there are many people in economics and business who are opportunistic; they are just doing it for the money, not following their dharma. This is why such peoples' activities are dangerous and potentially harmful to the business of business.

I have a fond wish. We the do-gooders of the world sometimes wonder why businesspeople are singularly disinterested in the well-being of future generations (the businessman Katsuhiko Yazaki [1994] calls this attitude "now-ism"). Perhaps if they knew about the scientific nature of reincarnation that we are discovering today, they would realize that they themselves would be part of the future generations, and their view of callous business practices would undergo a radical change.

Science Within Consciousness: A Summary

The basic elements of the developing science within the primacy of consciousness are as follows:

- Consciousness is the ground of all being. All objects, material or mental, exist as quantum possibilities in this ground of being. In other words, the laws of movement of all objects obey quantum physics.

- The quantum possibilities of consciousness are four-fold: material (which we sense); vital (the energy that we feel, primarily at the chakras and only secondarily involving the brain "molecules of emotions"; see Goswami, 2008a); mental (with which we think meaning); and supramental archetypes of physical laws, mental meaning, vital functions, and ethical discriminations (which we intuit). The material is called gross because we experience it as external to us; and the others make up the subtle domain of our experience that we experience privately and internally.

- Consciousness chooses from among its possibilities to make actual events of experience. What spiritual tradition calls downward causation by a nonmaterial agency (most often called God) is now recognized as the result of choice from a non-ordinary state of consciousness where we are all one and where the interconnectedness of all things allow signal-less (technically called nonlocal) communication. *No signals to mediate, no dualism*! Choice and collapse requires a tangled hierarchy that produces a self-referential identification of consciousness with a tangled hierarchical measuring device such as a living cell or the brain. In this way, quantum measurement enables consciousness to represent itself in living matter, a representation we experience as subject or self.

- Is there a criterion for the choice of nonlocal consciousness in making a collapse? The criterion is objective—to take purposive evolution of manifest consciousness further by allowing the evolution of better and better representations of the subtle. Right now, this evolutionary pressure is involved with evolving brain representations of the supramental archetypes through the intermediary of the mind.

- Contrary to Newtonian physics, in quantum physics, both continuous and discontinuous movements occur. Continuous movements reign in the movement of possibilities in what is called the unconscious (which is synonymous with the unmanifest nonlocal consciousness). Choice leading to collapse (transformation) of possibility into actuality is discontinuous. We experience such discontinuous movements (called quantum leaps) in our creative experiences of aha! insight. The aha signifies the surprise of the discontinuity and the newness of the insight.

- The subject/self experienced in a creative quantum leap has immediacy—we call it the quantum self. However, memories produce conditioning, and conditioned responses give rise to a continuous and predictable stream of consciousness, the experiencer of which we call the ego. In the conditioned ego, we have the limited choice between conditioned alternatives, which is useful in consumerism. There is also the all-important freedom to say "no" to conditioning.

- The three pillars of quantum physics that stand out in the new paradigm are: nonlocality, discontinuity, and tangled hierarchy.

- When consciousness chooses from the possibilities the actual event of its experience (with one or more of the physical, vital, mental, and supramental components), the physical (the manifestation of which is compulsory for possibilities to collapse into actuality) has the opportunity of making representations of the subtle. The physical is like computer hardware; the subtle is represented in it as software.

- Finally, the science within consciousness that the quantum worldview is gifting us is an inclusive, dogma-free science.

PART TWO

What Quantum Economics
of Consciousness
Can Do for Us

FOUR

The Conceptual Foundations of Quantum Economics

As the psychologist Abraham Maslow pointed out, besides our basic material need, we have an entire hierarchy of needs. The idea did not begin with Maslow, however; the discovery that we have an entire hierarchy of needs is very old. The Jewish Kabbala codified in the fifteenth century talks about our having five bodies, four of them nonmaterial, and each having function(s) that give rise to needs. Actually, the earliest reference is found in a story told in one of the Hindu Upanishads.

A curious boy wants to find out the nature of reality. So he asks his father—a wise teacher. Father is pleased. But instead of answering, he says, "Why don't you meditate and find out for yourself?"

The son meditates for a while, gets an idea, and goes to his father for verification.

"Reality is matter—the stuff of which my body is made, the stuff of the food I eat." The father approves.

"Yes," he says, "but meditate some more."

The boy goes away, meditates, and after a while, based on his experience no doubt, has another idea. "Reality is the energy that I feel," he declares to his father this time. The father approves but encourages him to meditate some more. The boy does what he is told; soon he has another idea. "Reality is mind, the vehicle with which we think and explore meaning, Father."

Father says, "Yes, but go deeper."

The son is perseverant. This time he meditates and meditates and finally discovers intuition, with shiver in his spine and all that and runs to his father. "Father, Father. I found it, I found it. Reality is stuff from which our sciences come, our values to live by." He is talking about the archetypes of course.

A smile breaks on his father's face. But he says, "Good. But go deeper, my son."

No matter. The son is really motivated now. He meditates again and discovers the oneness of everything, that reality is one and only, with no boundary. His being fills with joy and a certainty comes to him. This is it. He does not go back to his father anymore; he has no need to confirm this time.

The Upanishads refer to the boy's discoveries by the Sanskrit word "*Kosha*" that we have been calling bodies in previous chapters. The major shortcoming of the Adam Smith's capitalist economics is the ignoring of peoples' higher needs arising from the nonmaterial bodies in setting up the economic equation of needs and gifts—demand and supply, consumption and production. Following Maslow, but modifying his theory according to the insights of science within consciousness (see Chapter 3), we can easily see what these higher needs are. And in truth, the way our societies have evolved in the past sixty years, any person today can feel the need for more vitality—vital energy—no thanks to environmental degradation. Most of us feel the hunger for meaning; you can only consume meaningless mind-stuff and information so much. Even kids get tired of it occasionally. And although materialism has been preaching material values for all these decades, why are religions still alive in America and the world? In spite of scientific materialist bias in the education today, a significant portion of our young people are aware of their need for higher values. Obviously, our need for supramental and spiritual values transcends the efforts of materialist top-down attempts to prejudice us against them; it did not work for Soviet Russia, and it is not working for democratic America. Some people just know that—via intuition, what else—there are values whose pursuit brings us satisfaction, closer to wholeness and happiness.

Something does happen though, which is a tangible effect of all this propaganda in public schools, institutions of higher education, and, of course, the powerful media. What happens is value confusion. What happens is a distinct lack of intelligence directed towards the processing of nonmaterial values such as feelings, meanings, and archetypes. So we are aware of our needing some things, but we are so emphatically told in so many voices that all our experiences emanate from matter that we become confused as to their nature.

In the new science, we can recognize from the get-go that we not only should have physical needs but also needs in all the other dimensions of our experience—feeling, thinking, intuition, and happiness. Unfortunately, the worldview and cultural changes in America since Maslow's introduction of the concept of hierarchy of needs have created some camouflage of these needs. Also, don't forget that even the young man of the Upanishad story above had to meditate before discovering the higher needs. Today, you can recognize your higher needs through a little analysis with the help of scientific knowledge:

1. How do you know you are not satisfying your vital energy needs? As discussed before, feelings, the movements of vital energy, originate in the body at the chakra points. But face it! Except for rare occasions of crisis or creativity, you don't feel many vital movements in your body. The stresses of modern life make it difficult even to feel thirst or hunger, which, of course, are designed not only for us to be aware of our need for water or food but also, at a more succinct level, to be aware of our need for the vitality water and food provide. So one way is to develop sensitivity to the feelings in the body. This is the positive way. There is also a negative way. That we have the urge for the satisfaction of vital-energy needs (vital nourishment in addition to the physical) shows up in our negative emotional behavior. Negative emotions are a tell-tale sign that we have fallen deficient in satisfying our vital-energy needs at the three lowest chakras. Today's urban life is full of emotional stress that causes the negative emotions to erupt. Emotion is thought plus feeling, but unfortunately, most of us experience emotions as brain phenomena. Evolution has given us the instinctual brain circuits in the limbic brain. The feelings evoked by these circuits are what we ordinarily experience, contaminated with meaning given by the mind and codified in the neocortex as cortical brain circuits in experiences of negative emotions. When you develop sensitivity and trace your emotional experiences back to their visceral origins, you will begin to experience "pure" feelings without likes and dislikes attached to them. And then you will be acutely aware of the lack of vitality in your lower chakras, literally as if vital energy has run out of these chakras. So when you experience a negative emotion in response to a stressor, it is a cue to

acknowledge your vital energy need, and that is when you need to nourish these three low chakras the most. And implicitly you know this, too. When under emotional stress, who hasn't felt the need to eat chocolate or a snack? Obviously, when you eat a snack to deal with your anxiety, you are feeding vital energy to the third chakra; but because of the lack of clarity of the situation, you are trying to feed vital energy with non-nutritious food. For some people the tell-tale sign is weird horniness, which these people try to deal with using unhealthy addictive pornography. They are responding to the crisis of vital energy depletion at the second chakra. A depletion of the vital energy at the root chakra gives you fear for which the response often is flight. If you lack vitality in your root chakra, you are not rooted enough to stand still and fight.

2. Since millennia, we also have intuited, as part of our intuition experience, positive emotions that originate from positive "high chakra" feelings such as love, expressiveness, clarity, and satisfaction. Of course, the neocortical circuits give these feelings mental interpretations before they become experience. Our spiritual traditions and religions developed in part to help us cultivate these positive emotions in order to balance the negative. In fact, this has given us our civilization. Materialists can confuse you about the nature of your negative emotions—whether they are of material origin or not—but they cannot claim that these positive emotions have anything to do with the brain. In this way, what the kid in the Upanishadic story above discovered through meditation, you are discovering through opening your mind toward the new science. And we all will be better for it that today everyone can do so. Our future depends on discovering vital energy technologies to feed energy directly to our chakras. Our evolution depends on recognizing these positive emotional

needs and cultivating and harvesting them. This vital need is most basic to recognize for the aborning quantum economics.

3. Are you aware of the need for the pursuit of meaning, especially the pursuit of new mental meaning that requires creativity? Here the camouflage is the over-emphasis of information technology in our culture. Information processing has no end to it, it is addictive, and it can fill up all your spare time, or have you noticed? Trivial pursuits can keep you busy from boredom; but without new meaning, the energies of love, expression, clarity, and satisfaction go begging, their intuitions fail to grab you. Thus, the preponderance of dissatisfaction in our society, and thus the epidemic of depression. These are your telltale signs that you are lacking meaning processing in your life. Materialists will say that mind is brain, otherwise mind-body dualism. The new science, however, has resolved all the philosophical difficulty against acknowledging that mind is different from the brain, that mind is represented in the brain, and that the purpose of our lives is to make new representation of the meaning of the supramental archetypes. In this way, the new science helps you to argue your way around the materialists' clamor to the contrary and let you discover your meaning needs.

4. How do you go about discovering your need for the pursuit of supramental archetypes such as altruism, compassion, truth, beauty, wholeness, justice, and, of course, in the context of economics, abundance? Materialists deny the existence of these archetypes because they cannot explain them. Creationists deny evolution, in spite of fossil data, because they cannot explain evolution. Accepting evolution, they feel, will destroy their faith in the Bible. In the same vein, today's typical materialist scientist would rather give up the notion of eternal truth than give

up scientific materialism. But ask: Where is real science without the search for truth? Can there be real beauty without the artful observer? And how can prosperity come without pursuing the archetype of abundance? Can we truly explore health without the awareness of the archetype of wholeness? Can we follow ethics in business without cultivating goodness in people? These are hard questions for today's people to address, I know. But the new science is showing us the way. Meanwhile, all you do is recognize the validity of your own intuitions, via which the supramental archetypes talk to you even today, and the validity of the new science. And indeed, if your vital energy and meaning needs are satisfied, that is a definite help.

5. Finally, we must not forget the need for happiness. The confusion there is the insistent clamor of materialists that happiness is nothing but pleasure, that it is simply having a lot of molecules of pleasure in the brain. We have tried pleasure as a substitute for happiness under the aegis of scientific materialism. We have the Playboy mansion to show for it and the readily available porn on the Internet. Our movies and music and pastime readings are full of sex and food and other pleasure pursuits. But why then are we looking for committed relationships so much so that even gay people are being allowed to explore it with societies' recognition and approval? Because we know in our heart that "everybody needs somebody someday" to make him or her whole.

Your conceptual quandary is due to the materialist assertion that matter is the ground of being. And matter consists of independent separate objects. Wholeness is bah humbug! But is it? Quantum physics tells us otherwise: consciousness is the ground of being, not matter. And consciousness, beyond our ego-separateness, is one interconnected whole, albeit unconscious in us. It is separateness of subject and object, which manifest awareness is associated with, that is illusion. It is separateness that sometimes takes us away from wholeness—happiness.

The religions get this one better. In Christianity, separateness is called hell—suffering; heaven is where wholeness and happiness is. A Taoist story clarifies it for you. You are watching in hell invitees at a banquet with delicious food laid out, and people are trying to eat their food to no avail. Alas! Their forks are of table length! In heaven you watch with fascination invitees eating effortlessly the same food in the same layout. Each person is feeding the person sitting opposite at the table.

So here is the learned conclusion: In addition to the satisfaction of physical needs, capitalist economics must address the subtle and spiritual needs. Now that you have discovered the ladder of needs, recognize that this ladder of needs is not entirely hierarchical. There is feedback between the higher and the lower needs. If you satisfy higher needs, the urge to satisfy lower needs actually decreases. When Newton was in the throes of creativity, his sister had to remind him to eat his meals. And you don't have to be a Newton to realize this. The opposite is also true. If your lower needs are satisfied, the urge for satisfying higher needs increases. Try it and see the validity of heeding to the poet who wrote:

> *If you have five dollars, go get a hamburger.*
> *But if you have ten, oh connoisseur, buy some flowers*
> *To enjoy after your tummy is full.*

In this way, the strategy for a more suited quantum economics of consciousness for our time than the Adam Smith capitalism of the eighteenth century is to address all the needs simultaneously, not one after the other.

Adam Smith's capitalism was developed as an economics of physical well-being based on the satisfaction of our conditioned physical ego-needs. In contrast, quantum economics, being an economics of consciousness, must be an economics of holistic well-being based on the satisfaction of our ego needs of both physical and the subtle. And more. Quantum economics from the get-go must cater to the needs of the quantum self as well, and that means paying attention to nonlocality (as in cooperation), discontinuity (as in creativity) and tangled hierarchy (as in our two-way personal relationships).

This extension of capitalism to include higher subtle human needs (in addition to basic material survival needs) and the recognition of the needs of the higher quantum self (in addition to the consumer ego self) fits nicely with the etymological definition of economics. The word *economics* originates from two Greek words: *oikos* meaning place and *nomus* meaning management. In this way, economics is about the management of the place that we live. If you think about it, we don't live only in the physical world; we also live in the vital world of feeling, the mental world of meaning, and even take occasional forays into the supramental world of archetypal values such as goodness, abundance, love, justice, beauty, and truth. Naturally, a properly developed capitalism must include the management of all the worlds in which we live and which we visit.

Finally, where is the profit motive in the spiritual arena? Can we have capitalism without profits and profit motives? But there is profit! The religious culture of a bygone era has denied the acceptance of a material reward in exchange for a spiritual gift somebody shares with you. If somebody shares her exploration of meaning with you in the form of a book or a music video, you already enthusiastically pay for it. Right? Similarly, you happily pay for a masseur's vital energy gift of a massage; he is making a living sharing his gift, it benefits you, and you appreciate and pay, and both are happy. Why then the hesitation to pay for a sage's love? It's the culture! Money cannot buy love, money cannot buy happiness, we are told repeatedly. Who does not want to be rewarded for a good deed for which he or she is instrumental? And everybody needs to satisfy survival needs anyway. Doesn't that cost money? In the olden days, "sinful" people of power provided the money to the churches who supported the spiritual people. So the sage's love was not really free. Today, similarly, the Church supports a lot of highly spiritual people who provide you much needed help when you need counseling. But isn't the Church receiving tax breaks from the government, and who is paying for it? You, of course, but indirectly. Capitalism works better.

You can still ask: Are spiritual people motivated to make profit? When Jesus says that if you give, you get back hundred-fold, he is not talking about material profit. He is talking about subtle profit. People who produce "goods" in the subtle arena are much aware of the possible profits. They enjoy these profits, and as expected, the more they profit, the better they become in their production. So the gifted people in the arena of subtle production do not lack in motivation. We need only further motivate subtle production by supplementing the subtle satisfaction of the producer with additional gross monetary compensation so that he/she can devote to the task, not as amateurs supported by somebody else's philanthropy, but as professionals—full time. Our assumption has been that this will corrupt the system; so we create the intermediary of the rich benefactors and church-like organizations. But history shows that does not eliminate corruption. What will eliminate corruption is capitalism, capitalistic competition. We will pay only when we get benefit, not because an organization endorses it.

Micro Economics of the Subtle

Economics is about production-consumption, demand-supply, prices and all that. How does that kind of stuff work for our subtle needs? Let's talk about these micro details.

Production of vital energy can be accomplished in many ways: Forestation—plants and trees and their products—food grains, fruits, and vegetable—have abundant vital energy. We mainly get this vital energy from the food we eat; but some of it comes through breathing the same air that we share with the plant kingdom. In this way, even indoor plants and young pets can keep us supplied with needed vital energy. This is a level of production that we still engage in albeit unconsciously, but modern culture in the form of food extracts, excessive cooking, deforestation, environmental pollution, use of pesticides in agriculture, genetic engineering of our food grains supply, etc., is reducing this form of vital energy production. At this level there is plenty of opportunity for innovative and creative deployment of new forms and revitalization of old forms.

Water has a long evolutionary history with us humans; we were water creatures before we came to the land. Therefore, water remains a source of vital energy for us. And again, this source is being compromised today because of environmental pollution and the excessive chemical treatments needed to get rid of the material pollution. Unfortunately, the chemical treatment most likely removes the correlation of the water with the vital energy from which we derive our vital nourishment. Thus, revitalization of water is necessary to give us back this precious source of vital energy.

In the same vein, there are many products that we use today—diet food and nutritional substitutes, cosmetics, perfume, and such. Your vitamins and your Botox have their origin in organic substances. But the extraction of the material essence from the original gets rid of the vital energy that came with the original bulk—it is correlated with the bulk form, not the molecules. The new science says that the nutrition we derive from these products would take a quantum leap if we revitalize them. We already have the technology for such revitalization (see Chapter 10).

Of course, when we don't receive adequate vital energy nutrition, we may succumb to what the new science recognizes as vital energy disease (Goswami, 2004, 2011). Health and healing in the vital energy dimension is a major success story of alternative medicine practices such as Traditional Chinese Medicine (TCM), the Indian Ayurveda, homeopathy, naturopathy, Reiki, etc. There needs to be a lot of change in our mindset before we fully utilize this area of production and consumption.

We all can get into vital energy production not only enough for our own consumption in our "down" time but also to keep our environment vitalized by cultivating positive health in society. People of positive health radiate positive vital energy not only through breathing with others the same air, or using the same material stuff with them, but also through direct nonlocal transfer via consciousness. When is positive health? When your vital energies and their correlation with the body organs are in balance and harmony. If you are already healthy, the best way to cultivate positive health is to participate regularly in vital energy practices: yoga and pranayama (East Indian breathing practices), Tai Chi and martial arts, aikido, etc. This area of vital energy production is education-related and is already an economically active area. But there is enormous scope for expansion.

Is it really true that people of positive vital health radiate vital energy that somebody in their presence can get nourishment from? Yes. Measurements show that if a Chi Gong master "throws" (that is just another word for intention) good Chi on a plant, the plant's rate of growth is enhanced (Sansier, 1991). In this way, it should be clear to you that such people of positive vital health as a Chi Gong or Aikido or pranayama master are no less than valuable human capital.

This brings into consideration the very important third level of vital energy production—the recognition and cultivation of talented and gifted in this area. There are some infusions of Tai Chi and Aikido masters from China and Japan and kundalini yogis from India, and there is some local cultivation as well in economically advanced countries like the USA, but there is enormous scope here for entrepreneurial investment. In addition to teaching others, these people are literally human capital in vital energy because they can vitalize their local environment by their mere presence, a process called induction, which works through quantum nonlocality and maybe even through mirror neurons.

As for production of mental meaning, we already have some of the ways in place in the contexts of the arts, books, music, movies, and entertainment industry. All of these industries have the capacity of producing positive vital energy (positive emotions) as well. However, much of this industry has been bogged down in the negativity and existential cynicism of a materialist culture. If seeing a movie makes you depressed, it is not serving your higher needs, is it? But we *can* shift the emphasis from negativity to meaningfulness and positivity as we adapt to capitalism under a quantum economics.

The greatest challenge of a conscious economy is to create meaningful jobs for the labor force so that people can explore personal meaning on the job. You may have noticed that things are already moving in that direction. One of Adam Smith's historically useful ideas was division of labor that was used to produce the assembly line. This banished meaning from the life of the assembly line worker for quite a while, and then a miracle happened. In Japan, they found that most of the boring routine work of the assembly line could be done by robots, which new technology had made available. Even more important, they found that if a single person, by giving his or her work meaning and satisfaction, does the rest of the work that robots cannot do, the quality of the product increases substantially. "Quality is job one" became the mantra of industries so modified. (Of course, job satisfaction is underrated by many employers even today.)

The second development in this direction has been produced by the phenomenon of outsourcing of some types of routine labor jobs to developing countries, taking advantage of cheap labor available there. There is danger here, no doubt, of lost jobs in the developed economy from which jobs are being outsourced. But there is also opportunity. When routine jobs for producing consumer goods are no longer available, the challenge is for producers to innovate and develop new technology. You must have jobs for your would-be consumers to maintain demand; that is how capitalism works. Invariably, this creates meaningful jobs for the labor force, an opportunity. Is the labor in developed economy ready for the challenge these opportunities present? You bet. The Obama administration's emphasis of green-energy industries succeeded at least in part; both industrialists and labor were ready for the challenge. This is a clear example of the creation of meaningful jobs.

Traditionally, it has been the job of the educational institutions, schools, and universities to provide the labor force for business and industries to employ. When America was founded, these institutions doled out liberal education. The word *liberal* has the same etymological origin as the word *liberty* that means freedom. A truly liberal education frees the mind from the known and prepares one to explore the new. But with scientific materialism at the helm, meaning gave way to information, and creativity took a back seat in higher education, which was preparing a labor force for our businesses and industries skilled to follow other peoples' meaning, not explore their own. Who benefits most from this trend, and therefore, who are the most vocal supporters? The multinational corporations, of course.

Meanwhile, businesses and industries today complain about lack of innovation to no avail. The challenge is to free the higher education institutions from their shackles of not only scientific materialism but also tax exemption, endowments from alumni, big government research grants for big science, etc., that maintain the status quo and bring them to free market capitalism.

Once again, the question of cultivation of the talented and gifted to creative people of meaning production comes up, and we must recognize that with new science, we finally understand the creative process in full (see Chapter 9). Therefore, this area can expand like never before.

The production of supramental and spiritual energy requires renewed effort right now. In the olden days, spiritual organizations likes churches, temples, synagogues, mosques, and the like cultivated and produced supramental and spiritual intelligence in their leaders and practitioners. Nowadays, these organizations are more interested in influencing mundane politics than investing in the supramental. But make no mistake about it; it can be done although we may have to develop new spiritual educational organizations to do it.

In ancient Rome, the rich elite employed philosophers to feed themselves meaning. In later times, perhaps the most effective means of production (and dissemination) of meaning and supramental energy were traveling monks (called *sadhus* in India; in the West, troubadours are an example). This we can revive; to some extent the many new-age conferences on consciousness and spirituality are already serving this purpose but at a very small scale. In these conferences with or without group meditations, as some parapsychology experiments show, people can experience nonlocal consciousness and hence can take creative leaps to the supramental domain (Dean Radin, 2006). We are witnessing a new form of education that can easily be practiced even in workplaces.

We can move one step ahead. Suppose all sizable business and corporations set up a department of subtle energy production that will cultivate and employ creative people of positive health, people of positive mental health, and even people of supramental intelligence for the purpose of creating a positive subtle energy environment. Imagine you are a worker in such a corporation and are inflicted by mood swings of negative emotions. Suppose your in-house "doctor" can balance your negativity with his or her positivity simply by setting you in his or her proximity. How much productivity is saved! If accounted for properly, such saving of productivity could easily support such a subtle energy department. The good news is that Google may be already headed in this direction.

Now to the question of consumption. Because the vital and mental are representable in us, they can be consumed both by local and nonlocal means. For example, if we eat a fresh vegetable that is organically grown, we feel instant vitality. And if we see good theater, it cultivates the processing of meaning in us, sometimes even new meaning. When we partake in good meaningful entertainment, we also feel positive emotions; we are consuming both meaning and vitality. As we consume vital energy, meaning, and positive emotions regularly, life becomes positive in orientation; we become optimistic, and we look forward to things. Our consumption improves our health and well-being and our quality of life.

Then one day, a quantum leap of our attitude takes place; we begin to understand the differences between *pleasure, joy,* and *happiness.* We get pleasure out of a product or activity whenever the stimulus excites our pleasure centers in the brain. Pleasure is mechanical, predictable, and always arises in association with molecules of pleasure like the endorphins. Joy comes when we have a sudden positive feeling or discover a new meaning along with a positive emotion in association with an intuitive experience of the quantum self. And happiness is the experience of wholeness. As our subtle energy consumption occurs more in association with joy and wholeness, and less with pleasure, we realize that we ourselves have the potential to become producers and explorers of new meaning and positive emotions.

How does such a quantum leap happen? The vital energy practices as well as mental practices such as meditation have a side effect: these practices slow us down. Research is showing creativity is quantum creativity involving quantum thinking. Ordinary thinking is one-level thinking—machine thinking for hyperactive fast people. When we slow down, we partake in quantum thinking—two-level thinking. In between thoughts, we are unconscious, and our thoughts can expand as waves of possibility, becoming bigger and bigger pools of possibility for consciousness to choose from. Obviously with quantum thinking, our chance for choosing the new is greater (Goswami, 2014).

Meditation can be designed for another useful side effect—present centeredness. Ordinarily, "we live before and after and pine for what is not;" these habits create a lot of unfinished residue, cluttering up our unconscious and preventing effective quantum thinking. Meditation suitably designed, restores present-centeredness and frees up the unconscious once again.

Supramental energy consumption is nonlocal, but it requires local triggers. There are scientists who subscribe to the so-called

Maharishi effect according to which the spiritual and supramental energy generated by group meditation is consumed automatically in the local vicinity. Data is cited with claims of crime
reduction in big cities where TM (Transcendental Meditation)
groups perform such meditation. However, this is controversial,
and I am not advocating it without additional steps taken to
assure *triggering*. A purely quantum mechanical consumption of
your spiritual energy by me requires that I be correlated with you
by some means or other—triggering. For example, experiments
by the neurophysiologist Jacobo Grinberg and his collaborators
suggest that if two people intend together, they become nonlocally correlated, but it could be simpler than that (Grinberg et
al, 1994). There are many anecdotes of how people feel peace in
the presence of a sage. So just being locally present may trigger
nonlocal correlation and consumption. Experiments on distant
healing, where a prayer group's meditation on a list of names
enhances the healing of people at a distance who are recovering
from surgery, show how simple it is to correlate people enough
to effect healing (Byrd, 1988). But still undeniably, some local
interaction seems to be needed.

In Chapter 1, I spoke of Laughing Baba and the phenomenon of induction. I have experienced this phenomenon more
than once. Back in the 1980s, there was a time in my life when
I was very unhappy, and my unhappiness was affecting my mar-
riage. In short, my wife and I fought a lot. Circumstances sent
us to the ashram of an American philosopher named Franklin
Merrell Wolff situated in a small town named Lone Pine in California high up in the Sierra. Franklin was ninety-seven years old
at the time. When I tried talking quantum physics with him, he
refused. "It gives me headaches," he said. Since I liked him, and
there was nothing else for me to do to spend the long summer
afternoons, I just sat with him in his garden. He napped while

I vegetated. This went on for a while. Then I started hearing people talk about a "delightful physicist" on the grounds and became curious.

"I'd like to meet him," I said, and everybody laughed. I was that physicist! A little internal checking showed that I had had no marital disharmony for a quite a while. What produced the transformation? I am convinced that it was the local proximity of Franklin that triggered in me a quantum nonlocal consciousness whose wholeness made me happy. (Incidentally, as soon as we left the campus, within a few minutes, my wife and I started fighting, right in the car.)

Can we commercially produce people like Laughing Baba and Franklin? I think with the new science, we have the technology. In some people, the sex drive, even the drive for survival and self-maintenance, is very low. If we find these people, isolate them from negative emotional stimuli, and give them a crash course on inner creativity (Goswami, 2014), these people can go directly to self-realization and enlightenment without going through the arduous practices of psychological maturation. The East Indians have been using such a short-cut to enlightenment for millennia.

The best part of the story of subtle energy products is that they are relatively inexpensive and will remain inexpensive. The subtle energies have no limits; we can consume a sage's love all we wish since the supply is not going to diminish. There is no zero-sum game in the subtle. There may be a bit of material cost of production. And, of course, the ubiquitous labor cost. So one has to put a monetary price tag on subtle products to offset this, then add a reasonable profit to be sure, which may not be such a bad idea because it enables people to be more serious about their intentions when they consume subtle products. Here also is an opportunity for the government to subsidize the subtle industry. How will that happen? Perhaps entrepreneurs and philanthropists can initiate the subtle industry; eventually societies will recognize the benefits and use their vote to influence the government.

Can we even quantify holistic well-being? For the basic needs, the GNP (gross national product) or GDP (gross domestic product) is a fairly good indicator. Can we generalize the concept of GDP for the quantum economics of consciousness?

Redefining the GDP

To most materialists, science has to do deal only with the material world, because only the material can be quantified, can be measured reliably. We have to eradicate this prejudice. Can we measure our welfare or well-being from GDP? No. Both research in America and Japan in the 1960s show that the rate of GDP growth does not keep synchrony with the growth of well-being (Daly and Cobb, 1994). We need to complement the concept of GDP with an index of well-being.

We cannot measure vital energy, prana, or chi in the same sense that we can measure a quantity of rice, but it is not true that we cannot measure vital energy at all. For example, once you develop the needed sensitivity, when vital energy moves out of you, your feeling at the particular chakra will tell you the story, and the same is true of vital energy excesses. When vital energy moves out of the navel chakra, you feel insecurity, butterflies in the stomach. When vital energy moves in to the same chakra, the feeling is quite different, that of self-confidence or pride.

Similarly, meaning processing gives you a feeling of satisfaction in the crown chakra because vital energy moves in there. So we can quantify meaning in our life by the "amount" of satisfaction we derive from it.

Even the supramental can be measured. If we perform a good deed for someone, an example of altruism, we feel good. Researchers have found that giving consistently lifts even depressed people into lightness. This is not because there is any particular influx of vitality in any of the chakras, but because our separateness is gone for a time. With love, it is even easier to fall into unity and happiness because we not only feel the bliss of not being separate from the whole, but we also feel vital energy in the heart chakra. And both can be used as a measure.

Of course, this kind of measurement is not accurate in the sense material measurements are; they are indeed subjective and always a little vague. But if we give up the prejudice that only accurate and objective measurements count, what then? Then we can certainly establish criteria to judge a nation's net gain or loss of currency (feeling, meaning, godliness, and wholeness) in the subtle and spiritual domain. We must note that quantum physics has already replaced the doctrine of complete objectivity (strong objectivity) by weak objectivity in which subjectivity is permitted so long as we make sure that our conclusions do not depend upon particular subjects (d'Espagnat, 1983).

For example, we can send questionnaires to people to keep an ongoing tab on their feelings, meanings, supramental, and spiritual life (or lack thereof) as an economic person, *homo economicus*; in other words, when he or she is dealing with economic matters—consumption and production. When we tally all this for the entire year, we can calculate easily an index of vital, mental, supramental and spiritual well-being. This combined index then will complement the GDP—all goods and services produced in the material economy of the country, which is the index for our material well-being.

In the same way, we can estimate the contribution to the vital, mental, supramental, and spiritual energies from a particular production organization.

Some examples will show that well-being in the subtle and spiritual dimensions really does count, and we are missing something in our economics because we do not count it. In Hindu India (before the tenth century), the country and culture was fundamentally spiritual. The economy was feudal, of course, but according to all accounts (not only indigenous but also of foreign visitors) people were satisfied and happy albeit the prevalence of the caste system. What gives? Hindu India certainly had wealth but much less than today's America. In a spiritual culture, a lot of good vital energy, mental meaning, supramental values, and spiritual wholeness are cultivated; that is the reason. The subtle wealth reduced the need for material wealth and more than made up for the lack of it. The same is true for Tibet until the recent takeover by communist China. The communist leaders of China sometimes tout the rise in the material standard of living of Tibetan people under their rule. If only they were aware of the huge dip in the Tibetan peoples' happiness index! (Of course, they don't really care.)

Neither the Indian nor the Tibetan cultures were perfect because they did limit meaning processing by the lower classes, so evolution of consciousness eventually caught up with these cultures. But so much energy was generated in the subtle/spiritual domains in the ancient Indian culture that even today, when there is real poverty in the material domain, the Indian poor in the villages are quite happy because they continue to inherit and maintain their subtle and spiritual wealth. If Karl Marx had seen that, it might make him rethink whether the "exploited" classes are always unhappy!

Another example is the Native American culture of the old. There was so much of subtle wealth there that nobody even cared to own material wealth. They treated material wealth in the same way as subtle wealth—globally , collectively, without personal possessiveness, and without playing a zero-sum game.

Meanwhile, our efforts of quantifying subtle energy measurements are beginning to pay off. The next section is devoted to share the new research.

Truly Objective Measurements in the Subtle Domain

Can we measure vital energy with a physical instrument? The answer is no, by definition. Vital energy and physical instruments belong to two different worlds that do not directly interact. But there is a caveat.

The physical forms of an organism represent the vital body morphogenetic fields and are correlated with them. If we can measure these correlated physical forms as they change with the vital body movements, then indirectly we are measuring something about the vital body.

I think this is what the controversial technique of Kirlian photography really does. The Russian scientists Semyon and Valentina Kirlian discovered Kirlian photography. It involves the use of an electric transformer called tesla coil which is connected to two metal plates. A living tissue such as a person's finger is placed between the plates where a piece of film touches it. When electricity is turned on, what the film records is called a Kirlian photograph of the finger.

Typically Kirlian photographs show an "aura" around the object (fig. 11). Proponents of Kirlian photography claim that the color and intensity of the aura are descriptors of the emotional state of the person (whose finger is being used in taking the photograph). For example, red and blotchy auras correspond to the emotion of anxiety. A glow in the aura indicates relaxation, and so forth.

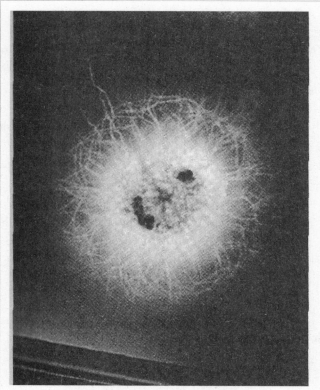

**Kirlian image of a fresh,
organically grown orange (Solomon, 1998)
Courtesy of Dr. Harry Oldfield.**

Figure 11

It is clear that some sort of energetic phenomenon is taking place, most likely physical. But it was verified early on that the energy involved cannot be controlled by the five senses; the energy is not material in origin. Some researchers thought that what we are seeing are pictures of subtle energy flow from the finger to the film via psychokinesis. But this could also be possible only if subtle energy is physical somehow.

An alternative materialist explanation was also given— that the auras are related to sweating. Indeed, the presence of moisture in between the plates affects the photographs creating controversy.

The reason I bring all this up is that it is possible to give still another explanation. Changes in vital energy (as in mood swing) do change the programs that run the organ representations whose functions also change, reflecting the mood swing. The photograph is measuring the change in the physical level, but because the physical level changes are correlated with the vital level changes, indirectly we are measuring the latter.

If this explanation is correct, then the physical correlate of vital energy that is being measured must be electrical in nature. Is there any evidence for that? Yes, for a few decades evidence has been accumulating that aside from the biochemical body, we have a bioelectrical body around the skin (Swanson, 2009).

Traditional Chinese Medicine has already shown how the morphogenetic fields correlated with the organs inside the physical body are connected to those correlated with the superficial parts of the body via what they called meridians—the approximate pathways of vital energy. (In quantum physics exact pathways are not allowed.) In this way, even a vital energy change correlated to an organ at a chakra deep inside the body will affect the superficial bioelectrical body whose changes can be measured with Kirlian photography or other means.

I have heard there is a Dr. Chauhan in India who is detecting very early cases of breast cancer by measuring the vital energy block of the patient at the heart chakra through Kirlian photography. His measurements have then been verified through biopsy and the patients treated successfully at that early stage of the disease.

A similar technique as Kirlian photography is being used to measure thinking by measuring its physical correlate. Can we tell if somebody is thinking? Yes. We look at activity in the brain with a magnetic resonance imaging (MRI) device.

A few years back, I was at a shopping mall in Columbia, MD with my granddaughter. When I saw a strange sign at a shop, I asked my granddaughter what the shop was selling. My granddaughter explained that if you place a helmet (that they give you) on your head, then you can experience how your thinking can move the helmet in ways that you can clearly discern. Instantly I figured this out. These people were using the electrical energy in the brain neurons that your thinking is associated with to affect the helmet you are wearing in discernible ways, employing something like an MRI apparatus.

MRI pictures can already tell us the quality of your thinking changes from mundane to creative processing of meaning. In other words, with some additional research we should be able to measure levels of mental wellness via the MRI imaging technique.

To summarize, as quantum economics is deployed, we can expect reliable objective quantification of subtle energy measurements to make subtle economics a viable one.

FIVE

How the Quantum Economics of Consciousness Solves the Problem of the Business Cycle

Economists don't have a very good popular image. Fortunately, many economists are quite aware of it. I heard this telling joke from an economist (blessed are people who don't take themselves too seriously!):

> Three professionals—a surgeon, a physicist, and an economist—are arguing about the world's oldest profession, the profession of God. The surgeon bats first. "God must be a highly-skilled surgeon to make Eve out of Adam's rib," he says smugly.
>
> The physicist pooh-poohs. "Ha! Everybody knows God is a chaos theorist to make order out of all that initial chaos."
>
> The economist smiles slyly, "Yes. But who created the chaos?"

I suspect this negative image of the economist is chiefly due to the fluctuations inherent in the presence of the business cycle which makes economic predictions difficult and economics look chaotic. In the nineteenth century, after some years of growth, capitalist economies regularly seemed to fall into a recession, and there was always the possibility of an even deeper stagnation called depression that eventually happened in the early twentieth century. It is to prevent this kind of fluctuation that the Keynesian, monetarism, and supply-side government intervention cures were proposed. With these cures, recessions still happen, but they are expected to be milder. Are they actually milder? No, the great recession shattered that expectation! Of course, some economists argue that the great recession could have become a great depression if not for the government intervention Keynes style. But is this rationalization or is this rationalization?

Unfortunately, all these cures notwithstanding, great recession notwithstanding, a perpetual expansion economy in the material sector continues. Because eventual recovery now depends almost entirely on consumerism, a perpetual drain of the planetary material resources has been created.

In the new paradigm economy, where we can invoke consumerism not only in the material sector but also in the subtle sector; and since production of subtle products is cheap, in recession times we can soften the blow by increasing demand in the subtle sector through government intervention. Increased demand would increase production in the subtle sector, keeping the economy going, and thus giving businesses time to regroup. And all this without any waste of resources in the material sector. The activity in the subtle sector would reduce the pressure to increase demand in the material sector that often creates unnecessary infrastructure jobs and depletes resources.

Creating demand in the subtle sector is the tricky part in this cure especially in the period of transition from a materialist economy to an economy of consciousness. But think. How do we create demand today at the onset of a recession? We create unnecessary public service jobs and also pay people unemployment insurance. As Keynes famously said, the unemployed might as well dig holes in the ground and fill them up. Quantum economics offers a better solution. Couple government-supported unemployment insurance and public service jobs with the incentive to consume subtle energies. The existing practice is for the unemployed to show evidence that they are looking for jobs in order to collect their unemployment insurance. The new requirement would be to offer proof that the unemployed are engaging with subtle energy education and practices under a skilled subtle energy master (producer). This will give the needed boost in subtle energy production and consumption and keep the overall economy going.

But most people enjoy the subtle and the transformative practices even if it comes virtually free only for a while. In a matter of a few months to a year, most initiates would reach a plateau and need a break. So by the end of a year or so, people of predominant *tamas* would have had enough transformation for now, and they would be ready to resume "real" work. People of *raja* would use the time of subtle consumption for recharging their batteries—time of incubation. People of *sattva* and inner creativity are, of course, the producers of subtle products: this would be their busy "do" time. In about a year, they, too, need a change to a more relaxed pace of doing. So, in effect, in about a year, both the producers and the consumers would be ready to switch to "normal times" just as material production companies have regrouped and are ready to produce at a normal level.

As the recovery from recession progresses the production of the material goods would increase, material consumerism will go up, and for a while there will be less subtle stuff produced and consumed. But only for a while. As the economy recovers and comes to full swing, peoples' material needs are satisfied, and they now, having already gotten a taste for subtle energies, would become hungry again for the satisfaction of their subtle needs whose production then increases to meet the increase in demand. And this has the effect of putting a damper on the inflationary pressures and tendencies of "boom" times in a capitalist economy. In this way, the addition of the subtle sector of the economy to the material sector more or less guarantees the maintenance of the aggregate demand along with aggregate production in spite of the fluctuations in the material sector. The important thing is that there is no appreciable depletion for the subtle stuff; there is no inflationary pressure in the subtle dimensions. Paying attention to the subtle production and consumption just enables the entire economy to soften the blow of both recessions and the boom time inflationary pressure. In other words cyclical variations of the economy would be much less severe, so mild that little or no government intervention (except in the very unobtrusive way mentioned above) can keep the economy in a steady state.

Note also how the business cycle works in harmony with personal and social transformation. Every recession takes people to a higher plateau of transformed living involving more and more subtle energy consumption. The *tamasic* people would have increased *raja*, and their meaning processing capacity would go up. The people of situational creativity would have more *sattva* and would learn to creatively enjoy more "be" time. For the people of *sattva*, the recession time of increased service would enable them to purify their *sattva*, further enabling a surrender of their ego to the demands of creativity. Changes can be expected for businesses as well as they, too, are run by the people so transformed. So after every business cycle, businesses will become a little more holistic, their products will be a little more meaningful, and so forth.

In this way, I am convinced that "spiritualizing" the economy quantum style, making capitalism conscious under quantum economics, is how to accomplish a stable economy that many economists have wondered if it is ever possible to achieve.

Previously, I used the term "classical economics" for Adam Smith capitalism plus government intervention—Keynes style. This was a step in the right direction because it makes explicit the concept of social good implicit in Adam Smith's thinking. However, as already discussed, the combination does not work, does not eliminate the boom-bust fluctuations of the economy. The inclusion of the subtle and spiritual sectors in the capitalist economy does the job; it truly establishes the great compromise between social good and profit motif in firm reality. This is why we call the new economics of consciousness quantum economics because, without the blessings of the quantum dynamics, the subtle and the spiritual would not be viable for manifestation.

For connoisseurs of quantum physics, please note that in the limit of negligible subtle sector, quantum economics would have to resort to Keynesian economics, smooth functioning or not. This is the correspondence principle between classical and quantum physics that Niels Bohr discovered. Obviously, the new formulation of economics is adhering to the same tradition.

Can We Forever Avoid Economic Meltdowns?

I have already introduced the subject of the 2007-2009 economic meltdown. When the meltdown was properly recognized, in the fall of 2008 in the middle of the American general election, did the world's governments take the right steps? If not, what could they have done better? What can we learn from the recent experience? Would such a phenomenon occur in conscious quantum economics? In this section, I will deal with these questions. But first, another quintessential question: What produced the meltdown?

One of the key things that went wrong is an element of the financial market. So we begin at the beginning. How did the financial market become a fixture of American economic life? Businesses have used stocks for quite some time to represent the value of their businesses in order to raise money from the public offering of stocks. This is quite conducive to capitalism's basic goal of spreading capital ownership and yet creating a large enough pool of it so that it can be effectively invested in economic activity. This idea was taken even further through the creation of mutual funds. Owning stock is good, but there is risk in whether the particular company whose stocks you own will succeed or not; or what is more relevant, whether the stock price will reliably keep going up over time or not. If you want to make quick money, you need a stock that will go up in value in short term. If on the other hand, you are saving money for retirement, you want a stock that will do good in the long run. In either case, there is risk involved, and then it makes sense to let the experts handle your stock. The idea of mutual funds fits this situation. You employ an investment company or an investment bank to invest your money. The company experts invest not only your money, but also the money pooled from many sources like you, in a plethora of stocks, thus spreading the risk that each of you take.

I have mentioned this already: one consequence of materialist thinking that originated in physics is the belief that the universe is fundamentally mathematical; mathematics is the language of physics. Naturally, under materialist influence on economics, mathematicians invaded Wall Street and convinced investors that there is a scope of mathematics in investment banking. You can degrade this by calling it the manifestation of physics envy, but that would not be appropriate. These mathematicians really could calculate short-term statistical effects to enable investors to accurately assess stock and bond prices, thereby making short-term investment in the stock market relatively risk free and making money on them easy. Once the financial investment banks obtained a footing in the economy, money became relatively detached from the material value it represents; and when smart mathematicians gave the financial banks models of investments, the banks then began to create very clever ways of making money. This led to newer and newer innovations of the basic idea of a stock giving more and more chance of making quick profit (with lesser and lesser transparency) such as futures (of commodity markets) and options (on stocks), hedge funds, derivatives, etc.

Eventually, the mathematical "wizards" of Wall Street claimed that they could even calculate the rate of default on loans backed up by collateral. Loans (from the point of view of the banks) are money tied up, often for a long time, such as 30-year mortgage loans in housing. But if a bank knows the default rate, and if the bank then puts together a whole bunch of loans from a whole bunch of sources to minimize risk of defaults, the loans can become assets against which the bank can issue securities. This is called securitization. The securities can be broken up in chunks, each chunk representing a different aspect of the security. This is what the bank sells as collateralized debt obligation (CDO). Somebody wrote an article in the *Newsweek* magazine comparing the situation of this way of creating the CDOs with how a cow is divided into different slices and sold upon pricing them according to the quality of the slice. Apt metaphor. Investors buy the CDOs and sell them again to other parties, thus creating more and more distance between a CDO and the original mortgage loans that back it up. Transparency is lost. The CDO", by the way, is a good example of what a derivative is.

Since politicians were equally influenced (duped?) by scientific materialism, it was easy to convince politicians of all denominations to change or suspend rules of investment in the name of the free market. This led to financial market deregulation opening up vast territories for the movement of investors' greed. Deregulation abolished the difference between investment banks and commercial banks, thereby widely deploying all these innovations that went against the grain of conventional production-consumption classical economics.

Some economists are of the opinion that these new assets of mathematical economics, the CDOs and the like, with the help of deregulation, "sat on Wall Street and it broke," causing the 2007-2009 meltdown. But to be fair, these assets were not the only cause.

Most economists agree about three factors. First, because of the dollar standard for foreign exchange, many net exporting countries tend to station their trade balance in dollars. This makes America very special, and during the period mentioned, there was a glut in capital availability. In the current materialist mindset, it is hard for people, especially *rajaic* people, to give up an opportunity to make money by investing easy credit. Traditionally, housing provides a safe haven for investment. So these investments based on easily available credit produced the housing boom. The boom was psychologically so captivating that many people thought it would   go on indefinitely. This created the second step of the problem—subprime mortgages, loan mortgages granted by banks at interest rates even less than the prime rate of bank-to-bank lending. The loan officers that handled the housing loans did not even properly check the creditworthiness of the borrower; instead, they depended on credit rating agencies who did not do their job either (so eager was everyone to close a deal and make money).

At the third step, there was the securitization process I discussed above. Derivatives called collateralized loan obligations (CDOs) converted the illiquid assets (that loan mortgages were before deregulation) into tradable objects. These came to wide use for investment because of the belief that the risk was very spread out and that the math that calculated the risk was very reliable.

Overall, the scheme was much like how the cartoonist Scott Adams represented it in his comic strip *Dilbert*: "I take your money and then use math to turn it into my money while destroying the whole economy." That sounds simple enough, but in truth nobody knew what he or she (mostly he) was doing. In a specially telling sordid episode, one investment company with its right hand sold CDOs while warning with its left hand against investing in CDOs. So what happened was that some people made money, but many more lost, and the economy overall went on a tailspin.

Experts still try to piece together how exactly the economy was destroyed, what the tipping point was. Something went wrong with the rosy scenario of indefinite expansion of the housing market. Perhaps it started with the subprime loan interest rates going up, so that lenders went into default at a higher rate than predicted. Perhaps some people became fearful that housing prices had reached their peaks and began selling off, as the result of which housing prices began to come down, thereby producing panic selling. Some buyers had made their house mortgage payments for a while with the hope of making a profit on "zero" investment. When the housing market collapsed, and their expectations did not materialize, buyers defaulted, and bank foreclosures resulted. These factors produced uncertainty in the value of the securities that backed up the CDOs. The situation was further complicated by the fact that the holders of the CDOs did not even know where the securities originated— the lack of transparency now became a huge impediment against properly pricing them. The net result was that these CDOs became toxic assets. Nobody knew how to price them.

Crisis and stagnation of financial banks resulted when these banks could not properly estimate their liabilities and therefore refused to lend money to one another. When lending stopped, the crisis not only affected Wall Street but also Main Street. The toxic assets in America had also already invaded the European financials banks. So markets everywhere in the developed economic world were threatened by the crisis. Then came government bail-outs, both in the United States and in Europe. The bailout worked to stabilize the financial markets. Of course, the fallout of the bursting of the housing "bubble" was a huge recession from which the recovery was very slow. President Obama took the classical approach of the Keynesian path to get us out of the recession—government spending, which would be paid for not by increased taxes but by deficit financing. Even with some help from the Fed in maintaining a steady money supply, this worked but very slowly, especially in the area of job creation.

Blame game went rampant. Critics generally harped on the lack of ethics on the part of several of the actors that contributed to the crisis. Should the loan officers of subprime mortgage organizations lend money to people without thoroughly checking that they were adequately capable of handling the loans? No, said the critics correctly; the fact that they did lend money is a sign of greed and unethical behavior. Critics also blamed the government for relaxing regulations that could have prevented the subprime loans. Critics also pointed out the moral hazard involved in government bailout. If big financial organizations know that government is going to bail them out because they are "too "big" to fail," they will continue taking undue risks in their investment practices (because they get to keep the profit), but government (the public really) bears the losses from such investments. This is obviously not fair because this further makes the rich richer and the poor poorer.

Financial bankers and the economists who help them produce bubble economies to make money had better take heed. The following take on a well-known story circulates on the Internet:

> A man was walking aimlessly. Sometime later, he walked into a curio shop and while looking, around he found a brass rat that caught his fancy. After some bargaining with the shopkeeper, he managed to buy the rat and left the shop. As he walked down the street, he heard strange noises behind him, looked back and lo! Thousands of rats were following him coming out of everywhere. In a panic, he ran to the end of the road and saw a river. There he heaved the brass rat into the river. To his relief, all the rats ran past him into the river. Now the man had an idea. He went back to the curio shop and asked the shopkeeper, "Do you have any brass economists to sell me?"

A less violent approach is to recognize that the critical analysis above was all right on, but incomplete. There is another culprit that went virtually unnoticed by economists and pundits in general. I am, of course, speaking of the prevalent materialist influence on economics. According to scientific materialism, there are no ethics where profit is involved, and there is no moral prerogative toward the movement of equalization of wealth. Nor is there, according to scientific materialism, any evolutionary prerogative for maintaining a healthy middle class with hunger for creativity and changing their economic station in life.

So let's take heart from the fact we feel disturbed about such lack of ethics or moral laxity, that we are not entirely convinced that the philosophy of scientific materialism behind materialist economics is right, and learn some lessons to act upon.

First, the crisis is making crystal clear the limit of the free market economy—materialist or even Adam Smith-Keynes classical style. The market can correct itself with little tinkering, a few bailouts, a little infusion of government spending in infrastructure, tax cuts, creation of money by the Fed, or adjustment of interest rates for a period. However, if we depend only on consumerism, in the absence of much real creativity, investment and job growth would be slow. And over a long-time scale, the market instability will always tend to grow to such proportion that the market cannot adjust itself back to equilibrium. In other words, something important is missing in classical and materialist economics. Earlier, I have discussed the missing component: it is the recognition of the spiritual and subtle needs of the human being. When these needs are included, we can enjoy virtually a steady-state economy in the material sector while maintaining continuing expansion in the subtle sector.

The second important lesson of the recent crisis is this: it is too dangerous to gamble with our finances. It is not the sub-prime loans that caused this crisis per se. What caused the crisis is the packaging of the mortgages, making them more attractive for speculation and less transparent to mid-term correction. Many economists have pointed out the dangers of the expansion of the financial sector of the economy, but nobody knows on what basis one can control it. The economics of consciousness gives rich people and corporations with sitting money more outlets for expansion—infinite outlets really if we are creative enough. This new expansion would create not only new vital energy technology but also an avalanche of exciting cultural capital and unprecedented new human capital.

Should We Tax the Gains from Financial Investments?

Idealist quantum economics has another clue in the search for fresh answers. In ancient spiritual societies it was forbidden to charge interest on loans. Even in more recent times usury has never been encouraged when the religious worldview dominated our economics. The reason is the recognition that money should be connected with meaning; it should result from the toils of honest labor, production of goods, or giving a service. But in capitalism, in order to grow capital, it is necessary to pay people interest for their investments. And then it also seems logical that if people want to speculate on the future values of the stocks themselves or commodities, they must be free to do so. How else can we say that the market is free?

Actually, some decades ago, the economist James Tobin, a professor at Yale, no less, proposed the imposition of a small tax on the profit from short-term financial speculation. But this would make speculative financial markets unprofitable, cried the rich and powerful quite predictably. At the time, the "Tobin tax" as it came to be called, was against the grain of capitalist economics, influenced by scientific materialism as it was.

But when quantum economics becomes the going paradigm of capitalism, one can argue differently. Economics is the management of the place where we live, and that means the physical world, the mental world of meaning, the vital world of feeling, and the supramental world of archetypal values, even the spiritual world of quantum consciousness—the ground of being. In this way, economic transactions even in the material sector should be transactions of meaning and value, not devoid of them. Since money has no inherent meaning or value, we should conclude that such transactions as making money on money that are devoid of meaning and value are antithetical. To the extent that for a while some people are going to engage in such practices anyway, given the negative emotionally-wired human brain, we probably have to deal with this as we deal with other unhealthy practices like gambling and drug use (for example, alcohol and cigarette addiction): via taxing. And as business people begin to see the relevance of the new quantum economics in their businesses, lives, and society, they will be able to accept the taxation.

Some Final Thoughts on Preventing Future Economic Meltdowns

What happens if we discard the lens of scientific materialism and look at the situation in 2007-2009 from the point of view of the quantum economics of consciousness? The housing bubble was created in part to bring us out of the 2001-2002 recession. In view of the last section, firstly, quantum economics is a steady-state economics for the material sector, and bubbles would not be necessary to deal with recessions because there would be little or no recession in the first place. In part, the housing bubble was created because it was assumed that business people make their decisions rationally in keeping with mathematics. So secondly, in quantum economics, never do we need to assume that humans, businesspeople included, are capable of making rational decisions. Thus, under quantum economics, we would not put too much reliance on the predictions of mathematical models to make business decisions especially in the long term.

In science within consciousness, feeling and meaning are on the same footing. If anything, we have negative emotional brain circuits that take us astray from rational behavior. Our evolution has not as yet produced circuits of positive emotions in our brain to balance the negative emotions. In the quantum economics of consciousness, the subtle sector of the economy actively strives to produce energies of positive emotion (such as inspiration, compassion, and cooperation) to balance the negative tendencies (such as greed or excessive unfair competition) of people doing business.

Would quantum economics, implemented immediately, have rescued us faster from the current recession? In 2009, I actually wrote an open letter to President Obama to that effect and, of course, received no response, not that I expected any (Goswami, 2011). We will never know. Seriously, we all must accept that a conscious quantum economics cannot be implemented overnight anyway; there are many new innovative ideas for subtle technology, but what is lacking are the many creative people—entrepreneurs and business leaders—to deploy subtle energy technology even if the politicians and the government went for it by some fluke. What we can do is make a good beginning all around, involving academics, business leaders, gifted producers, and grass-roots consumers as soon as possible, and that should help our economic future.

Actually, the Obama administration did do something that a quantum economist would approve. Aside from investing in "bridges to nowhere" to create jobs, Obama did divert some of the government-rescue attention toward the overhaul of health care. This is halfway quantum economics because investment in health care is meaningful, not empty consumerist consumption. In full-fledged conscious quantum economics, this particular investment would involve both conventional and alternative medicine as well as subtle-energy practices of preventive medicine. The government can still do that and perhaps will at some future time (but prodding will be needed).

Obama's idea of investing in renewable energy technology also involves meaningful economic investment. People who find employment in these renewable energy companies will be processing meaning, creatively finding satisfaction, and thus producing subtle energy in profusion.

For moving further away from future meltdowns, we could divert some of the government spending on education and research from meaningless materialist projects (such as the vain pursuit of sending people to other planets) to developing new subtle-energy technology. Inhabiting Mars is not cost effective now nor is it going to be cost effective in the future, even for the very rich, marketing techniques notwithstanding. But a revitalized perfume that promotes romantic love between couples is guaranteed to be cost effective and useful for everyone. Similarly, we could revamp our philosophy departments in the academe; we could establish chairs of quantum physics and for consciousness research. We could free up the academe from the tyranny of scientific materialism and big science in the service of weapon building. Instead, following the precedent of President Kennedy's moon project (which, in view of the cold war, was appropriate then), Obama or a future president could initiate a ten-year research project to establish scientific consensus for the existence of the subtle worlds and for the causal potency of consciousness in the form of downward causation. In a peaceful world (except for regional skirmishes) that we are moving toward now, this is the appropriate direction for science, nay, academic research in general. The guidelines for such a research project are already clear (Goswami, 2008a, 2011).

All this would be part of the project I call quantum activism—large-scale effort by all quantum aficionados to change self and society using quantum principles (Goswami, 2011). Isn't it time that we implement the worldview dictated by the newest physics that has been on the horizon for almost a hundred years and that is promising to give us a dogma-free approach to reality that integrates all previous polarized approaches to reality?

Eventually, we have to recognize that the institutions of higher education are already in the business of selling meaning. They do it, however, in a more or less irrelevant and often downright noncreative way within the straightjacket of scientific materialism, taking advantage of the monopoly they enjoy because of tradition. In the long run, (it could be sooner), we have to be rid of the monopoly that the institutions of higher education enjoy today in the business of selling meaning (see Chapter 10 for further discussion).

The quantum physics way to consciousness is analogous to what Easterners call "*gyana*" (wisdom) path to spirituality. In the short run, we could try to revamp Christianity and other religious traditions (as a part of quantum activism) by encouraging them to adapt the new science of spirituality in their practices to make themselves more effective and efficient producers of positive subtle and spiritual energy. In the long run, we should rid ourselves of the monopoly that religions enjoy in the business of values. In this way, with insight and effort, we could pave the way to a future sector of subtle economics that would be in place before the next great recession happens.

What is the Nature of Invisible Hands of the Free Market?

There is a light-bulb joke about conservative economists of the old: How many conservative economists does it take to change a light bulb? The answer is: none. If the light bulb needed to be changed, the invisible hands of the free market would have already done it.

But today's conservatives approve of supply-side economics and government intervention in the form of tax cuts for the rich. They also don't mind that the Fed keeps the money supply going by creating money and keeping inflation, as well as interest rates, low. Liberals also like government intervention, but Keynes style, with a lot of materialist ideas of consumerism. How many liberal economists does it take to change a light bulb? you wonder. The answer is: all of them. When more are employed, there is more aggregate demand and consumption.

Governments today tinker with the free market with the supply-side "trickle down but never does" economics or Keynes-style "building bridges to nowhere" demand-side economics, depending on which party is running the government. The governments also intervene with the market in a few other ways than mentioned above that Adam Smith may not have approved: they make bureaucratic regulations, bail out big companies "too big to fail" from bankruptcy, give tax incentives to segments of the economy for political and not economic reason counter to the spirit of capitalism, etc., etc.

Can we have economics without government intervention? Even with the quantum economics of consciousness, the discussion so far shows that a little government intervention may be required. So is the supposedly free market destined not to be free in practice, but free only in the ideal?

There is so much mystique about the "invisible hands" of the free market because nobody, no economist, understands it. Scientific materialists wave their hands: it must be an example of emergent self-consistent field of some kind. But no model is ever offered, promissory materialism.

When you don't understand something, you can only joke about it. I really like this one. "We economists are armed and dangerous. Watch out for our invisible hands."

The truth is that nothing is wrong with government intervention per se if we give up the idea that the free market has to
be free. Adam Smith himself was quite aware of this. He suggested government intervention to reduce *unjust* income distribution, to ensure that the entry to the free market is really free,
even for the small entrepreneur (regulation against monopoly,
for example), and to provide liberal education to everyone par-
ticipating in the market.

I will tell you my hypothesis. You know that materialists say
that it is the competition between businesses that keep the free
market free. This may have some validity, but the business cycles
make it clear that this alone could not make the free market free.
I think that so long as what the businesses do, what the government does, what the consumers do, are all compatible with
the evolutionary movement of consciousness, the economy runs
okay. Right now the challenge of evolution is to spread meaning
processing to all people. So long as the economy serves the job of
expanding the processing of meaning among people, it remains
stable. But if the economy runs for long without creative innovations, or if peoples' negative emotions (such as greed) come into
play in the working of the economy in a major anti-capitalist
way doing violence to social good, or if income disparity tends
to eliminate the creatively-striving middle class (striving to fulfill
their "American dream"), then the economy becomes unstable.
What I am really saying is that it is time we acknowledge that
the "invisible" hands are nothing but the hands of purposive
evolutionary movement of nonlocal consciousness.

More recently, the freedom of the market is being invaded by
truly anti-capitalist ways. This has been the result of the wounding that scientific materialism has produced in our collective
psyche. The wounding has released the powerful among us from
helping their fellow humans with the search and exploration

for mental meaning and instead has led them into the slavery of instinctual greed, avarice, and competitiveness. One of the effects of this is the gross corruption of the practices that keep the stock market relatively free. The current practice is to legalize corruption away (the law against insider trading is an example); yes, these laws are important, but laws alone would have very limited success. There is another effect that is more subtle.

There is now an active counter-evolutionary anti-capitalist movement for taking away meaning processing from large segments of people. Right now, this is more of an American phenomenon, but it may soon spread to other developed economies with strong currency.

A dollar standard creates this new problem for capitalism. All trade surpluses tend to be stationed in dollars, creating a vast amount of money supply in America that can support a lot of deficit financing on the part of both government and private sectors. Is deficit financing desirable? Shouldn't money always be used to make more money? Adam Smith's capitalism was not designed to deal with such issues. It is another sign of the influence of materialism that gives affirmative answers to both of the questions above.

Americans have been in a unique situation since the gold standard shifted to dollar standard. Americans can borrow money to buy resources and goods from other countries almost indefinitely because those countries have not much option but to reinvest their money in the American dollar and American economy. The American government has then the ability for large amounts of deficit financing, and it has used this deficit financing for cutting taxes for the rich and getting into dubious wars. This is not immediately detrimental to the economy because the rich are the biggest consumers, and they are also big investors. And wars in the past have been known to help expand the economy. But these practices make the gap between rich and poor larger and tend to eliminate the middle class. In this way, market share becomes more concentrated in the hands of the rich, and a new class system is created leaning toward old feudalism. Cynics can say that the rich are unconsciously threatened by a prosperous middle class who may want to share their power, so they manipulate matters to shrink the middle class quite deliberately. But can even materialist economics function when the capital becomes concentrated again as in feudalism/mercantile economy?

In the quantum economics of consciousness the remedy of all this would be a part of a universal revival of idealist values. In quantum economics, we do not deal with the symptoms of the materialist wound such as corruption but rather we heal the source of the wound so the symptoms disappear.

For example, take the case of deficit financing. I commented above that right now with most of Bush tax cuts still in place, deficit financing is being used to increase the wealth gap between rich and poor contrary to the spirit of capitalism. Even worse, deficit financing removes the very important economic constraint against nations with aggressive ideas. George W. Bush's Iraq war would not have been possible if deficit financing was not permitted. So should we be against deficit financing in idealist economics? Not necessarily. How does quantum economics deal with government creating income disparity between rich and poor or aggressive war? After all, it is people in leadership positions who declare war, and it is these people who decide on tax breaks. In an idealist society, the root cause for the government actively creating income disparity or war—negative emotion—would be addressed by electing only leaders who have an adequate supply of positive emotions to balance their own negative ones. How is this ever possible?

In quantum economics we can use deficit financing to create and/or expand the subtle sector of the economy as necessary and as far as practicable without affecting the proper functioning of the economy—national and international (that is, so long as the deficit remains only a few percentages of the GNP). The consumption of the subtle transforms people—it is movement away from the current information-based economy toward a transformation-based economy. When people value transformation, they elect transformed leaders.

One final comment before we leave this chapter. Some economists think that the success of the Chinese economy so far shows that controlled capitalism is better anyway than free market capitalism. But we would be too hasty to conclude that. The point to see is that so far the Chinese have used their government control in synch with the evolutionary movement of consciousness: removing poverty and raising the standard of living for all to open up meaning processing to many more people than before. But watch it! People who are free to process meaning are sooner or later going to demand their own hand in choosing what meaning they process; they are going to demand democracy to elect leaders of their own ilk. That will be the day of reckoning for controlled capitalism—Chinese style. At that point, the Chinese government will discover that they have to deal with peoples' actual needs, not what the government dictates. The Chinese have to innovate, not just produce what developed economies outsource to them because of low labor cost.

SIX

How Businesses and Consumers are Changing in Synch with the Movement of Consciousness

There are movements in business practices in this country and elsewhere that are in synch with the evolutionary movement of consciousness. There is an eco-friendliness that is trendy. Some businesses have begun to care about the ecosystem; they want to reduce environmental pollution, and they want to deploy sustainable sources of energy. Is there profit in that? Sometimes. Other times, the nudge of government incentives is helping the movement.

Sometime in the recent past, production of solar panels to heat a building became profitable, and American businesses were there to build solar panels and make good business out of it. The Chinese eventually bid them out of the game, but that's a different story. They probably got a lot more nudge from their totalitarian government. In any case, there is now a growing robust sustainable energy-production program benefiting our planet.

Another heart-warming story for the environmentalist is the electric car, a car running on electric batteries. The impossible became possible partly because gas is so costly, but mostly because of traffic laws in some crowded cities in California, where driving regular gas-guzzling polluting cars is restricted.

In this chapter, I will talk about this one and how to take it further in the spirit of the quantum economics of not only consciousness but also of integral well-being. From eco-friendliness through deep eco-friendliness to integral eco-friendliness if you will.

The other movements I will explore in this chapter have received much publicity in the press and played a major role in the recent great recession in the job sector. I am speaking about globalization and outsourcing. Many economists present them as evil while others accept them as inevitable. I say these are movements quite in synch with the evolutionary movement of consciousness; naturally, they are huge openings toward deploying quantum economics.

Environmental Pollution, Shallow Ecology, and Eco-friendliness

There is this pressing problem with materialist expansion economics—environmental pollution. This is a tricky one. In the short term, if cleaning up is a must, then production of pollution helps expand the economy by creating pollution cleaning-up sectors of the economy. Believe it or not, the Exxon-Valdez oil-spill disaster in the 1970s actually produced an economic boom in Alaska. And recently, hurricane control, or protecting New Yorkers from a polar vortex, have become sources of some economic gains! Or in a few decades, when the rise of sea level tries to drown Amsterdam, and even New York city, could we see another economic boom with mushrooming business activities busily protecting such cities? I am being facetious, of course; but undeniably, in the long run, uncontrolled environmental pollution in a finite planet environment is bound to end up with a doomsday of reckoning. Global warming produces global climate change. Many environmentalists think that global warming has already reached doomsday criticality resulting in a 2.5 degrees Celsius increase by the end of the twenty-first century.

Another little known fact is this: Environmental pollution—especially air and water pollution—reduces our access to vital energy. This is in addition to all the other well known health risks of air and water pollution.

Liberal economists have suggested some good solutions for global warming such as carbon tax, taxation based on how much net carbon dioxide a company releases in the environment. Quantum economics has a better solution.

In the quantum economics of consciousness, material consumption is reduced, thus automatically reducing environmental pollution. And there is further fallout from this. Much of our material consumption is prompted by our negative emotions (anxiety, jealousy, greed, lust, egotism, boredom, etc.). If a negative emotion hits you, one way to regain control is to go shopping. Unfortunately, shopping in this way can very quickly become an addiction. In a quantum economy, if are hit by a negative emotion, you have a healthy choice: Use a subtle energy product that will lift your mood. And overall, the reduction of the dependence of our economy on material consumption reduces the production and advertisement of these unhealthy material escapes from negative emotions as well.

Do you see negative emotions as pollution? You should. Don't they pollute your internal environment? In addition, in the economics of consciousness, we pay attention to production of subtle energies of positive emotions by you, in this way creating the possibility of emotional balance and emotional intelligence. With emotional balance, we begin to take responsibility for our actions—individually and collectively. We get rid of our ostrich-like tendency to avoid the truth (the style of Fox News and Rush Limbaugh and scientific materialism and Richard Dawkins.) All this substantially contributes to our ability to live in a sustainable economy.

One encouraging development of businesses in the direction of gaining economic legitimacy for peoples' well-being is the "green" business that grew up from the ecology movement. Haven't you heard? Green is the new black. The green business has two components. The first is the realization that ecological considerations can be used for economic gains, for making profits, and this is basic. An example is recycling; the Xerox Corporation made a ten-fold return on its investment in recycling toner cartridges. And the second is the realization that in the long run, ecological sustainability—harmonization of the business activity with what the earth can support—is a good thing to aim for. Sooner or later it is going to be imposed by governments or by nature itself, whichever comes first.

What is ecology based on? On the idea of the web-like relationship between life and its environment—living and nonliving. To be sure, ecologists are talking about local connections alone. But from ecology it is a small leap to realize that the connection of life and its living environment is much deeper. The connection is not only through material, local signals, but also through vital energy;, and ultimately, through consciousness itself, through a quantum nonlocal connection which even includes the nonliving.

So you see, ecological businesses are also moving us beyond the mere satisfaction of ego material needs toward the satisfaction of more subtle needs of higher consciousness, subtle well-being. Ecologically sustainable businesses are literally increasing our global vital energy output.

A Wisconsin company, BioIonics, uses electromagnetic power to transform human and industrial waste, shit and sludge, into fertilizers for agriculture and horticulture and hear this, cleans up after itself. A chemical company in Oceanside, NY, has invented household cleaners so user friendly that if you swallow it accidentally, it will not harm you, and what's more, you may even like the taste (Smitha, 2011). That is eco-friendliness!

Let me emphasize the etymological origin of the word *ecology*. The prefix "eco" is common to both economics and ecology, and it comes from the Greek *oikos* meaning place. Since "logy" originates from the Greek *logos* meaning knowledge, etymologically ecology is about the knowledge of the place that we live.

Now realize that we not only live in the external material world that is the domain of shallow ordinary ecology where we study our relation to the physical environment, but we also live in our internal subtle world. When we include in our ecology the knowledge of our relationship to the internal world(s) as well, we get what the sociologist Erne Ness called deep ecology. Since etymologically, economics comes from *oikos* meaning place and *nomus* meaning management, economics is the management of the place we live. The quantum economics of consciousness with its subtle sector is deep economics and goes hand in hand with deep ecology. As we engage with the subtle economy, as we consciously consume and produce more and more subtle energy, we clean up our internal environment, we transform. This is the key to the concept of sustainability, about which many businesses are asking questions. Is sustainability ever possible to achieve?

Sustainability

Building designers and architects have a long history of mavericks paving the way to ecologically sustainable architectural designs of buildings, including buildings for industrial use, starting with the dome houses of Buckminster Fuller. Now there is also the visionary futurist designer Jacque Fresco who has written a book *Future by Design,* which promotes a future so sustainable that not even money will be necessary to make transactions. Another designer William McDonough (and his collaborator Michael Braungart) printed their book on paper which is "treeless," made from plastic resins and inorganic fillers that are recyclable material. The same designers were designing eco-sustainable buildings in seven cities in China—a much ballyhooed project. In a report of *Newsweek* magazine (2005), even the first phase of the project has gone awry.

So these are exceptional ideas, and they can only go so far as workable projects, which makes us wonder how we can ever achieve sustainability since it smacks of reducing our standard of living. Doesn't it involve sacrifice? As we know from the dismal failure of the Marxist economics, unless people have the selfish motive of living a better life (that American dream again), they will never work hard enough to make capitalism work. And what is a better life without the capacity for enhancing personal material comfort and pleasure? Could it be that there is a sustainable answer consisting of enhancing overall personal satisfaction in the subtle sectors to complement a more streamlined and efficient approach to material comfort and pleasure?

But have you noticed that after a certain standard of living is reached, objects of pleasure become more and more a question of availability and not of necessity? After all, our pleasure centers tend to saturate; you can only eat so much, enjoy so much personal space at a given time, and have so much sex! Your car may have the potential to drive at 240 mph, but to use that capacity, you will have to spend time to find special places where such driving will not endanger others. It becomes counterproductive after a while unless you are one of those people who has security only when you have unlimited availability. Those are the people who get into the game of power. Power being an aphrodisiac, this game becomes addictive.

The truth is, as people's higher needs are met even partially, as is the case with people living in a quantum economy, their physical needs reduce, thereby reducing the demand for material consumption, and thus reducing the wastage of limited material resources. Even more importantly, when there is love and satisfaction in your life, conditioned *tamas* in the service of the often-unconscious need for security gives way to creativity and risk taking, and you are—believe it—able to give up some of the need for availability. You gain an uncanny sense that things will be available when you need it; you don't need to secure it now! The spiritual savant Ramana Maharshi used to say to his audience, put your luggage down. You are on a moving train. Buddhists say, surrender to the flow of the current; don't resist it. In new-age parlance, this translates as "go with the flow." In explicit religious parlance, you are deferring to God's will instead of always depending on your ego-will. In Carl Jung's language, you are beginning to court with synchronicity—meaningful coincidences. With the change of mindset in this direction, the society can move toward a sustainable standard of living.

The quantum economy still expands, of course, but in the subtle planes where the resources are unlimited. There is no limit on love and satisfaction and hardly any discernible limit anytime soon on the number of human beings to make representations of the subtle in their being! There is no discernible limit on revitalizing organic products. There are hardly any limits on the cultural capital created via the representation of meaning so long as we keep creatively exploring new meaning and use recyclable material to disseminate meaning. There is no limit in producing human capital—human beings of emotional and supramental intelligence.

I have used the term "supramental intelligence" before, for which the Sanskrit word is *buddhi*. Supramental intelligence is intelligence that is gained by the creative mastery of the archetypes. In other words, supramental intelligence is the result of continuing your journey of manifesting positive emotional brain circuits of archetypes. As you do it, you become human capital; your proximity has value to others.

People like Ramana Maharshi and the earlier mentioned Franklin Merrell-Wolff lived as recently as the last century. Today, there is the Dalai Lama. In the presence of such human capital, it is common experience that peace and happiness reigns.

Earlier, I mentioned the 1999 conference of new-age scientists and thinkers meeting with the Dalai Lama. Before we discussed our ideas with the Dalai Lama, we thought it might be worthwhile to discuss what we would present among ourselves, get a consensus. For two days we tried. We couldn't reach consensus. Instead, we fought, sometimes bitterly. When we had the audience with Dalai Lama, and Dalai Lama was told about our behavior, Dalai Lama defused all the tension with just laughing. It was an amazing presence. You can see it all in the documentary film *Dalai Lama Renaissance*.

There is no limit even for producing human capital of enlightened people. When we cultivate the subtle, as we move deeper and deeper toward inner transformation, in the material plane, we move toward an ecologically sustainable economy. What was unthinkable and unfair sacrifice before, now becomes voluntary simplicity. In this way, quantum deep economics promotes deep ecology, which then promotes shallow ecology, less material consumption at a sustainable level. We will have lowered our standard of living, but who cares? We will have gained quality of living, and our index of well-being would be up. We would be wealthy in a sustainable way.

From Standard of Living to Quality of Life

Let's now take up the subject of another counter-evolutionary tendency of materialistic expansion economy—loss of the worker's leisure time. In response to the problem of rich-poor divide under capitalism, almost to the extent the divide was in feudal times, some economists counter, "Oh, but the poor have such a standard of living today!" Capitalism under materialist influence and its continuing economic expansion in the material plane produces higher and higher standards of living, true; but wages do not keep up with it without producing inflation. To meet the demands of a higher standard and its higher cost, people are forced to give up their higher needs such as the need of children to have one non-working (or part-time) working parent or leisure time to pursue meaning. Thus invariably some of the basic promise of capitalism is shortchanged by the nature of the beast itself. In the economics of consciousness, this problem does not arise.

The economics of consciousness has a built-in constraint on expansion in the material plane, as already noted. So the standard of living does not have to move up and up at rates faster than wage increases. Even more importantly, the economics of consciousness values other needs and their satisfaction that require leisure time. So in an economy under the aegis of this economics, standard of living is defined differently and increases not in the material dimension but in the subtle dimensions and without compromising the worker's leisure time.

From Eco-friendliness to Deep Eco-friendliness to Integral Eco-friendliness

A huge step is to begin integral eco-management—managing the well-being of both our shallow and deep ecology. Economy must preserve shallow ecology—this much we already know. Quantum economics that empowers subtle businesses and industries will promote deep ecology as well. Promoting deep ecology further promotes shallow ecology and so forth; and very soon we will have an integral eco-management.

There are already hints for the importance of acknowledging the subtle in not only for eco-business, but also for all business. For example, indiscriminate use of the objective theories of mathematics (for example, game theory, see later) to gauge the mind-set of the business entrepreneur in economics does not often work because business decisions are colored by peoples' feelings and intuitive hunches. The behavioral consumer economics similarly does not work either, except in short term, creating bubbles in the economy that eventually burst.

The fact is that subtle influences the gross; there is no way around it. Should it be part of good economics that a consumer product be good for your subtle well being? You bet. Once we open the door to subtle energy to become part of the market, the market forces will decide anyway whether this is beneficial or not to the economy. Should you demand that the businesses produce subtle energy goods for you to use so you can build up a reservoir of subtle well-being, positive health? You bet. Is it legit when you accept a job to demand that your work environment has good vital energy, that your job is meaningful, that it brings satisfaction and the energies of wholeness? You bet. Scientific evidence is already growing to show that vital-energy infusion in workplaces enhances productivity.

To integrate shallow eco-friendliness and deep eco-friendliness, we have to cultivate both and develop a society of integral eco-friendliness in businesses. We begin with the idea of eco-friendliness but face difficulty because we are not ready to make the needed sacrifices yet. We work on deep eco-friendliness; after a few back and forth feeding and working with both, we learn voluntary simplicity; and we are now ready to begin integral eco-friendliness.

We can do this because we know that we are not separate from either our external or our internal ecosystems. In developing eco-friendliness, we know already that there are business-people who are turning recycling and re-using into a profitable industry. For reducing, we have to delve into a deeper journey of moving from negative to positive emotions. For reducing, we also have to move away from an information-processing society and bring back meaning processing.

From Negative Emotions to Positive Emotions

Businesses intuitively know about the importance of the subtle. For example, businesses know that a customer uses a product based not only on an objective appraisal of the sensory uses of the product but also how he or she feels about it. Look at the ads the automobile industry puts out for selling their product. If the considerations behind these ads were purely physical, the ads would talk about physical aspects only, mileage per gallon, durability, maintenance cost. Instead most ads talk about "sexy" stuff," how much speed you can get, how fast the car accelerates, how much pleasure you can get out of it; and sometimes more directly, the ads point out the sex appeal of the car.

Remember our earlier discussion of chakras? The new science explains them as the places where physical organs and their vital blueprints are simultaneously brought to manifestation. It is the movement of the vital energy at these chakra points that we experience as feeling. Movement at the three lower chakras is responsible for our base feelings that become instinctual negative emotions with the help of brain circuits: fear, lust, envy, jealousy, competiveness, egotism, and so forth. Many businesses (the auto industry is an example) try to sell their product by appealing to the lower chakras and the self-centered emotional brain circuits. They just have not gotten around to good vital energy, the positive emotions confused by the claims of the scientific establishment that there is no such thing!

But the human condition is not limited to the low chakras and negative emotions.; There are also the higher chakras, starting with the heart where the movement of vital energy (with the help of the meaning-giving mind) can give rise to noble or positive emotions—love, exultation, clarity, and satisfaction. The problem is that there are few positive emotional instinctual brain circuits hardwired in the brain through evolution. Higher emotions mainly come to us if we are sensitive to our intuitions.

The society thus needs to amend its education of the producers and consumers. And it must begin with you, the individual. Educate yourself about vital energy. Go to a yoga retreat, a Tai Chi master, or an institution of martial arts training, or at least a masseuse who is a connoisseur. You will be amazed. Of course, for the masses, for large-scale awareness of the efficacy of the subtle, we will probably need government intervention. I have proposed in the previous pages government intervention in the form of the use of alternative subtle energy medicine for Medicare and subtle energy education for the unemployed if they want to collect their unemployment insurance.

Knowledge is everything. For example, if a car ad says that the car covers 60 miles of distance for a gallon of gasoline, it does not sound sexy and will tend not to appeal to the run-of-the-mill person; but to an environmentally-aware person, it could very well be an inciting and satisfying ad. Similarly, an automobile ad that projects love and beauty would appeal to a consumer who has opened up to his or her intuitive dimension.

Today's people would pay a fortune for Kim Kardashian's used tee-shirt! Will a day come when you realize that a used automobile regularly driven by a Chi gong master has acquired correlated positive vital energy from the driver, and it is now there for any user, and what a sense of vital well-being driving such a car would bring to you? Or to own a house which has been similarly inhabited by a spiritual master? It is all in the mindset, isn't it?

It is usually said that in order to get ahead in a company hierarchy, employees must compete with one another. We are constantly reminded that it is a dog-eat-dog world as far as businesses are concerned. Negative emotions again. But is that all? When the Japanese ways of running production lines (in which a single worker is responsible for a single finished product) became popular along with the slogan "quality is job one," businesses worldwide recognized the importance of job satisfaction that an employee derives from seeing his or her handiwork in a finished product. There is massive scope for higher emotion in businesses after all!

From Information to Meaning and Transformation

For developing the interest in the exploration of meaning in business, we have to change our perspective from machine creativity to human creativity, from mere manipulation of the known for the pursuit of wealth and fame to a curious and sensitive exploration of new meaning, with the purpose of discovering the archetype of abundance and developing new representations of it. To do this, we need to believe in the positive possibilities of the uncertainty of exploring new dimensions. In the consciousness-based worldview, we acknowledge from the get-go that creativity consists of discoveries or inventions of new meaning of archetypal value and making full-fledged innovative products of the discovery. When you recognize this, clearly you must realize that creativity in business is more than exploring an innovative product to make more profit. Profit motive does not need to be given up, but it has to be complemented with motivation toward social good and subtle well-being. Knowing that wealth is abundant gives that confidence in you to share wealth.

Look at the great innovations that begin new trends in business and industry. They all—from fluorescent electric bulbs to *post-it* stickers—contribute to our capacity for meaning processing directly or indirectly—and therein is their value. The material profit is a by-product.

In the industrial age, the necessity of mass production made the job of ordinary people repetitive and monotonous. Practicing well-being by being well both materially and emotionally, while working on the assembly line, is easy to talk about but not easy to carry out. However, in advanced economies such as the United States, Europe, and Japan, we are just about ready to get out of the industrial age to a technological age that will relieve us from mass production through increasing use of robotics in the workplace and through outsourcing (Friedman, 2007). That and other factors such as ecological awareness are increasing the scope for meaningfulness and creativity on the job as never before. With this the future for well-being in the workplace is taking a quantum leap.

Well all right, I will acknowledge we are not there yet. There is indeed movement still in the opposite direction. Beginning with the 1980s in the last few decades, businesses have discovered that there is profit in information processing, much more than there is in meaning processing. At least it seems so in the short term. So today, the book-publishing business is in jeopardy, retail sales of books are down, the recording industry is going through a major re-visioning, and so forth. Young people don't have the attention span any more, we are told. Make audio recordings and videos and accept the fact that they will be pirated and be available free on the Internet. So a vast amount of cultural capital has gone down the tube!

Noted scientists of materialism began writing about the pointlessness of the universe. Who can blame businesspeople who were trying to market household desktop and eventually laptop computers with video games for kids? No meaning in them! But there is information to share with other kids who are also watching them. Soon the technology of the cell phone caught on so a kid not only could play video games in all his or her spare time (in whatever was left of it), but then they could exchange video game information on the cell phone.

There is more. A professor at some place like Harvard by the name of Alan Bloom wrote a book saying that it is more important for a college-educated guy to know about Plato and the gist of what he did than to read Plato. Information is what counts for education; the rest is available on the Internet if you need it. Don't clutter your brain with meaning; clutter it with information.

A few decades of this, and what happened? Information pollution of our kids' brains took place to such extent that attention deficit hyperactive disorders have become epidemic. Recently, a British study revealed that when three-year-olds are subjected to preschool training (which means a lot of information processing, what else?) such kids have a twenty percent chance of contracting ADHD.

There is evidence. In 2008, researchers at the University of Michigan discovered that processing too much information tires the brain out. At Stanford University, researchers have found that heavy use of multimedia leads to trouble in filtering out irrelevant information and focusing on the real task (Agus, 2011).

Businesses have to become aware that information is not natural to our internal environment, but meaning and feeling and intuition are. Information is pollution for our internal ecology. A little of it we can tolerate; we have to because meaning processing requires information. But too much of information pollution of our internal environment is as disastrous as pollution of the physical environment. IT enthusiasts, please note what the computer guru of an earlier time, Norbert Wiener said, and I am paraphrasing: let computers do best what they do best (information processing), let humans do best what they do best (meaning processing).

In this way, the power of the quantum economics of consciousness is fully revealed when we combine shallow and deep ecology. As we transform following the dictum of deep ecology, we see the whole world of consciousness as us, and we become keen in protecting it. The boundary of our self becomes enlarged. Then only shallow ecological considerations—caring for our environment— manifests from possibility to actuality in our thinking and living. Then only can we reduce our standard of living, seeing that it is not really a sacrifice; it is actually increasing our quality of life

Small is Beautiful

At first look, economics—management of place—does seem to refer to the local place that we live as the eco-activist Satish Kumar (2008) has argued. At both ends of production and consumption, if the economy is kept local in the main, the people involved will be responsible for their actions, and then economics can be compatible with ecology. When we try to generalize the concept of place to include the internal worlds, we recognize that for these worlds, the local boundaries are defined by culture. Ideally then, economy should be mainly local, geographically and culturally as Gandhi and more recently E. F. Schumacher have envisioned (Schumacher, 1973). And I believe that with the economics of consciousness in place, eventually we may be able to achieve that ideal with a lot of trade between localities, of course. Remember the Internet is here to stay and it is a part of the movement of consciousness. Just as it is being misused to replace meaning processing with information processing and peddling pornography, it should not close our minds to the possibility that it can be used and is being used for meaningful communication (nobody can deny that the Arab Spring was meaningful!) as well.

But right now, the reality of the economies all over the world is a phenomenon called globalization (see below). Jobs from advanced economies are being outsourced to developing economies. In other words, the trend is quite the opposite from the above ideal. Is globalization in or out of synch with the evolutionary movement of consciousness?

Globalization

Globalization is the breakthrough technology of outsourcing that caught on because of the development of multinational corporations. It is the major reason that the world is rapidly becoming an economic flatland, to use Thomas Friedman's metaphor (Friedman, 2007). Is globalization good or bad? Is it going to be a permanent fixture of capitalistic economics?

Trade between countries has always existed for a variety of reasons. Initially, trading was confined to goods only, but technology made it possible to trade also services resulting in outsourcing. This is one way that economies became global contrary to its original premise, that and the creation of multinational corporations due to relaxed trade regulation, tax advantage, etc.

As an example of outsourcing, consider the call centers of India that cater to Americans. Workers at the call center attend the telephone and answer questions of Americans about problems with a business or industrial product. These workers try to talk in an American accent and attend to problems devoid of any local (ecological or cultural) importance. In this way, the job does not serve the workers in processing any personal or cultural meaning. Eventually, it very likely can alienate a worker from his or her own culture, as captured beautifully in the popular novel by Chetan Bhagat named *One Night at the Call Center*.

Multinational corporations have been criticized for many reasons. They have access to cheap labor in underdeveloped economies, and this they use by shifting manufacturing to underdeveloped countries. This is also a form of outsourcing. One major criticism is that the multinationals exploit the cheap labor of underdeveloped third-world countries; sometimes they even employ child labor, for example. There are also charges of tax evasion that are bound to be true going by the revelations about Apple's tax set-up.

A more sophisticated criticism is this. The labor in the multinational's host country has no leverage of wage increase through negotiations with management (commonplace in advanced economies) since the labor laws are very different in underdeveloped countries because of economic necessities. The labor of developed countries lose leverage, too, because of increasing fear of outsourcing of jobs.

But I think the argument is also valid that globalization is here to stay so long as labor cost differential exists between nations that make outsourcing profitable. In that case the important question is: Can we put globalization to use to further the purpose of capitalism and the economics of consciousness—spreading meaning processing among all people? Yes, we can. Multinationals are, after all, creating new employment in developing countries. This can be a good thing, if we make sure that the development that follows becomes an entry to increased freedom for the labor in those countries (Sen, 1999). This can be assured through government intervention and the insistence that the labor used gets guaranteed liberal education through night schooling. Note that this solution additionally benefits the local subtle economy.

In the same vein, the adult holders of outsourced jobs can be encouraged to provide meaningful service to their own culture and contribute to the subtle sector of the local economy. This will go a long way to prevent alienation.

The case of management-labor relation is more complex. In order to subject multinationals to uniform management-labor practices, obviously we need to move from nation-state economies to more and more enlarged international economic unions. This can be used to the good in the economics of consciousness. In other words, the tendency anyway of the economics of consciousness would be to move toward one international economic union, within which the individual democracies will function with political and cultural uniqueness, and sovereignty even, with their own currencies but with increased cooperation. This is because science within consciousness recognizes quantum non-locality of consciousness from the start which is fostered through cooperation.

What about Jobs in the Developed Economy that is Outsourcing?

Of course, outsourcing does take away jobs from the developed economies of the world. Politicians in the developed economies sometimes make a big case of this against outsourcing and talk about tax incentives to corporations that would bring back manufacturing jobs to the economically-developed country. As the developing country improves in economic performance and the cost of labor there increases, this even becomes more and more feasible. This is already happening in the case of outsourcing from USA to China; and indeed, some of the manufacturing jobs there outsourced from America are coming back.

But the problem remains. There would always be other underdeveloped economies in the world for companies to outsource for quite a while. So how do we provide jobs for the labor in the outsourcing country's economy?

Get a clear grip of the situation. Manufacturing jobs are mostly assembly line routine jobs. When you undertake such a job for an eight-hour shift, after your job is done, all you want to do is flop before the TV and veg out. No incentive for meaning processing is left. Such labor, although its powerful labor unions may be able to negotiate good pay for the labor, does not constitute middle class with leisure time to process meaning. All you can say is that they make room for the American dream for their sons and daughters. So bringing back manufacturing jobs does not contribute to the middle class in the short term.

Now look at the flip side with an open mind. Outsourcing offers a challenge and an opportunity to the developed economy—an opportunity for its labor force to take up more meaningful jobs, even though such jobs may have to be created. Is the labor in America and other developed economies ready for such challenges?

The answer is a resounding yes. In the aftermath of the 2007-2009 recession, jobs were coming back to the economy very slowly. And the jobs that were being created were low-paying meaningless jobs (like waitressing and pumping gas), and well-trained middle-class people were not willing to take on those jobs. *The New York Times* columnist David Brooks commented that this was because people were looking for more meaningful jobs.

We have to come out of the machine mentality of scientific materialism and accept the fact that once a person has tasted meaning processing and the joy of processing meaning on the job, it is difficult to give that up even under the threat of physical survival. With government intervention, these people can easily be encouraged to create small businesses of the subtle sector and meaningful jobs for themselves.

Outsourcing does have another serious problem. Does the outsourcing corporation reinvest its profits back in its home country's economy? Rarely. Here is where tax incentives should be given. Investment capital will become available when the case for a subtle-energy industry is well articulated especially if tax incentives are given. Once this happens, we can count on peoples' creativity to start up new subtle ventures for economic expansion, if only as a society we disengage from the straight-jacket of both scientific materialism and religious dogmas. The first keeps our creativity limited to computer creativity, and even that only for the material domain, while the second tends to bring back the old feudal economy.

Thus I think that outsourcing could be a very desirable trend and in consonance with the evolutionary movement of consciousness. Eventually, of course, when all the different economies in the world become materially developed enough to make their labor force expensive, outsourcing will cease. By that time the new worldview and the new economics will be firmly in place, and we will have the challenge of reshaping manufacturing jobs in sustainable local economies, Gandhi/Schumacher style.

The Elimination of Poverty

The elimination of poverty has two different contexts. First (and the more pressing one) is that of the underdeveloped economies in which the bulk of the people live in material poverty, even in hunger. The second context is of a little surprise: in fact, the elimination of poverty has been a stubborn problem of economic development even for economically advanced countries. Even in the world's advanced economies, there is a core of a few percent of the people that are homeless, that cannot hold a job, and that, in general, can be called "dropouts." The communist countries of the old such as the Soviet Russia had one legitimate criticism of capitalism that stung: If capitalism is so great, why can't it eliminate poverty? They were using this second context.

A lot of people think that these "poor" in America are unfit. But one can also argue that living in America in the proper way is economically too burdensome when you are old, when you are sick—mentally or physically, when you are unlucky (for example, to lose your job without any unemployment benefit), and when you have no family to lean on.

Consider the first context first. Redefining wealth and economic well-being in the way of the economics of consciousness go a long way to equalize the true economic situation between so-called developed and underdeveloped countries. In fact, this redefinition brings to light how important it is that the so-called third-world countries, while allowing free trade, outsourcing, and multinational corporate investment, do not allow their innate spiritual cultures to be destroyed by the ideology of scientific materialism that come with these things. Fortunately, as the new consciousness-based worldview replaces scientific materialism; and as the economics of consciousness replaces Adam Smith's capitalism, the intrusive destruction of spiritual cultures by the more aggressive materialist cultures will be arrested, thereby initiating a much needed return to a way of life of humans in intimate relationship with nature (see also, Liem, 2005).

In this way, in the long term, the effect of the economics of consciousness will be a worldwide economic prosperity, of economic well-being in the new sense that has never happened before. This will happen in parallel with social good. People will have a higher sense of mutual concern for their fellow travelers in the society as they pursue their own selfish economic agenda. In the short term, however, our work is cut out for us; never underestimate the opposition of the elitists.

And of course, the most pressing problem of poverty is hunger. It is within our current capacity to eliminate world hunger and every politician knows it. Unfortunately, until the worldview changes, the politics of the situation will prevail. When the worldview changes, however, world hunger will be gone forever.

How about poverty in the second context that I mentioned above? This may be a fundamental problem of human nature. There may always be a small percentage of population whose *tamas* (conditioning) is so strong and *raja* (propensity for situational creativity) is so weak that they cannot hold a job. There may also be the true unlucky due to traumas of various origin. In addition, there is the problem of people in poverty being pushed into criminality.

Spiritual cultures like India had a solution for this that we may be able to revitalize. Until recently, India's very spiritual culture supported a small group of spiritual dropouts called *sadhus*. Some of these *sadhus* were true wandering monks in search of spirituality; however, there is no doubt that a substantial portion of *sadhus* was more like what we call in modern times "hippies"—people of *tamas* taking advantage of the tradition. What is interesting is that although these people faked their spiritual search to a large extent, overall they contributed positivity to the society. Compare this to the negativity the sight of a homeless person in America and Europe arouses in us today! When our poverty programs not only provide soup kitchens and shelters in the winter but also education in subtle-energy consumption, the dropouts regain their dignity because they gain some economic value; they are on their way to become human capital. If we can recycle garbage to make electric power, why can't we recycle wasted human beings into human capital? The good news is that the members of the recent Occupy Wall Street movement actually engaged the homeless and encouraged them to exert themselves in positive ways.

Finally, let's discuss the problem of the poor youth being pushed into criminality. Let's take one pressing example made possible by today's pleasure-oriented culture in the form of what is most often a rich peoples' problem—drug addiction. Suppose a poor kid starts with making easy money being a peddler of crack cocaine. At some point, he himself succumbs, and gets a prison sentence when caught in the drug mess for possession or peddling, doesn't matter. These kids are driven by the same information culture as others, so they have picked up hyperactivity on the way. So conventional methods of education with subtle energy that requires slowness won't work here. How do we deal with these kids that are crowding the jails everywhere in the West? Decriminalization is a partial answer. Do you know that the main opposition to marijuana decriminalization comes from private prison owners? But can we keep hard-drug addiction contained if we decriminalize them? I don't know except that that way is too risky. Addiction to pleasure goes back to scientific materialism being our worldview.

Quantum economics suggests another way. If we put these kids in the spiritual presence of a master, the induction will slow them down, and then they can be educated with subtle energy techniques which in the future will enable them to slow down by themselves and learn. So in this way, a combination of intelligent use of human capital and subtle-energy techniques can go a long way to solve the problem of the growing number of prison populations in this country and elsewhere. Talk about the efficacy of integral eco-friendliness!

Implementation: When and How?

How will the quantum economics of consciousness replace capitalism? When? You may think that the economics of consciousness sounds good. It brings together spiritual values and what is best in capitalism. But how is it going to be implemented? By the government? By social revolution as in the case of the Marxist economics? By a paradigm shift in the academic practices of economics?

How did capitalism come to replace feudalism/mercantile economy? On one hand, it was the brainchild of Adam Smith, no doubt. And indeed it helped that academics welcomed Smith's research as it opened a new paradigm in academia, economics itself. But today's academic situation is quite different from the days of Adam Smith. Some time ago, academic economists chose to pursue not a real world economics but an economics of certain ideal situations so that mathematical models can be used for economic prediction and control. Also today, the entire world of academia is gung-ho that all scientific research must be done while wearing the "straightjacket of scientific materialism."

For example, a very recent economic theory was heralded as a breakthrough because it applied a new innovation of game-theory mathematics to economics. Previously, economists were handicapped in their application of game theory because they had to assume "perfect rationality," that every economic player can figure out the best money-maximizing strategy combination used by the competition. But obviously perfect rationality is impossible in practice because there are so many possibilities. What we have is "bounded rationality"—rational decisions made on the basis of incomplete information about the money-max-imizing strategies of the competition. The new breakthrough is considered a breakthrough because it uses information theory formulas to figure out an approximate description of a set of strategies even with the assumption of bounded rationality. But this still is not the real world. Pleasure-centered materialism has so eroded our pursuit of rationalism; and today we are so subject to negative emotions in our decision making, so bombarded are we by media campaigns that appeal to our negative emotions, that any theory that ignores the emotion component of an eco-nomic decision of the competitor is not going to be of much use.

A game-theory joke that I have read. Two policemen are deep in discussion for a problem of catching a certain bandit. One of them wants to get busy and calculate the optimal mixed strategy for the chase. He is a game theorist, you see. The other policeman is practical, "While we calculate, the bandit is making his escape."

"Relax," says the game theorist. "The bandit also got to fig-ure it out, don't he?"

Actually, the implementation of capitalism happened not because academics welcomed the idea but because capitalism served the purpose of a modernist adventurous people. It was during a time that people were exploring new adventures of mind and meaning which feudalism lacked the manpower to do. Meaning exploration had to be opened up for the masses as science broke free from religious authorities. As meaning explo-ration opened up, scope had to be prepared for the implementa-tion of the fallout of this exploration by making capital available to innovative people for new revolutions in technology and keeping it available. Hence capitalism was inevitable.

And now modernism has given way to post-modernism and post-materialism. The old-fashioned exploration and expansion in the material world are practically over. The old frontier is gone. However many times you see reruns of *Star Trek*, outer space is not going to emerge as mankind's final frontier to play out one final episode of defunct materialism.

Now the society has to deal with the shortcomings of materialist economics with little opportunity to expand in the face of finite resources and challenges of environmental pollution. In addition, the society has to heal the wounds created in it by materialism.

Unfortunately, the elitists will recognize a challenge to their power and construct obstructions to ushering the new worldview and the new economics every step of the way. I believe that we will have the best chance to achieve success quickly through the widespread emergence of centers of quantum activism around the world whose goal is to create positive examples of holistic living and livelihood.

In the 1970s, when I was transitioning from the old physics to the new physics, I read a lot of science fiction. I came across a statement by a science-fiction writer who said that there are only two frontiers left: to open the sky or to open the mind. Materialists still pursue the former, but reality will stop us there sooner or later. I think there is only one new frontier. The new frontier belongs to the subtle dimensions of the human being, and we need a subtler economics to ride in order to explore it.

So the economics of consciousness is inevitable for implementation because our society needs it. As our society moves beyond our competitive ego needs, as we begin to explore the benefits of cooperation en masse, the old competitive capitalist economics has to give way to the new economics, where competition exists simultaneously with cooperation, each in its own sphere of influence.

To understand this, we need to look at how any economics is really implemented., What are the elements that implement it? These elements are the businesses, of course. It is how business is done that provides the drive for the change in economics. And vice versa. The change in economics helps businesses along. Each is essential to the other.

So what will enable the economics of consciousness to replace the current materialism-influenced capitalism? Ultimately, it is the need of the workplace, the businesses. And there, if you look, you will find ample evidence already that business is changing its ways as some of the discussions in this chapter illustrates.

Yes, competition will continue to exist without which there is no market economy. But in the workplace, inside how a business is run, there is increasingly a different philosophy and a different aspect of the human being which are at work, as I have shown in this chapter. In our businesses, we have discovered the value of meaning and creativity, leisure, love, cooperation, and happiness.

With this in mind, in Part 3, in Chapters 8-10, I will explore ideas that you personally can follow up, as a consumer and as a business person, to help usher in the new era of quantum economics. But first, let's acknowledge that government and politicians could help a lot here. In a democracy, macro-economic policy making always depends on politics.

SEVEN

Politics and Economics

Economics is coupled with politics. People elect politicians, expecting help in their pursuit of the American dream. But today politicians are beholden to a variety of vested interests, including economic elitists, because of campaign finance requirements, apart from the fact that they themselves may belong to the elitists. This makes things complicated.

But as should be very clear from the previous pages, to bring about some of the changes that can save capitalism, we need the government to act which, in a democracy, means a lot more than an executive action. Right now our legislative branch in America is polarized. We cannot straighten out economics without doing a similar job of straightening out our democracy. The founders of our democracy were neither blind followers of religious dogma, nor were they materialists. Amazingly, they were integrationists; they recognized the cogency of both mind and matter, and even spirituality. Unfortunately, when they wrote the Constitution, they left their spiritual principles at best implicit. Today, we must include the subtle and spiritual dimensions explicitly in the pursuit of democratic ideals as I am proposing it for economics. But even this is only a beginning.

Democracy is much degraded today because of our unabashed tendency toward negative emotions and because we choose our leaders in such a way that takes no recognition of the leaders' emotional intelligence. This has to change, but the job of the quantum approach is cut out for this one. We also need to bring people of *sattva* in the political arena, but the current domination of the political arena by media and money makes it very difficult. Whose money? Money of big corporations and individual elitists. So we have to change the mindset of some of the elitists; a difficult task, not impossible. Additionally, we have to change the way big corporations are run, trying to influence politics to serve their greed. Can corporations wake up to the energies of love? We will discuss that issue in Chapter 9.

We can bridge the polarization of politics in America and elsewhere by ushering in the quantum worldview and the science within consciousness. Are there signs that such bridge building is not far-fetched?

The Politics of Worldview Change

In America and many other countries, right now there is a huge polarization between people based on worldviews, the root of the political divide. First, the old worldview of religion/spirituality/values lives on. In this country, the religious worldview is the popular Christian worldview. Most conservatives, Republicans for example, subscribe to this, at least by words if not by deeds. The opposing worldview is that of scientific materialism, mainly propounded by academics, fanned by so-called liberal media, and is unofficially the dogma of the Democratic Party with some humanism thrown in. And, of course, in America, no politician dares to admit publicly that "God is dead."

The Christian worldview is simplistic to the extreme. The God of popular Christianity is still a bearded, fat, and majestic white guy, sitting on a throne in heaven with a magic wand, judging people on Judgment Day, and thereby sending people to heaven or hell, according to their earthly deeds. The academics pooh-pooh these simplistic ideas; but unfortunately, to a religious person, the ideas of scientific materialism are equally simplistic. How can this complex world with purposive, living human beings, be simply a cause-driven machine? How can such a world come into being without God's creativity? All creative acts come with meaning and purpose. What is the meaning of a human life if not to serve the purposive values of the act of creation of a higher power that brought us here? How can we not recognize that overindulgence in certain activities, like sexuality, takes us away from God and must be regarded as sin while other acts of value, such as love, takes us towards the divine and therefore must be regarded as virtue?

Because both sides are an exclusive dogma, neither side can see any validity whatsoever in the ideas of the other side. Pragmatism, which used to be an American virtue, and still is to some extent, demands otherwise. Science has given us not only its undesirable-to-many worldview, but also experimentally verified theories that are the basis of much important technology that everybody uses. How can we deny this aspect of science? On the other side, spiritual traditions of which religions are a popular rendition, have given us the archetypal values, without which civilization disappears. And indeed, as we have argued in this book, our economies go awry.

But scientific people are afraid that given a little inch, the religions will take a mile and bring back the unthinkable Victorian age of sexual suppression. Human beings do have those instinctual brain circuits that for most people cry out for the freedom of gratification. How can we call what comes naturally "sin" and deny them even when we do not have adequate readiness for denial? Of course, you cannot trust people who don't believe in evolution anyway, so the scientists turn their backs on religionists.

And religions are equally afraid that given an inch, the atheists also will take a mile and take us to Sodom and Gomorrah and civilization will suffer. After all, scientists do seem to act like the proverbial fool who was seen cutting off the very branch of a tree on which he was sitting. Science is a search for truth whose pursuits make sense only if there is absolute eternal truth—the laws of science. If truth itself is relative, how can we do science? Yet, under scientific materialism all archetypes are under the attack of relativism.

You cannot trust people who do not believe in absolute truth, grumble the religionists. Of course, that does not stop them from hypocritically using relative truth to malign scientific findings about global warming!

The good news is that the polarization, at least in America, is not really 50-50, but more like 1/3, 1/3, 1/3. The last third are a relatively dogma-free pragmatic people who see value in science but do not subscribe to the metaphysics of scientific materialism. They also see the value of archetypal value, and so they can see the pragmatism of following a middle path between the conditioning of the brain circuits and striving for values.; They can see that the simplistic images of God have become a relic and can easily be given up, and they can see that just as easily the dogma of scientific materialism only unnecessarily puts a straightjacket on the human potential and limits it.

The sociologist Paul Ray has called this last segment of American people "cultural creatives" (Ray and Anderson, 2001).

When Ray wrote his book, the number of these people constituted about 20 percent of all Americans. I call these people quantum activists, because perhaps without consciously trying, they are already transforming their own lives and their society following the principles of quantum physics. In my experience, in this country they are about 70 percent women, about 70 percent middle-aged, creative people all, and highly concerned about pursuing a life of meaning and values.

From the materialist side, this group of people has moved on to post-materialism, looking for post-materialist science paradigms. From the religious side, these people differentiate between religion and spirituality and have moved on to what I call post-secularism.

This group recognizes the value of science but does not subscribe to everything-is-matter philosophy. This group recognizes the value of spiritual transformation, but does not abide by the particular dogma of any particular religion. They are multicultural, they see value in all religions; they do not see why religions should be antagonistic to science defying the "fact" of scientific data and usefulness of scientific theories to sort things out. On the other hand, they do not accept the dogma of everything-is-matter as "fact." And they don't like the exclusivity of this dogma.

As I said, these people are de-facto quantum activists. They already use quantum creativity to guide their lives but blindly. The movement of quantum activism is designed to give direction to this adventurous group's creative meaning and value-seeking pursuits.

From an economic perspective, this group can be divided in the usual way: business producers (management and labor), and consumers. The producers of the new ilk are looking for a livelihood that will bring meaning and satisfaction in their lives. The consumers are looking to satisfy their higher needs. They want to enjoy vitality to feed their optimism, they want to explore meaning beyond mere entertainment and information gathering, and values for inspiration; and above all, they want transformation.

Can even a sizable minority as these cultural creatives influence politics? The case of waking up politicians of both parties to archetypal values is not completely hopeless. Democrats already are open to human values in words and often in deeds. Republicans at least give lip service to spiritual values. The saving grace is that quite a few politicians in both aisles are intelligent; they are painfully aware that there is only a minimal validity to their party lines. They all have been waiting for the real story of the universe and its journey in the past, now, and in the future. They all hope that their most favorite beliefs will be included in the grand story of the universe. As we saw in Chapter 3, quantum physics is giving us an inclusive story, and therein is its persuasive power.

So if you are one of the open-minded politicians who wants politics to be moving again and economy to prosper again, simply realize that you have a new science protecting your back while you persuade your colleagues to talk again. Simply realize that you do have a huge latent support among the populace. I hope knowing that will help you to support the quantum agenda for economic change.

You Want a Real Economic Change, Mr. Politician? Here is the Quantum Manifesto for Economic Change

Dear Mr. Politician,

One of your campaign slogans has always appealed to me; you are for *change*. Recently, Obama used this slogan to an art in 2008: *change we can believe in*. But almost every one of you talks about change in election time. Senator McCain, Obama's opponent, surely did. At his convention acceptance speech, he downright tried to scare lobbyists with his change talk. But the lobbyists who try to influence the government on behalf of their clients are just a symptom that our democratic political system is not working. The government is not really doing what it should be doing. And politicians who oppose big government are not doing what they should be doing either. This is why nothing is working, politicians have become irrelevant, and our democracy in America is on the crossroads.

The same situation prevails everywhere. The economic meltdown that gave us the great recession is a symptom showing that there is something very wrong at the base; the economic models we are using aren't working. And politics (in the way we are used to) is not working either.

Perhaps the political model you are using is equally wrong? In the olden days of Thomas Jefferson and Abe Lincoln, people sought political power to use their power to empower people. The whole objective of democracy is for people to participate in the pursuit of "life, liberty, and the pursuit of happiness." If you call this aim the "American dream," clearly it is not just acquiring a house (here politicians do try to help people with tax breaks); a car (no tax break there; but politicians bail out car companies in trouble in order to maintain a steady flow of production, and that's something!); or a nice family (no thank you; Americans don't need your help there). Additionally, people need prerogative and empowerment to use their liberty in search of creative exploration of meaning and value to them. And people need a good internal environment to be happy and to eventually even achieve spiritual wholeness. They can use help to empower themselves. Instead (you excepted, of course), most politicians are using their power to dominate others, don't you see that?

Yes, the economy, our businesses, need to provide jobs for people. But we have evolved since the days of Adam Smith when peoples' well-being meant only material well-being. Now people want more—they want meaning and value in their lives. The definition of the American dream has changed and you have not noticed.

What have you done lately to help people in their exploration of meaning and values? If you are a Democrat, you will say that's a job of higher education. You will proudly point out your party's commitment to student loans so higher education, in spite of the sky- rocketing costs, can get enough students. But do you keep track of what the students are getting for their money? Job training yes, jobs they can do for a few years. But after that? The universities do not teach people general principles of meaning exploration anymore, nor do they create any understanding of the archetypes that are the driver behind all human occupations. Blinded by scientific materialism, they teach short-term stuff, material and machine ways to deal with material technology and human beings. Meanwhile, we are running out of ways to expand technology in the material domain; there is not enough energy, and material resources are also short in supply.

Being Democrats, I know what you are thinking. We will create a government-funded commission to study the question. Eventually, you or some other democratic leader will want to expand government in higher-education business.

No, we don't need to worry. Republicans will oppose you; that is what they do best.

If you are a Republican, as a group you don't approve of the "higher education" that colleges and universities dole out today. So you will pass on meaning education and may lamely point to Glenn Beck's television show for value education. And maybe even churches, except you probably know that that, too, is a Pandora's box. That will never get traction—secularism, you know.

Behold! The solution is here, with quantum economics. Exactly the way you have always wanted it. Let education be freed up— from the higher-education establishment that has given up on meaning and values because of their sellout to scientific materialism, and from the organized religion establishment because what they teach about values will never pass the test of secularism. Allow free market forces to do the rest. This is what quantum economics says.

Well, churches may get angry with you, but are you so attached to dogma? Can you get elected without a coalition with churches? Yes, you can, if your bold step solves the problem of education and the problem of the economy all in the same stroke of genius.

The same thing goes for you, Mr. Democrat Politician. Are you so attached to the dogma of scientific materialism? You like science. But we can do science without that dogma! If you join hands with Republicans to make both meaning education and value education free from their monopolistic domination by establishments of their respective fields and allow free market to enter, the market forces will take care of the rest.

I know you don't particularly like the tone of that; that is a Republican line. You want a role for the government here. There is a very important one. To initiate quantum economics, government can do certain things. I will talk about it in the next section.

There is another biggie that needs fixing, and that is health care. Health care in America is not even universal like in other advanced economies. But even so, health care costs keep going up and up, Obamacare's tinkering notwithstanding. This is also a symptom that something is fundamentally wrong with our health science itself. It's not individually the fault of the hospitals, the doctors, nor even the insurance companies and the pharmaceuticals. There is only one party to blame: the AMA, the medical establishment with its stranglehold on how medicine has to be practiced. And they side with material machine medicine—allopathy—exclusively.

Mr. Politician, for some time we have known that in most situations, conventional allopathic medicine only gets rid of the symptoms, but does not really heal because the disease is at the subtle level produced by a mismanagement of vital feeling or mental meanings. In particular, allopathy does not work with chronic disease; in fact, the use of it to alleviate symptoms, because of side effects, may actually harm the body in the long run. The older people don't have much immunity left! When the disease is caused at the subtle level, doesn't it make sense that it is the subtle that we have to set right? There are already alternative medicine systems in place; they are legal and popular in this country thanks to President Nixon's trip to China and thanks to President Clinton's creation of the office of alternative medicine.

Now here is my puzzle with you. Are you so scared of the allopathic lobby, AMA and the like, that you are missing the simple fact that alternative medicine is much cheaper than conventional medicine? That its emphasis is on prevention so insurance companies would not be pressed as hard with costly claims as they are now? Most importantly, intelligent use of alternative medicine heals for longer periods, so recurring expenses will be avoided.

Mr. Politician, there is now in place a paradigm of integrative medicine that establishes the perimeters of both conventional and alternative medicine and that is cost-effective. The best part of integrative medicine is striking—it empowers the patients to maintain health and even heal themselves. If one uses this integrative system, health-care management will become tractable. Why not use your political power to bring integral medicine to health care?

If you are a Republican, help alternative medicine to get a level field by allowing free market in part of medicine, the part that is optional. And join hands with Democrats to allow compulsory medicine, general, and preventive care to be mostly the territory of alternative medicine. In Chapter 1, I suggested this for Medicare; but really the idea applies to the whole population with the proviso that in emergency and a few other situations, allopathy will prevail. This is the solution to medical costs and it is so in hand for us to institute.

Mr. Politician, you complain about polarization. If you are a Republican, you blame Democrats for always wanting to expand the role of the government. I agree with you, the bureaucrats will generally take us down the garden path. But wake up! Without ethical transformation, the rich and famous aristocratic elite will also take us down the garden path. To get capitalism going, to get the government going with the right balance as to its size and scope, we need the elite to transform by exploring the same subtle products that will transform the 99 percent. That is the message that you need to heed, Mr. Politician, irrespective of your political color.

Scientific materialism tried to replace the earlier worldview of religious elitism where an elite, consisting of the rich and powerful and the religious oligarchy, ruled the economic roost—feudal economics. Capitalism was designed to break away from that. But driven by the greed unleashed by scientific material-ism, a new elitism is created consisting of the religious rich and famous and scientific meritocrats. Most of the economic gains go to the new elite, and the gap between rich and poor becomes greater and greater. Wouldn't you call that a step backward from capitalism toward a new feudalism? Long gone is the optimism of the 1970s. Middle class is visibly shrinking now. Cynics are already saying that this is due to a deliberate strategy of the elit-ists who see the meaning-seeking middle class as a threat. If you are a connoisseur of how capitalism works, I know you support the middle class. But can you resist the political power of the new elite? You need new moral authority.

Mr. Politician, it is time that you recognized scientific mate-rialism for what it is: another system of dogma much like a religion. In fact, I sometimes wonder if teaching scientific materialism in our schools and institutions of higher education violates the constitutional separation of church and state. It would be interesting to see what courts have to say about that!

The era of modernism gave us the three pillars of modern civilization: capitalism, democracy, and liberal education, and we are just beginning to establish a fourth great pillar—institutions of integral health, both physical and subtle well-being. Scientific materialism, as it promotes elitism through economics, also tends to destroy democracy via a frontal attack on feeling, meaning and higher archetypal values. Under democracy, ideally political power is to be used to make meaning accessible to bigger and bigger portions of humanity. But if meaning itself is dubious, why pursue it or promote it? Why not indulge in pleasure instead, which feeds the negative emotional brain circuits that are the real thing, not ideas? And while you are doing that, why not make sure that others should cater to your pleasure, too? Use your power to dominate others, power for power's sake! And the new elite, the "pointy-headed" professors of the higher-education academia will help you by routing out all opposing worldviews. With 200+ IQ you can count on them to be great experts in sophistry by which the light of truth can appear dark, or at least grey enough to confuse people.

So it is this materialist version of capitalism that you have to root out. And replace it with the spirit of the original version modified according to the dictates of the newest discoveries of science. And that means to bring back meaning and values, even feelings in the economic equation. As Maslow said, we have a whole hierarchy of needs, not just the material need for survival. If you care to look, Google the words *consciousness* or *quantum physics* on the Internet, and you can readily come across an alternative paradigm of science based on the quantum worldview.

Among other things, this worldview irrefutably posits consciousness, not matter, as the foundation of all being and easily gives us a science that includes all our experiences, both material and the subtle—feeling, meaning, and archetypal values. There are already plenty of data to support the quantum worldview and this new science. If you want more data, just divert a little of your huge science budget in this direction.

Behold! This quantum-based paradigm validates our subtle needs—need for love, need for the exploration of meaning, need for justice and beauty, and goodness. These needs don't much come from our brain circuits or our genes. They come from nonmaterial subtle worlds, and consciousness mediates their interaction with the material world. So please help to make them part of the production-consumption equation. Can we do it? Yes, we can. There is a fallout from it that you will like. The subtle economy, in contrast to the gross material one, is not a zero-sum game! So investing in it intelligently actually gets rid of those vicious business cycles with little government intervention (inexpensive, to be sure).

All our institutions need leadership. Yes, democracy is important, but so is it important to see that *tamas* dominates large segments of people who are not truly individual persons but followers of other people who are true individuals. Who is a true individual? You have to be a creative, an originator of an opinion, to be an original individual. I believe (we have to believe) that there are many individual persons of this ilk in politics, and you are one of them. Go one step ahead and become a leader with the avowed goal of getting rid of the polarization and elitism.

You cannot institute instant worldview change. You don't have enough support for that. But economics and the economy are pragmatic subjects. If you can show that using subtle technology, jobs can be created, peoples' well-being can be improved, and eventually that even drug addiction can be reduced as can prison population, then you have a chance of a break through. It all begins with small steps. A research grant here, a research grant there, giving this business a tax break, tinkering with Medicare a little, tinkering with Obamacare a little. Here, I have a whole list for you.

The Role of the Government: a Summary

In the aftermath of the great depression, government intervention was used in the form of Keynesian economics. The economy did not recover, but since then the Keynesian tactic of government intervention has been used a few times to bring the American economy out of mild recession with mixed success. After the deflation of the economy in the 1980s and the failure of the Keynesian remedy, our government tried rescue with supply-side economics. It did not work and taxes had to be increased again. It was a downright disaster when George W. Bush tried it because most of the tax relief of the rich went into the financial sector of the economy instead of the production-consumption economy. As you recall, the genie of the financial speculative investment had been released from the bottle of government control a few years back, in 1999.

This is the thing that our traditional economists are reluctant to admit. Capitalism crucially needs consciousness and creativity to get out of recession. Consumer demand has to be stoked by new creative innovation, and it is the latter that is lacking lately.

We have to face the fact that the material age of our civilization (which East Indians call *kali yuga*) is over. We are entering the age of the subtle vital energy now (*dwapar yuga*) according to some thinkers (Chandra Roy, 2012). There is wisdom in this ancient thinking as this book amply proves.

If the answer to the 2007-2009 great recession were in the form of government intervention to bring about subtle economics and rapid deployment of vital energy technology, much of the economic problems we face today could have been avoided.

To their credit, the Obama government did take some preliminary steps conducive to the coming age of subtle energy and "small is beautiful" economics of consciousness. The government has encouraged solar and other renewable energy. It has introduced measures to reduce energy consumption. This is all from the negative side: reduce (the excesses of material consumption). It is the positive side that is lacking.

During the election campaign of 2012, President Obama took a wonderful initiative step for an economics of consciousness. He emphasized the subtle energy of hope into the economic equation. But the next steps for a subtle economics require much more boldness. This is what the government can do in the short term:

1. The government should give research grants, tax benefits, and other incentives to any business that extends to subtle-energy production in ways I spoke about in an earlier chapter—yoga, Tai Chi, martial arts, massage, acupuncture, and all that.

2. There is still huge unemployment if you count those people who have given up looking for work. And face it. In the absence of innovation in the material sector, businesses will continue to sit on their trillion dollars or play with it in the financial sector. But unemployed people should be given unemployment benefits irrespective of how long they have been unemployed whenever there are not enough jobs to go around. Then they could be required to spend this time in subtle-energy enterprises and to educate themselves to open up to their subtle energy needs. This will create consumer demand to the producers above.

3. The government can start a national laboratory to investigate the subtle and confirm some of the findings already made and make new discoveries leading to new vital energy technology. In particular, government-sponsored research would be the quickest way to establish rigorous quantifying devices for subtle-energy measurement.

4. The Medicare program for the elderly should invoke quantum integrative medicine in which alternative medicine gets to play the leading role to bring the cost down and eventually saving this program from going bankrupt. The Medicare program should surrender its costly prescription drug benefits for people who are dying; instead, it should initiate death-with-dignity programs, which again by bringing in the latest progress in science within consciousness into gerontology, allows huge financial savings.

5. The Medicaid program for the poor similarly should include "dignity" programs. The use of holistic integrative medicine will do that.

6. Government should immediately initiate research looking into the vital energy aspect of genetically-engineered agricultural products (such as Monsanto rice) and take appropriate steps depending on the new research findings.

7. Last but not least, the government can immediately start vitalizing its various workplaces. This would certainly improve the efficiency.

These are all at the Federal level. At the local level, municipalities, instead of inane and controversial fluoridation programs, should get into water revitalization programs, especially in large urban areas.

PART THREE

The Implementation:
Quantum Activism

EIGHT

Preparing the Mindset
for the New Economics

So finally, let's get down and dirty: What is the plan of action to usher in the new economic mind-set among first, the consumers, and second, business investors and professionals—the producers? When the field is ready, the players will come. Right now, we have the beginnings of a new paradigm; we also have quite a few people of gift in the subtle arena, left over from old spiritual/religious traditions. There are a quite a few consumers, too. There are 700 million yoga practitioners, according to some counts, in a world population of 7 billion—which is a significant percentage but obviously not enough to attract capital investment from the business entrepreneur to provide financial backing to the gifted people to start a subtle economy that counts.

The first issue for you the reader is to wake up to the importance of your own subtle well-being, subtle health really, as a consumer and/or as a producer. You have been duped by the

allopathic-health establishment, by the higher-education establishment, and even the religious establishments, that your well-
being is not a fundamental right protected by the Constitution,
that your well-being is not an economic issue at least. It is time
you called their bluff.

Consumers and Businesspeople: Changing the Mindset to a Quantum Integrative Worldview

In 1995, a couple of years after my first book (*The Self-Aware
Universe*) on the new paradigm was published, I had already
gained some entry to the new paradigm lecture circuit. While
giving a lecture, somebody in the audience made a comment
that puzzled me. "You talk a lot like Stephen Hawking," this old
lady was saying.

"But dear lady," I objected, "Steven Hawking is the staunch-
est materialist I know of. And my work demolishes the Hawk-
ing-favored philosophy of scientific materialism. I must not have
done such a great job in explaining my work," I lamented.

"But you both talk about the mind of God," the lady explained.

Scientific materialists are extremely clever sellers of their
philosophy; they have to be. After all, they have managed to
convince a whole generation of scientists, philosophers, and
humanists, among them people of 150+ IQ, that they, in spite
of their high intelligence (often accompanied by a considerable
amount of creativity), are walking computers (zombies really).
And more. That the brain is nothing but a neural network; and
everyone, they included, are people of all conditioning and no
creativity other than computer creativity, which is but a special
conditioned propensity to look into the deep caverns of the neural network not accessible to normal people. And more. That
their consciousness and free will are operational accompani-
ments of the neural network probably arising from Darwinian

evolution and the gene's struggle to survive and so forth. But these scientific materialists co-opt ideas like the "mind of God" to denote the mysterious laws of cosmology or elementary particle behavior that these scientists are deciphering, therein giving the impression that their work signifies deep spirituality, whereas in actuality, they do not even subscribe to the idea of meaning-giving mind. They equate mind with brain; so when Hawking talks about mind of God, is he ascribing God a brain?

Okay, I am being facetious in part, but there is truth in what I am saying, and this is one reason scientific materialism is so difficult to challenge. The majority of even educated people rarely know what scientific materialism is really about. In America, there is a tradition already against pointy-heads and ivory-tower people debating free will and stuff like that. Educated persons incessantly ask questions about the meaning of their lives and values they try to live (and want others to live, too) and yet are unaware that scientific materialism has no room for meaning and values.

Scientific materialism, like the Christian worldview that it tries to replace, denigrates anything it cannot accommodate. This includes (in addition to mind and meaning) also feelings and intuitions. Of course, being good experimental scientists, these people do not deny that we have instinctual brain circuits, and that is okay because it is just brain wiring that is giving you a behavior, and why not exploit that behavior! Just don't ever ask for an explanation of where those instincts come from, or if you do, be satisfied with a vague utterance about Darwinian evolution and survival necessity.

This behavior manipulation of your instinctual negative emotions gave businesses some of the power of selling anything by marketing techniques making consumer behavior mathematically predictable. The challenge now to both businesses and consumers of the subtle is to develop the ability of rising up, at least when the occasion demands, to positive feelings, meanings, and intuitions that are not already wired in the brain.

The immediate challenge to the consumers in this age of cell phones and digital messaging is to first, shift from information to meaning, and second, shift from the tyranny of the instinctual brain circuits of emotion to the visceral experience of feelings (in other words, to embody themselves). The novelist James Joyce wrote about one of his characters, "Mr. Duffy lives a little distance away from his body." Today we all have a tendency to live away from our body. Have you noticed how you feel tired after attending to emails on your laptop for a few hours, and this without any physical exertion at all? You feel tired because all your vital energy is now associated with your brain; check it out and feel the blood flow there. The rest of your vital organs have detached from the vital body and lack vitality—vital energy, stuff that gives us feeling, and the very thing you are avoiding in this machine culture.

The brain circuits are there, of course, so your base feelings come back in a hurry when confronted with appropriate stimuli. What you lack though is the capacity to feel the higher feelings, feelings like love, exultation, clarity, and satisfaction—the higher chakra feelings that are not wired in the brain and, therefore, do not come easily without effort.

Fortunately, women have some built-in safeguards against such total isolation from higher feelings which men of our society face. First, women are not so conditioned against feelings as they grow up; after all, they are future mothers. Second, motherly love is one of those instinctual wirings in the female brain and is a positive emotion. So women have access to one noble emotion at least. Thus potentially women can lead us all to the promised land of subtle economics, and the good news is that to some extent, they are already doing it.

Now the bad news. The women's lib movement of the 1960s began with the high promise to finally lead humanity in the new age of appreciation of women's values, such as the importance of the noble emotions. But scientific materialism has long since corrupted and co-opted the women's movement into the men's power game.

Waking Up to Higher Emotions

And so the challenge remains not only for the consumer but also for the businessperson who dares to venture into the new land and start a business. You have to know your commodity. What can you do to meet the challenge? Again, the good news is that it takes only some easy practices to wake up to your higher emotions. Here is a sample:

1. The prerequisite is to become viscerally sensitive to your feelings, and the first problem you have to overcome is that unless you develop sensitivity, you always experience feelings mixed with thoughts— emotions. So begin with body awareness training.

2. Recreate a loving scenario, some incident that aroused feelings of love in you. If you have to back all the way to your childhood for such an incident, so be it. Recreate the incident in your mind's eye. Carl Jung called this active imagination—very effective for this sort of thing. Pay attention to the details. As you do this, keep attention to your heart chakra. You will feel some vitality there, maybe tingles, or at least a feeling of warmth or expansion. Okay, this is heart chakra energy. When you were not so taken by the mechanical gadgets of your youth, you used to feel this regularly. Devour it now. Repeat the exercise

at least once a day, or as often as you can handle it. After all, you cannot allow yourself to be mushy, can you?

3. This one is for the bathtub where because of reverberation by the tiles, anybody can sing. Sing a love song (just one line will do) like, "All we need is love." Sing with gusto! Feel the energy first in the throat chakra, and then as you continue, notice that the energy is spreading to the heart chakra, and eventually even to the crown chakra, giving you deep satisfaction. Not bad, huh?

4. Focus your attention to the brow chakra and try to understand what just happened. It's huge. You have the capacity to invoke higher emotions even though you do not have brain circuits of automatic recall. As this clarity dawns, feel a warmth at the brow chakra.

5. Rub your palms together and then separate them slightly as you have seen East Indian people do the gesture they call "namaste" when they greet people. You should feel a tingle—vital energy. This energy is easily transferred to other areas of the body by taking your activated palm to that area with (hands on) or without touching (hands off).

You are doing well. Keep it up. In the arena of vitalized consumer goods, you have to judge the feeling you are getting; so, how can you judge without developing the sensitivity? Similarly, for the businessperson, how can you produce vitalized products without developing some sensitivity to vital energy? True, we have to develop objective instruments, too, and such instrumentation is arriving, but nothing beats direct experience.

When you become energy sensitive, you will have a personal gauge of other peoples' energy to tell you if somebody is really protagonist or just faking it. This is very helpful in a business transaction regardless of your role—buyer or seller.

Waking Up to Intuition

Ultimately, higher feelings are representations of the archetypes in the medium of feeling. So the greater challenge of developing subtle nuance is to wake up to intuition. If you have been persuaded by scientific materialists that intuitions do not exist, suspend your disbelief.

How do you distinguish between ordinary and intuitive thought that is really an instant representation of something deeper, namely intuition? Since intuition is a direct experience of a supramental archetype, it always contains a modicum of truth, so it comes with a feeling of certainty. But since the encounter is fleeting, the certainty likewise, the resulting conviction is shallow, not enough to overrule an already present belief system otherwise. Thus disbelief will follow; and that is what I am asking you to suspend every time it comes up.

Since intuition connects us to the supramental which cannot be directly represented in the physical body, there is no direct memory of it to cause any conditioning. So there is no ego in this experience; it is a direct encounter with your quantum self. Hence, it naturally comes with a cosmic feeling of oneness of everything, but the feeling closes down quickly. So be as quick to appreciate it.

Get used to expecting this unexpected visit from your quantum self. The more ready you are to receive your uninvited guest, the more it comes to you, inviting you to the investigation of this or that archetype. Heed what the psychologist James Hillman said: It's not you pursuing the archetype; it is the archetype pursuing you.

If we each choose a course in life to trust our intuitions more, even though we cannot fully confirm their wisdom intellectually, I believe our process of working collaboratively with the archetypes and with the evolutionary movement of consciousness will flourish into a new holistic way of life.

Evolution of the Concept of Self-Interest

There is a lot of inertia associated with the human situation, the reason that negativity and materiality tends to dominate and the "small voice within" of intuitive urge for satisfying higher needs gets lost. We need a sociocultural push to overcome the inertia and move toward a broadening of what we call our self-interest. Let me elaborate.

"Greed is good" is selling as the mantra of capitalism today. Even the respected journalist Fareed Zakaria used the phrase in a 2009 *Newsweek* magazine article supposed to lay down the manifesto of capitalism. He should have made it clear that it is the capitalist manifesto under the spell of scientific materialism. In Adam Smith's original formulation influenced by the philosophy of modernism, not materialism, Smith was very clear that he distinguished between self-interest and greed.

It all depends on your worldview. In modernism, mind, meaning, and ethics are all valued. And you cannot practice ethics without relationship to others. So your self-interest covers at least your local societal environment.

Under the influence of materialism, your self tends to become just you, your physical body, and what is conditioned into your brain by your genes and environment. Let's face it; you become narcissistic. Since the brain is sort of a computer and rational thinking is computable, this narcissistic self is supposed to be the rational you, but guess what? Materialism and rationalism cannot change your nature that is guided a lot by your instinctual brain circuits of negative emotion of which the greed circuit is a major one. So it is not surprising that you identify with self-interest and greed whenever it suits you. For example, as CEO of a big corporation, it is "normal" behavior for you to demand and get a hefty raise irrespective of the interests of the stockholders, or irrespective of whether your company is showing a profit. In those moments you suppress your higher needs, even rational thinking, in favor of greed.

Growing up in a consciousness-based worldview, it is different once again. Once more, your broader self-interest recognizes your higher needs with ease. This prompts you to try to balance your negative emotions with positive ones. And if the social norm demands that you should be ethical, you don't consider it a "sacrifice" to give up your greed more often than not and behave ethically.

There are other striking differences, too. The "self" of materialism is entirely operational and behavioral. Thus it is not surprising that under the aegis of materialism, business and corporate CEOs tend to do their empire building not through innovations, but through acquisitions. In a consciousness-based worldview, the self is once more recognized to have nonlocality and creativity. So nonlocal expansion of the self to include others takes place and creativity, as in Adam Smith's era under modernism, can once again thrive in businesses.

Attuning to the Movement of Consciousness

The new science tells us that consciousness in the long term is always evolving toward making meaning processing accessible to more and more people (Goswami, 2011). When your business is tuned to add a meaningful product or service in your society and environment, it is in tune with the evolutionary movement of consciousness. When this happens, then your intention (of a successful creative business) is backed up by the entire power of downward causation of nonlocal quantum consciousness. Will this not create greater prospects for success in your business endeavor? Think.

So remember that in terms of consciousness, aside from the profit motive, there are two additional purposes for your business whatever the content may be. It is to spread positive emotions and meaning processing to people. When this purposiveness is clearly expressed in your business dealings, they cannot fail. The invisible hands of the free market, the movement of nonlocal consciousness itself will come to your aid.

How to attune yourself and your business to other peoples' positive feelings and meanings? You have to engage in business not with the exclusive purpose of making money but with the idea of exploring the archetype of abundance. Remember, abundance is not just about material wealth; it also includes mental meaning, vital satisfaction, and spiritual happiness. You cannot follow the archetype of abundance with a closed heart; the archetype won't let you.

Business producers, be aware! Ask, did I choose my profession because I see meaning in making money more than anything else? Then go deeper. Am I in business to just make money, or am I also interested in the broader questions of the archetype of abundance that include both material and subtle well-being? Is this way of making a living a suitable vehicle for my creative exploration of abundance? Does it make my life more meaningful?

The co-founders of the New Dimensions Radio, Michael and Justine Toms, put it this way: "In the Thai language there is a word, *sanuk*, which means that whatever you do, you should enjoy it." (Toms and Toms, 1999) Processing old meaning is computational, machine-like, at best joy-neutral, usually boring.

How does joy enter meaning processing? When new meaning is processed, when our intuitive facility is engaged, then the brow chakra and crown chakra vital energies (of clarity and satisfaction) are also engaged. When you process new meaning that you love, then additionally you engage the heart chakra, your consciousness becomes expansive, and you experience bliss or spiritual joy.

The next question we ask is this. Are the practices of my business and the products I help create serving the purpose of evolution? If not, are you willing to change the ways of your business? If you are, you have made another quantum leap in making your business conducive to the economics of consciousness

In our current materialist culture, material accomplishment is everything. When one acts with accomplishment of material orientation, any action, even those that are seemingly selfless, always tends to strengthen the ego-centered narcissism—the accomplisher has to look after numero uno in a zero-sum game, has to compete and control. When we stop measuring our accomplishment in material terms and learn to enjoy our subtle accomplishments, we no longer have to be numero uno, we no longer have to seek power to dominate others, even though they are employees; and only then can we seek meaning without violating our values. No longer do we take ourselves too seriously.

In one of the issues of the comic strip *Mutts*, one of the canine characters says to another while looking at some birds flying, "How do birds fly?"

"Because," the other canine responds, "they take themselves lightly."

Recoupling Meaning and Money

When we reward gifted people of production in the subtle arena with money, in the process we change the "color" of money; we infuse money with meaning. Let me elaborate.

I have been a physics professor at a university for most of my professional life, so higher education is an area I know first-hand. I have heard from my older colleagues how it was before the "Sputnik" revolution. Even scientists did not have government grants those days; and talented academic scientists accepted very low remuneration relative to their industrial peers in clear recognition of the fact that they were "paying a price" for the freedom to pursue meaning in their research in whatever way they liked. When I came on board in the 1960s as part of the Sputnik revolution, this was already changing. Scientists were getting (mainly government) research grants and demanding higher salaries than their humanities colleagues who did not have such grants. In the next fifty years, as modernism gave way to materialism, and Adam Smith's capitalism was gradually replaced by materialist economics, money was quickly decoupled from meaning, even this changed drastically. As meaning became decoupled from money, academics claimed and got comparable salaries for people of similar qualifications everywhere and, of course, a star system was created at the same time. This is one of the factors why we see the cost of higher education going up in this country at a rate much higher than the rate of inflation. Greed again.

Can the economics of consciousness recouple money back to meaning? You bet. And this has very serious positive implications for business and industry.

Originally, money was created to facilitate meaningful economic transactions. Money acts as a catalyst. Now if you remember your basic chemistry, catalysts are not meant to accumulate. It is the failure of materialism to distinguish between need and greed that leads to the accumulation of money for the service of greed and power to dominate others. Up to a point, accumulation of money, it can be sensibly argued, will lead to investments into economic production and serve basic capitalism. But since without creative innovation, production is limited by the equation of demand and supply, very soon accumulation serves only the purpose of acquisition: not only acquisition of unneeded goods and services that can be relatively benign but also acquisition of other businesses, and especially acquisition of power.

The Greeks understood this perfectly. Explains the biologist Brian Goodwin:

> The confusion between money as facilitator of trading transactions and as something with intrinsic value comes from a failure to distinguish between *oikos*, the Greek root for economic, and *krema*, the Greek word for individual wealth which is purely about acquisition.... the "krematistic" accumulation of money in individual hands was condemned by Aristotle as destructive of community wealth and the intrinsic health of resilient trading and exchange systems (Goodwin, 2007).

We have argued in the previous pages that the decoupling of meaning and money has been disastrous; for example, it contributed to the current economic meltdown. Goodwin agrees. "It is the development of an economic culture based on pure money making and acquisition that has shaped our monetary and economic systems ... so that they are intrinsically unstable and destructive." I believe that this came about through the use of money as power to influence policies that accelerated the acquisition of more wealth by a few, and very few of us were sufficiently equipped enough to prevent the avalanche of chaos that resulted.

Let's get back to the question: Can the economics of consciousness rescue us from acquisitory accumulation of money? Built into the economics of consciousness is the idea of production of transformative subtle energy of positive emotions. Also built into it is the scientific validity of ethical principles. Together they should be able to balance greed in the long run and economic transactions will return to meaningfulness. In the short run, during the transition between paradigms, it may be necessary to use taxation to achieve that goal. A creative and articulate alternative media is also a must.

Transforming the Energy of Money

From the advent of its first use, money has always been regarded as a representation, a symbol of something of meaning and value. But with the denigration of meaning and value, many economists began to treat money having intrinsic value of its own. Thus was born monetary economics.

Nowadays a quasi-governmental organization controls the money supply by controlling interest rates that banks charge for borrowing money. In America the Federal Reserve serves as the agency of this control. The idea is to avoid recession. If the economy shows signs of slow-down, the Fed can increase money supply by reducing interest rates. Likewise, when the economy heats up showing signs of inflation, too much money chasing too few goods, the Fed can raise interest rates to cool things down. Does this manipulation keep recessions out? As I argued earlier in the book, this is highly debatable.

Trade between nations raises the question of the exchange rate between various local currencies. Previously, we always had a reminder that money is a representation of something of value; a gold standard was the reminder. It is another sign of the influence of materialism that the gold standard was abolished in preference to a dollar standard so the exchange rate became a floating concept.

A major influence of the materialist attitude of money having intrinsic value was the creation of economic transactions completely devoid of normal economic transactions of production and consumption. This has the potentially disastrous consequence that most money transactions in the exchange market today are devoid of any meaningful connection to the goods and services economy; instead, they are speculative, resembling gambling in a global casino. Comments the monetary economist Bernard Lietaer (2001):

> Your money's value is determined by a global casino of unprecedented proportions: $2 trillion are traded per day in foreign exchange markets, 100 times more than the trading volume of all the stock markets of the world combined. Only 2 percent of these foreign exchange transactions relate to the "real" economy reflecting movements of real goods and services in the world, and 98 percent are purely speculative. This global casino is triggering the foreign exchange crises which shook Mexico in 1994-5, Asia in 1997 and Russia in 1998. ... Unless some precautions are taken soon, there is at least a 50-50 chance that the next five to ten years will see a global money meltdown, the only plausible way for a global depression.

As the 2007-2009 great recession shows, Lietaer was right in his prediction. Without anyone monitoring the procedures of this global casino, a few rich people can play their games. As discussed earlier, this transaction-of-money-without-meaning philosophy combined with overreliance on mathematical prediction and control, additionally combined with the general lackadaisical attitude toward ethics that comes with materialism, eventually led to the great economic meltdown of 2007-2009. Materialist economics finally lost credibility. A financial columnist for the prestigious *Financial Times* Martin Wolf declared flatly, "Another ideological god has failed." The original "failed god" of economics is, of course, Marxism.

So the question is: Is money the evil? How do we change the energy of money? Should we look for alternatives to money? Many well-intentioned economists think we should give up the use of money and go back to something like the old barter system. But as I have pointed out from the get-go, this is impractical, and it will never happen with the scale of economic transaction as global as it is already.

We have to change the energy of money. One of the ways is to rethink the subject of making money on money. One of the evils of how we run businesses today is the rise of the financial institutions that deal purely with money and no other business product. Businesses that make money speculating on money have no scope for fundamental creativity; and because there is no intrinsic value involved, there is no creativity, or even situational innovation. What results are cleverness and greed and catering to the worst of human instincts. So this is one thing to remember when you consider changing the energy of money: keep yourself away from money-from-money business. From your new point of view, money business is monkey business! It will make you dizzy jumping around from here to there, but it won't enable you to fly.

And as you get into subtle economics and venture into subtle business still using money in your transactions, you will find that the energy of money will no longer seem incompatible with the energies of love. You will perceive money instead as creative energy helping you to create new meaning and values.

Similarly, when your money brings you closer to wholeness via investments in happiness, your money acquires sacred energy.

And the same is true when we consume more subtle energy. You will find that you can use your revitalization to acquire any level of abundance that you desire.

Eight New Ways to Consume

We humans are habitual easily conditionable creatures with negative emotional brain circuits as added burden. Because our old ways are habitual, we have to consciously practice to develop new habits of consumption. Fortunately, not all subtle energy products that you need to consider for consumption to give subtle economy a boost are entirely new. Moreover, for some of the new products, the reward comes quite fast. Other products require our slowness, and their consumption helps us to develop our much desired quality of slowness. So here is a list:

1. Learn to consume organically-grown foods; they are rich in vital energy. They have been available for a while and you can easily find them. But they are not as popular as they should be because the average consumer is too lazy to take the extra trouble to find them, or take the extra time to get to like them as opposed to their more refined cousin. And if you rightly think they are also costlier, compensate that thought with the realization that you will need to eat less of them. Additionally, mass increase in consumption will surely bring the cost down.

Do a little experiment. Taste a firm fresh vegetable like a green bean side by side with what you buy from the supermarket and notice the difference. You will see what I mean. The same thing goes for organic brown rice vis-à-vis regular white rice.

2. Often our chronic ailments come to us in a gradual way; we can catch their presence at a very early stage if we watch for them as we approach middle age. Learn to act at the early stages and treat them not with allopathic medicine but with alternative medicine. You will really need to interrupt your current addiction to the quick fix of allopathic medicine. And get used to Traditional Chinese Medicine, Ayurvedic, naturopathic, and homeopathic medicine. You will be surprised with their healing efficacy.

Warning: I said earlier that they are less costly. They may not appear to be. But they should be for obvious reasons, and again mass production is certain to bring their cost down.

3. The first two above are easy, and they are not really new ideas. This next one—vital energy practices—is also not new. But your motivation in view of what you are trying to develop in yourself—slowness as opposed to fast—because you want the quantum and the subtle, transformation (not information) is the new key factor.

Yoga, stretching exercises from the East, is now very popular; unfortunately, most of the popular forms have adapted to the fast culture. So you have to make an effort to find slow yoga. The Chinese (and Japanese) origin practices—Tai Chi, Chi Gong and martial arts—are slow. The East Indian breathing practice of pranayama is also slow.

Besides these traditional ones, there are other simple practices for chakra massaging and cleansing that you can do with a little effort. You can even learn them from written instructions, they are that simple. And they will grow on you so your lifestyle will change. Read my book *The Quantum Doctor* for an intro to a very effective chakra cleansing practice.

4. A very effective way to rekindle your interest in meaning is dream analysis (Goswami, 2008a). Dreams are purely mental experiences and they convey to us an ongoing report of our meaning life. The dream objects and characters have mostly your personal meaning; in some cases, in what Jung called "big" dreams, they convey collective meaning from the "collective" unconscious.

5. Change your sex habits when you are a teenager, but you can do it at any age—better late than never. For teens, this one will likely need the help of skilled teachers and parents. The fast way of living has given us a massive increase in promiscuity: sex for conquest. It is gratifying to conquest, no doubt. But give romance a chance, wait for a romantic partner to appear in your horizon before you have sex, and you will be surprised by the difference between the two kinds of sex. How do you know it is romance? By paying attention to your heart chakra movements of vital energy—those heart throbs, tingles, expansiveness, and all that. A new self has entered your awareness—the self of the heart. More on this later.

What you were getting before was pleasure, the brain circuits were active, and there was involvement of the neocortical self, the reasoning self. When you engage in romantic sex, however, you are making love, and you will see why these words apply so vividly that you will be surprised. Also, in romantic lovemaking, the slowness will come to you quite naturally, whereas conquest sex is always fast.

With this change, you will obviously appreciate new vital energy products that boost your romantic attraction. You may want a perfume or an after-shave vitalized with romantic energies. No, we don't have such things in the market yet, but hey. If you create a demand, the supply will come. Never doubt this economic law. Don't worry, the technological know-how is already here (see Chapter 10).

6. After learning slow sex and love making, you graduate toward exploration of other archetypes such as goodness, beauty, justice, and abundance—call it the exploration of soul energy. Remember to always explore them in both meaning and feeling dimension. For example, watch for the movement along your spine while you practice to be good and do good with a friend, or discover the beauty of the face or overall demeanor of a person of the opposite sex rather than get caught in sexual kicks that the person's protuberances bring you.

7. The exploration of abundance is most important in your quest for becoming a consumer of soul energy. When you feel the energies of the archetype of abundance in fullness, all your higher chakras, the heart, the throat, the brow, the crown will be active with tingles and expansiveness and you will want to sing out thus (paraphrasing the poet Rabindranath Tagore):

> *I have looked*
> *And listened*
> *I have explored soul energy*
> *In this manifest world*
> *Looking for the archetypes.*
> *And I sing out loud in amazement.*

Don't hesitate to give vent to your new-found tendencies to sing out. This is what hard tiled showers are for. Now you are ready to support a lot of old and new soul businesses that will spring up. The old ones are books and records and art videos for which you will happily pay instead of looking for free downloads; you will want to support the artists of the soul. You know why? You will discover that the downloads don't have soul energy that you are looking for. The downloads are for information seekers, not for people who want transformation. The new ones will be new products created by people who help you with soul retrieval whatever that means using whatever gadgets they create and bring.

8. The last practice is the practice of wholeness. When your soul energies are active, you begin a lot of singing and dancing even if you were never good in them. Watch your level of satisfaction. Watch how that smile never leaves your mouth and eyes. And of course, depression never hits you anymore. You will need help with this one from people of human capital that I have talked about throughout this book. If you and others create demand, businesses will begin farming for the production of such "enlightened" people whose presence can induce wholeness in us. Otherwise, we have to depend on spiritual communities; that, too, will encourage new businesses.

Seven New Avenues of Producing

- The most prominent field for investing new venture capital is vital energy; and among all vital-energy enterprises, technology is available already for what I call revitalization—putting back the vital energy that gets thrown out in the manufacturing process of much stuff of organic origin that we consume today.

- Integrative medicine: health management services emphasizing both alternative and conventional medicine as appropriate.

- Vital-energy management of workplaces.

- Production of human capital in the field of vital energy. Okay, we already have some people who qualify as human capital of vital energy, the Chi Gong masters and so forth. However, using the creative process of quantum creativity to raise "kundalini" (the Sanskrit name for the creative potentiality of vital energy) is new, and when used en masse, will produce an explosion in the production of human capital in this field.

- Another old field of activity from Roman times that will be rejuvenated with new quantum understanding is philosophical counseling.

- The same goes for the idea of production of human capital for supramental values. We now have the knowledge of how to do it in massive scale. Do you see how that will change fields like psychotherapy and psychological education?

- Finally, the production of enlightened people—human capital in the form of people of embodied wholeness.

If this seems like too short of an intro, don't worry. I will give adequate details in Chapter 10.

NINE

Business Leadership, Quantum Style

What's wrong with this picture (fig. 12)? Nothing, of course. It is a perfectly good photograph of Mitt Romney, the billionaire who was the Republican Party's presidential candidate in the 2012 election. Am I being facetious? Not quite. What is wrong is that the American culture has changed so much in recent years that this man became the role model of roughly fifty percent of all Americans in the year 2012. And his main qualification, in fact his principal accomplishment of life, is how he accrued his billions as head of a private equity company (which includes acquisitions and breaking up businesses for profit) called Bain Capital. He made part of his money by acquiring businesses that he systematically dismantled by partly firing people, selling off profitable parts, and taking advantage of the tax code. And on top of it, he outsourced the money thus earned to Switzerland and the Cayman Islands. Even in the 1990s, a movie called *Pretty*

Woman became a hit by making a caricature of a similar busi-nessman. The plotline was how a prostitute helped rescue him from his straightjacket of business mediocrity! And just in a mat-ter of two decades, almost fifty per cent of Americans believed that Mr. Romney could rescue America from the great recession!

Figure 12

Go back to a concept developed in Chapter 3. In East Indian yoga psychology (which includes reincarnation) the concept of qualities called gunas is considered important: gunas tell us on the average what kind of profession a person will choose. The gunas are but three ways that we can process meaning. We can process meaning by engaging fundamental creativity——-creativ-ity consisting of the discovery of new meaning in a new con-text. Engaging fundamental creativity is *sattva* guna. We can also process meaning by engaging situational creativity in which we look to invent a new meaning but only within known contexts. This quality of the mind is *raja* in Sanskrit. Finally, we can also process meaning within what we know, within our conditioned memory, without seeking new meaning. This is the guna of *tamas*, the propensity to act according to conditioning.

Fundamental creativity, being discovery of new meaning in a new context, is the hardest of the lot; its processing requires both being and doing. In this way people of *sattwa* engage in a lot of *tamas* in the pursuit of being. So naturally, they are also accepting of people of *tamas*. So *sattva* is necessary for people skill.

Raja, the propensity for situational creativity, which consists of the horizontal movement of meaning consisting of invention in already known contexts, on the other hand, requires doing often for the sake of doing itself; it is necessary for empire building.

Tamas is just the tendency of remaining where you are; it is inherent in all, and necessary for proper functioning of *sattva*, but not as necessary for *raja* and, in fact, is often seen as a hindrance for the pursuit of *raja*. Hence, people of *raja* do not tolerate *tamas* in themselves and are often intolerant of people of *tamas*.

In traditional societies, people who make their living in service jobs mostly engage the quality of conditioned *tamas*, their conditioned repertoire is all they need and all they are encouraged to use. Blue-collar labor consists of predominantly *tamasic* people. Some of the people who earn their living in business and trade, traditionally are mostly driven by the conditioned instinctual emotion of greed for increasing their material possessions (in other words, love of money). Today, many more are at least partly driven by *raja*, the tendency to expand. So businesspeople are dominated by *tamas* mixed with a modicum of *raja*. They are situationally creative in making money and building conglomerates by acquisition, but they use their creativity in the service of conditioned brain circuits of pleasure. In the past, businesspeople always had problems with uncontrolled greed; in olden societies their greed had to be restrained by the people of *raja* (the aristocrats) and the people of *sattva* (the spiritual leaders), and this proved useful.

People of politics are traditionally people predominantly driven by the quality of *raja* and they use it to build their empires. In the olden days, people of politics also had a modicum of *sattva*. With this they brought to bear their power at the service of people to enable them to process meaning and values. But when their *raja* is tainted by *tamas*, they engage their power to dominate others, in the service of egotism.

People of predominant *sattva* engage in the professions of teaching—worldly knowledge and spiritual, the profession of healing (excluding cosmetic healing), and, of course, in professions requiring fundamental creativity explicitly—arts, science, literature, music and dance, and mathematics.

I mention Mitt Romney to make the point that today the difference between leaders of business and leaders in politics is blurring. Both business leaders and politicians have given up on *sattva*—fundamental creativity—confused by scientific materialism, probably. Or maybe they just lost their way while searching for meaning and values. The net effect is that greed is rampant; it is seen as a quality even in the pursuits of those people who still serve *sattva* (the scientists, for example).

In another time, a different type of businessperson captured the imagination of the culture. In the movie, *Executive Suite*, the hero fights (and wins) his battle against the Romney-type unimaginative businessman through his bold and creative risk taking. This is the role model—business honor—we need today to change our materialist ways. What is honor? It is the prerogative to stand up for your personal dharma, which for a business leader is to produce in a creative way using gifted people to satisfy what the consumers need. We need business people in the ilk of Thomas Edison, Henry Ford, Steve Jobs and the like to take us in the centuries ahead when the subtle economy will be our frontier. Furthermore, spiritual leaders are not influential any more, nor does democracy allow them much voice anyway to keep greed under leash; business leaders have to do it on their own.

In other words, leadership in which the CEO does all that is needed to follow Martin Friedman's dictum that corporations exist "purely to make profit," will not do to usher in the new economics. Greed, when unrestrained, never works in the long term. Traditional managerial profit seeking works well for the material arena, but when your search for abundance deals with the subtle as well, then human beings come into the picture. Human relationship becomes important and it's not mechanical, nor is it arithmetic any more. There is no doubt about it. Business leaders of today have to develop *sattva*, and they have to engage in fundamental creativity themselves (in order to develop an appreciation for *sattva*, in the least) so that they use their predominantly situational creativity at the service of *sattva*. Then only they will be able to be aware of the creative potential of their fellow workers and even nurture and mentor them.

Lee Iacocca, who is credited with saving Chrysler Motors in the 1980s, said that "once leaders lifted us up and made us want to do better." Iacocca had a nine-step recipe for this kind of lifting leadership, the nine C's. It is worth listing them:

Curiosity: the ability to look for new opinions and new ways, even new contexts for doing things.

Courage: to explore new ideas.

Conviction: enough to follow through the ups and downs that exploration of the unknown often brings.

Creativity: the ability to think "out of the box."

Common sense: not airy fairy but pragmatic wisdom.

Competence: solid ego, strong ego with a lot of proven experience to get things done.

Character: Patterns of ego-habits and learned behavior, the ability to discriminate between right and wrong, for example, and having the "guts" to do what you think is right.

Charisma: to inspire people to want to follow you and your ideas.

Communication: the ability to give it straight to people who trust you.

This is a good list, and some of these qualities are hinting at *sattva*; but in this quantum age, you must engage explicitly the "quantum principles" of leadership. What are they?

The Quantum Principles of Business Leadership

Remember the basic quantum principles: downward causation that comes with nonlocality, discontinuity and tangled hierarchy? A quantum business leader must engage these principles and inspire his followers/associates to do the same. The quantum business leader knows the importance of intention and the science of manifestation. The quantum business leader knows the creative process of quantum creativity—the importance of both doing and being, do-be-do-be-do. You have to have conviction that enables you to defy the world; that kind of conviction comes only from a quantum leap to the supramental land of truth. The quantum business leader always remembers the value of "walking your talk" if you want others to walk them also. The quantum business leader not only brings common sense to a situation but also "uncommon sense," that comes from paying attention to feeling, meaning, and intuition too. Finally, a quantum business leader pays attention to contingencies and opportunities they create; he or she always looks for synchronicities. Let's elaborate each of these aspects of leadership.

New Paradigm Business is a Balancing Act

Many businesses begin with creativity, somebody's innovative new idea for a product or a service. And as everybody knows, no innovation is forever as the central motif for running a business. New ideas replace old ideas; new innovations stir new trends. Paradigms shift in science and technology and our societies change worldview—and businesses have to reflect those changes. All of this requires creativity in business in an ongoing basis.

Organizations, and businesses are no exception, require structures and hierarchies, as well as reliance on past experiences, to avoid chaos. This necessitates a lot of conditioned movements as well on the part of the personnel of a business.

Creativity and conditioning: businesses need both and it is a balancing act. Like balancing yang and yin in Chinese medicine. Understanding the nature of creativity and conditioning is essential for doing the right balancing. But it is much more than that right now. Discovering how to elicit the *sattva* potential in each of us requires a certain disposition supported by a new lifestyle based on new paradigm thinking.

A need for new paradigm thinking is coming to business. It was not too long ago when environmental pollution by business and industry were taken for granted as a necessary evil for the economic necessity of job creation. And businesses were quite satisfied with the assumption of infinite resources on which the current materialist economic paradigm is based. What prompted businesses to look for alternatives is the arrival of two undeniable emergencies: global climate change (a direct effect of environmental pollution) and the soaring price of oil leading to increased production cost for virtually all businesses. Now increasingly businesses talk about eco-friendliness and sustainability. What is needed now is to see that sustainability is not possible while staying within the gross materialist arena.

Businesses have to extend their balance sheet of creativity to the subtle arena of human experience. Likewise, our economics has to be extended to deal with not only the gross but also the subtle.

Balancing the Qualities called Gunas

I said above, business people are dominated by *raja*. They get a creative idea to start a business, and then they hire a few people of *sattva* for further acts of innovation, a few more people of some *raja* but mostly *tamas* for management positions, and finally a lot of people of *tamas* for labor. This has been the tradition. However, as a new paradigm business-person, it would behoove you to begin developing a modicum of *sattva* and practice balancing your three gunas—*sattva*, *raja*, and *tamas*—as soon as possible. It would behoove you to provide leadership in this area also for your creative and management people.

For developing *sattva* in a *raja*-dominated person, what it boils down to is to learn to relax, giving up the do-do-do lifestyle of *raja* dominance and make do-be-do-be-do one's living mantra. Only then does fundamental creativity open up to you, the door to feelings and intuitions opens wide, and the beacon of conscious evolution becomes clearly visible.

To the naïve, business is "busy-ness," being in business means being in busy action. Businesspeople are supposed to be always on the run, with do-do-do as their motif of operation. Businesspeople also have the image of needing to be in control all the time; they are supposed not to entertain the new (even in possibility) because of the fear of losing control. These are stereotypes of popular perception and not universally true. The creative businesspeople are exceptions to all this stereotyping.

Look at it in another way. The bottom line of businesses is to make money, to make a profit. The fear of losing money gives you butterflies in your stomach, haven't you noticed? So the tendency is to analyze your past actions incessantly or to project the future so as not to repeat your mistakes. In other words, being in business seems synonymous with anxiety. Isn't the best way to cope with anxiety to do something? Non-doing means inviting thoughts and thoughts beget anxiety. Right?

Not right. One of the great discoveries of the new age is that there is an antidote to the anxious mind—the relaxation response. To learn to relax is a better way to cope with anxiety. To learn to relax is to learn to be—being in your own company without judgment, without incessantly creating the past or the future. Somehow the creative businessman is an expert in living Zen—this being in the moment. Stanford professors Michael Ray and Rochelle Myers (1986) wrote a book, *Creativity in Business*, in which they quote a businessman, Robert Marcus of Alumax, famous in the 1980s for business success, to make the point:

> We're an efficient company in terms of people per dollar. Although we're a two-billion-dollar company, we have only eighty-four people in headquarters. Which isn't too many. We're doing the same thing, but we are not as big as Alcoa or Alcan. We're about a third of their size, but we have a tenth of the number of people in headquarters. It seems to work pretty well, so we're going to stick with it. . . .
>
> I will tell you some of the things we do. We don't have a lot of meetings. We don't write a lot of reports. We make quick decisions. You know, if it takes you a long time to make decisions, if you have a lot of meetings and write a lot of reports, you need a lot of people. We communicate very rapidly. We do it all by word of mouth. I don't write letters. I don't write reports. In fact, I don't know what I do. . . . We play squash often. . . .

I don't let time I allocate to some big parts of my life interfere with each other. I confine my business time, which is pretty much nine to five. . . . I go out to play [squash] three times a week. And I don't feel really pressed by business.

(Quoted in Ray and Myers, 1986, pp. 144-145.)

This (creative) businessman learned to relax; he developed a kind of equanimity about time. He learned to complement the conventional do-do-do of the business mind by a be-be-be attitude. Being complements doing with unconscious processing of many possibilities at the same time. And this is the secret of creativity.

So maybe being in business does not mean being busy all the time; instead it means how to be busy as needed and relax at other times, how to combine in tandem busy doing with relaxed being.

However, giving up the emphasis on outer accomplishments is against the grain of the business culture; this is why materialism has taken root there so fast. The only reason that businesses can even entertain change now is because the zero-sum game is over, the limits of material growth have caught up with us, and the paradigm shift is upon us. Nevertheless, you the quantum aficionado have to lead the rest of the culture in this respect, and you have to change the social systems so subtle accomplishments are valued.

An important aspect of developing *sattva* is diet. As you know, the body proteins are our promoters of action. In this way a protein-rich diet promotes *raja*, the empire-building quality and the pursuit of power with the objective of dominating others. No wonder, several years back, a protein-rich diet touched a popular nerve in America where most people covet *raja* and actively cultivate it toward the pursuit of power. For a businessperson who is interested in balancing the gunas, a diet with only moderate protein intake is helpful. In other words, not only keep away from fat (which grows *tamas*), but also keep away from excessive protein and develop a diet rich in complex carbohydrates, fruits, and vegetables. Moderate protein intake, by making room for *sattva*, allows you to channel your power to positive use, such as empowering not only yourself but also other people to engage in meaning processing.

Finally, the million-dollar question. Can people really change from one station (*tamas* dominance) to another station (let's say *tamas* plus *raja*) to still another station (balanced *tamas* plus *raja* plus *sattva*) of conditioning? Well, I will tell you an inspiring story, a true one, but it was also made into a movie for all to see. This is the story of Christopher Paul Gardner

Born in a family plagued by poverty, Gardner received very little education in his childhood. As an adult, his wife left him; and afterward, he lived the life of a homeless person, with a little son to complicate things further. What drama he lived! Even spending a night in a bathroom at the San Francisco Bay Area railway station with his young son. No doubt, he was a man of dominant *tamas*.

But synchronicities come to people who are ready for a change. Gardner's life changed when a stockbroker named Bob Bridges came into his life, a man literally in a red Ferrari. Paul became a trainee in a stockbroker firm, made a whole bunch of people rich, and even passed his licensing exam to become a full-time employee of the firm he worked for. He had arrived at a second station of life with a balance of *tamas* and *raja*.

Eventually Paul owned his own stockbroker business and ran it successfully. If this is not enough proof of his growing *sattva*, there is more. He became a philanthropist in his later life, donating millions of dollars for the betterment of the life of homeless people.

By the way, the movie (*The Pursuit of Happyness*) is good, the actor Will Smith playing the role of Paul Gardner.

Moving from Short-term to Long-term Thinking

In the *Bhagavad Gita*, Arjuna, the hero of the Indian epic story of Mahabharata, is given the teaching of karma yoga—the yoga of how to act appropriately. The mystery, said Krishna the teacher, is to learn to exercise our right to act without implicitly believing that we have the right to the fruit of the action. You can see the relevance of this teaching to the new subtle economics. The problems (economic meltdowns, for example) that we purport to tackle with our economics are all not only short-term but also long-term problems. Solutions likewise require actions that will bear not necessarily any immediate fruit, thus the reluctance of today's politicians to attend to the solutions.

You may wonder if Krishna's advice is an easier way to partake in the economic activism required to tackle today's problems. Why develop *sattva*—the capacity for quantum creativity that does not come easily? Do we really need quantum activism—quantum creativity in changing our practices of economics and businesses—when such a simple recipe of giving up the right to the fruit of the action is available? But we do need *sattva*. When we engage with problems with predominant *raja* where the motivation is empire building, we cannot let go of short-term gains and fruits of our action. Try it and see. But with spiritual purification when *raja* give way in part to *sattva*, we can dedicate ourselves to long-term projects even though there is no immediate fruit of our actions in sight. It is no secret that this is how our greatest scientists and artists operate in the pursuit of their great science and great art. Einstein, for the last thirty years of his life, looked for a theory to unify all the material forces. He didn't care much that his work did not bear fruit during his lifetime (that is, his disappointments did not divert him). Indeed, the fruit came only after his death.

A thorough reading of the *Bhagavad Gita* shows us that Krishna was quite aware of this kind of consideration. *Bhagavad Gita* begins with what sounds like a simple recipe: acting without the guarantee of the fruit of the action. But toward the end of the book, when we get the entire teaching, Krishna says that to accomplish that simple goal of fruitless action, one has to cultivate *sattva* and balance all the gunas—*sattva*, *raja*, and *tamas*. In other words, one has to combine simple busy-ness with creativity, do-be-do-be-do.

This fixity of match between a person's guna and the profession he or she engages in is very resistant to change. But as quantum activism becomes more prevalent in our societies, people will balance their gunas more and more, and people will engage in all these professions with all three gunas. Only in this way shall we be able to come out of the guna stereotypes of these livelihoods. Only then can winds of change engulf the arenas of our livelihood (our workplaces), and mental evolution can proceed en masse.

Thinking Out of the Box: the Nine-Dot Problem

I have heard a joke about the degrees that our universities, mostly driven by conventional and conditioned knowledge systems, bestow upon us. I am talking of BS; you can guess what it means. It takes four years of accumulation of the stuff to get the B.S. degree. Another two years of *more of the same* to get an M.S. Finally, spend another five years at accumulating it; now the stuff is *piled high and deep*, so you get a Ph. D.

To get an idea of what I am talking about, consider the following problem, called the nine dot problem:

What is the smallest possible number of straight lines that will connect the nine points of a 3 X 3 rectangular array (fig. 13a) without taking the pencil off the paper?

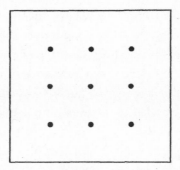

Figure 13a

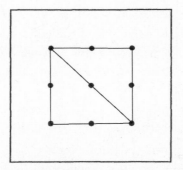

Figure 13b

It may seem that you need five lines (fig. 13b), doesn't it? That's too many. Can you see right away how to get a smaller number of straight lines to do the job?

Perhaps not. Perhaps, like many people, you got stuck thinking that you have to connect the points while staying within the box defined by the outer points of the rectangular array. If so, you have defined yourself an unnecessary context for solving the problem, you are thinking in a box, and this is not the right box.

So you have to move out of the box to find a new context in which a smaller number of straight lines will do the job (fig. 13c). This is a simple example of discovering a new context. This idea of extending the box beyond the existing contexts—thinking out of the box—is crucially important in creativity. Creative people beware! When the implicit context for your problem may not be working, you may have to find a new context.

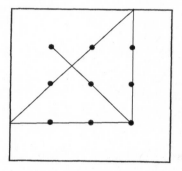

Figure 13c

There is a story that circulates in the Wharton School of Economics. A person is walking along the countryside when he encounters a shepherd with a flock of sheep. "Here's a hundred dollars against one of your sheep that I can estimate the exact number of your sheep.

The flock is large, so the shepherd does not hesitate, "You are on," " says he.

The man says, "973." "

"Amazing!" says the shepherd. "OK, take one of my beasts."

The man does as he is told and begins to leave.

"Hey, wait," cries the shepherd. "Give me a chance to win my animal back. I will bet double or nothing that I can guess your profession. The man thinks, there are so many professions; he would never guess.

"All right," he allows.

"You are an economist," says the shepherd.

Now it's the economist's turn to say, "Amazing!" which he does and adds, "but tell me, how could you guess?"

The shepherd says, "Put down my dog, and I will tell you."

Fortunately, there are creative people in businesses, and they are way ahead of this stereotypical economic thinking. Consider the case of the post-it stickers, an invention by two creative guys by the name of Spencer Silver and Arthur Fry. Silver was a senior chemist at the 3M Company where in 1968, he invented a high-quality low-tack adhesive. The adhesive, he noticed, was good for temporary attachment to things and could easily be pulled off without leaving marks, but what is the use for such a thing? Out came Fry who was tired of having to keep bits and pieces of paper from falling off his hymnal in choir practice. The new context for use: Use post-it stickers as temporary markers of a page that you want later, like we use them today for any office document. The rest is history.

Opening Up to the Archetype of Abundance

Of course, solving the nine-dot problem is not real creativity for humans; it does not involve any archetypes. As we release economics from the straightjacket of scientific materialism, the next challenge is to introduce the idea of economics as the pursuit of the archetype of abundance which includes both material and subtle wealth.

Previously we spoke of opening up to our intuitive facility. An intuition is a glimpse at an archetype. What eventually leads to a creative exploration of that archetype and ultimately (if you follow the creative process) to a discovery of a new context of thinking involving that archetype, is the creative process.

The Stages of the Creative Process

The creative process has been studied for almost a hundred years now and most theorists, following an original suggestion of Graham Wallas in 1926 (Graham Wallas, 2014), accept four stages of it: preparation, unconscious processing, sudden insight, and manifestation. Quantum physics supports this classification with a little fine tuning, which my own experience confirms:

Stage 0. *Intuition*. Creativity begins with intuition, a summons of sort from the quantum self to tell you that an archetype (archetypes) is (are) demanding your attention. For businesspeople, one of the archetypes is usually abundance. The other ones will vary depending on what you want to manifest as your particular business venture this time around.

Stage 1. *Preparation*. You read up on what is known, what other people have to tell you. Retain all, but always with the attitude, not this, not this. Finally, end with a mind that is open to something new; old just will not do! Now work on making your question intense, a burning question.

Stage 2. *Unconscious processing*. Relax, be. Done enough. Let your unconscious take over. Don't worry. Quantum possibilities of meaning, being waves, will expand, becoming bigger and bigger possibilities from which to choose. Every once in a while, the pool may contain the new. Who knows?

Stage 2a. *Do-be-do-be-do*. Alternate doing and being. It is hard to maintain intensity if you relax too much. A pragmatic strategy is to alternate do and be—relaxed intensity.

Stage 3. *Sudden insight*. This is the coveted creative experience of the discontinuous quantum leap of which the suddenness reveals as a surprise—aha!

This time, you get to look at the archetype for more than a fleeting moment. The insight comes with conviction—I *know*. Now nobody can tell you otherwise. You have become your own person—an original. If you are an entrepreneur going into business, you have discovered what you are looking for, your venture. Go for it.

When Thomas Edison went ahead with the idea of using the carbon filament for his light bulb, there was much opposition. But because the idea came to him as a result of a quantum leap, he went ahead anyway and paved the way for the future. His support of the direct current communication network for electricity transmission, on the other hand, was an example of stubbornness, and he was proven wrong.

Stage 4. *Manifestation*. Manifest your insight into a full-fledged business.

Stage 4a. *Do-be-do-be-do and further mini-insights*. The manifestation stage usually requires further mini insights for which again and again you have to invoke do-be-do-be-do. If you are dedicated to be a creative businessperson, make do-be-do-be-do your modus operandi.

When do-be-do-be-do is incorporated in the businessperson's modus operandi, a time comes when the gap between doing and being becomes so little that the shift is hardly noticeable.

And if the being comes with a sense of surrender, in which the doer refuses to resolve the usual conflicts of work problems with mere logical step-by-step thinking, and when the businessperson truly avoids the small business's three worst enemies(thinking too big, thinking too small, thinking too much), something special happens. The sense of the doer disappears, and the doing seems to happen by itself.

This easy, without effort, way of (creative) action is, of course, the flow experience. When one achieves this creative way of working, business itself becomes pleasure. Listen to what Paul Cook whom I have mentioned before is saying:

> I am having the time of my life. I wouldn't change it for anything. I'm doing what I have always wanted to do, and it's every bit as exciting as I thought it was going to be when I wanted to do it. It is a thrilling experience, doing new things and leading the new technology to create new products for society. I couldn't want anything more.
>
> (Quoted in Ray and Myers, 1986, p. 113.)

And of course, creativity will involve some risks. I will tell you the case of Jamsetji Tata, the founder of the Tata business dynasty in India. Jamsetji succeeded in colonial India despite the many constraints on native businesspeople that restricted what they could or could not do. And yet, Jamsetji succeeded in establishing business venture after business venture, textile, management, steel, and even hydroelectric power. When he went into the last two areas, the prevailing wisdom was that the existing British laws would never open the door for Tata. Jamsetji took the risk. He was creative and he succeeded.

Today, we similarly face the opposition of not one but two worldviews from the past. Subtle businesses will have to take risks, no doubt. But their creativity will wean through all the barriers.

Empowering the Ego

I hope you have noticed that although creativity is a gift from the quantum consciousness of which we are unconscious, the receivers are the dynamic duo of the quantum self and the ego. Creativity is an encounter of the quantum self and the ego. Don't worry about the quantum self; just be open to it. But to be open and to receive the quantum self's ideas and give these ideas form, you have to have a strong but malleable ego. This is empowering.

Openness and intensity are the key. Giving up control of the unconscious is the prerogative only of a strong ego. Giving up control so the new can come. Sometimes the new comes in the form of a dynamic person for which you the leader have to make room. Only a strong ego can do that.

Take the case of Henry Ford II and the previously mentioned Lee Iacocca. Iacocca was the creative engineer behind the very successful Mustang that Ford produced. But Ford II's weak ego could not handle Iacocca's success; he let him go. This is business history in America since Ford's loss of Iacocca became the rival Chrysler's gain. Iacocca produced for Chrysler the very creative minivan that met the approval of the times, among many other accomplishments.

The ego is excluded from processing the new. Are you strong enough to accept exclusion? Some time ago, I was at a workshop where the workshop leader was truly great and facilitating the creative aha! for many of the participants but alas, I was not one of them. When I complained, the teacher said, "I can only open the door, Amit. Can you leave yourself at the door and enter? Trust me?"

I blurted out, "But I want to be there when it happens!"

Everyone laughed, and only then I realized my mistake.

How do you empower the ego? Learn to take risks, to make mistakes. Make failures acceptable. The great physicist Richard Feynman used to say, "I have been wrong before; and I will be wrong again." What is the big deal about being wrong if you don't make it a big deal?

Heed the poet Robert Frost's advice—take the path less traveled. Synchronicities will guide you. A general sense of satisfaction will guide you when the shoe fits. As the mythologist Joseph Campbell used to say, "Follow your bliss."

How to Begin a Creative Business

I said before that businesses begin with a product. This statement is not quite accurate and needs to be modified. The correct statement is businesses take off when there is a creative product. Actually businesses begin with a conviction-carrying idea that there will be such creative products.

There is a great movie on the American game of baseball called *Field of Dreams* in which there is a great line (I am paraphrasing a little): when the field is ready, people will come. This is true of businesses too. All you need is a faith in possibilities, quantum possibilities of your interior flute—your psyche—and your ability to harness them.

The co-founders of Apple Computers, Steve Jobs and Steve Wozniak, consulted with lawyers, venture capitalists, and all that it takes to set up a business, without knowing exactly what they were setting up. Strangely, this openness of their minds was crucial to the profundity of the actuality they eventually established. In the same vein, Paul Cook, the founder of the Raychem Corporation said, "When we started, we didn't know what we're going to do. We didn't know what products we were going to make."

In this aspect creativity in business is no different from all other expressions of creativity, which all begin with questions, not finished answers. For example, an important question is: Can I contribute to meaning through establishing this business enterprise, meaning for myself, my employees, and for the people who use my product (or service)? Contrary to common sense, creative businesses begin with a seed of an idea—an intuition, a field of possibilities open to the new.

To Make the Transition Complete

What more does it take to make the transition complete from capitalism to the economics of consciousness? We still have some ways to go. And I think that businesses can and will lead the way to this transition.

The goal of the economics of consciousness is to maximize the profit not only in the material output, but also in our vital energy output, mental meaning output, and supramental output that include ethics. Even with creativity, ecology, and ethics included in the workplace in the ways mentioned above, we have only made a dent in the possibilities.

At the next stage, we can encourage creativity not only for the management or the research people, but also for everyone. True, only a professional can make quantum leaps of creativity that will produce a product in the outer arena, but everyone can be creative in our inner arena. I have called such creativity "inner creativity." Suppose, as already suggested, all business corporations of sufficient size open a division of subtle-energy production. If the corporation encourages inner creativity (a major component of which is transformation of negative emotions to positive ones) for all its employees and allows all employees to open to their souls under the guidance of the subtle-energy department, what happens? The entire environment of the corporation becomes a happy one full of vitality and meaning. Is this valuable? Of course. It contributes directly to the production outputs in our subtle dimensions. And it is a fact that happy people produce better products. And more. Inner creativity can increase the outer creativity of already outer creative people, the backbones of an innovative corporation. So ultimately, the practice will even improve material productivity and profits.

In some ways, some of the high-tech companies of the Silicon Valley are already partway on this stage. Take Google for example, the inventor of the Internet search engine. Google offers employees free nutritious and delicious meals, swimming pools, massages, pool tables, all this for easy access to vital energy, and even quirky toys for exercising the mind. Employees can even bring their pet dogs to work for an instant supply of the energies of love.

At the next stage of conscious development, we bring in the concept of tangled hierarchical relationship between the management and the labor of a corporation or a business in which the "self" of the organization will emerge, with which everybody will identify. Can you imagine the creative potency of such an organization?

From ecological sustainability, the next step is the awareness of the evolutionary movement of consciousness. Not only we demand ecological sustainability but also we ask: Is my business contributing positively to the evolutionary movement of consciousness, or at least, not harming it? This is when we put explicit attention, not implicit, to making tangible production in the vital energy, mental meaning, and supramental value sectors of the human economy. This is already implicit in some of the new wave of business especially in property development.

Of course, much has to happen before businesses take these remaining steps. The paradigm shift from primacy of matter to primacy of consciousness has to take root in the academe and in the society. Our politics has to change from the politics of power to the politics of meaning. The is already happening, but the elites are protecting their turf as in the case of sabotage of Obamacare that President Obama has suffered. Our educational institutions have to stop their preoccupation with job training and revamp meaning and soul in the classrooms. Our religions have to give up telling people how to vote and influence politicians and return to the pursuit of godliness and teaching that to people. And so forth. I believe all of this will happen soon and some beginnings are already in sight. Such changes will be resisted by those whose jobs are threatened by it.

Adam Smith's capitalism played a crucial role in where we are today (until materialist economics took over), and as Smith himself envisioned, small businesses are the backbones of capitalism and the free market. In the same way, the path to the economics of consciousness will also be paved by small businesses. So we should not lose heart that the big multinationals of today are corrupted and very far from practicing what I discussed. It is not unlike the corruption of the mercantile economy of Adam Smith's days. But corrupted mercantile economy disintegrated when a better way of doing business that is more conducive to peoples' needs became clear. The same thing will now happen to materialist economics. It will disintegrate before our eyes, making room for the economics of consciousness. There are evolutionary pressures, the real "invisible hands," that are guiding this change.

Creativity in Big Businesses under the Economics of Consciousness

In a recent documentary *Corporation* the filmmakers demonstrate that modern corporations have all the symptoms of being psychopathic. So the big question is: How can normality, even creativity, be restored in big business corporations? The succinct answer is: by allowing them to expand to the subtle sector. The answer is crucial.

Converting to the economics of consciousness implies that there is a shift in emphasis in how a business is run. A business is no longer an organization with one bottom line—material profit. Now it can be explicitly recognized that:

1. A positive showing in the production of subtle products also has value. Corporate interest in value increases employee retention (Barret, 1998).

2. Labor can be paid not only in terms of gross material remuneration but also in terms of the subtle; for example, by the gift of more leisure time, meditation break during work hours, company of spiritual masters, and so forth. (Good news is that Google is already offering many of these benefits to its workers.)

3. With labor expenses thus under control, outsourcing can be considerably reduced, and meaningful employment can be restored in economically-advanced countries.

4. Meaningful jobs can also be created in the subtle sectors of the economy to which corporations themselves may contribute directly or indirectly. If the corporation deals with organic products, the long-ignored vital components of such products will have to be restored; this is an example of direct contribution to the vital energy economy. Hiring consultants toward the increase of positive mental health of employees (which has demonstrated value for increasing production and employee retention) is an example of indirect contribution.

5. Step 4 restores meaning processing in peoples' life once again in economically advanced countries, opening them to creativity. This will greatly contribute to employee retention.

6. A big corporation can take further advantage of its creative labor force by including the labor force in quality production, in research, and in other creative activities as much as practicable. In this way, the corporation itself becomes creative. This will require some re-education of the management.

When big business becomes producers of positive subtle energies, even indirectly just through increased employee job-satisfaction, the whole society gets a creativity boost.

One can ask: Will this development not affect the developing countries adversely? Not necessarily. Don't forget that developing countries also need to convert to the economics of consciousness right away. Furthermore, developing countries need capital and market share for their exports. So long as attention is given to these aspects, developing economies are better off if freed from the relatively meaningless labor jobs that the current form of outsourcing provides for.

Is It possible to Humanize Corporations?

The Republican presidential contender in 2012, Mitt Romney, famously said, "Corporations are people." Many people in America would object to this kind of characterization of corporations as they are run now, but it is good to ask: Can corporations be humanized, endowed with human qualities so that this kind of comment would not be mere hubris but reflect some truth?

The economist Milton Friedman said (on the other hand) that corporations exist "purely to make profit." If that is so, it is hard to see corporations as people. If people existed purely to make profit, there would be no relationship between people, not even any acknowledgement or allowance to the subtle side of themselves. So as long as corporations remain glued to their profit motive in the material arena, there is little chance to humanize them. But if their interests include the subtle, what then?

If corporations "liberate their corporate soul" and align their worldview with their employees', the employee retention goes up (Barret, 1998,). There is already some tentative data (Jaz, 2012) that if employee well-being is looked after by corporations via vitalizing the working environment, employee productivity increases. I think similar productivity benefits are bound to follow if corporations actively went into the business of subtle-energy production as I am suggesting. And nary less important, this certainly would make corporations into becoming more human.

The board of directors of an old-wave capitalist corporation always watches over their businesses to ensure the selfish gain in the material profits of the corporation's shareholders. The board of directors of a few new-wave capitalist corporations are not only increasing the material profit for its shareholders, but also are literally contributing to the vital energy and meaning profits for everyone. This is already a good beginning of the new era of quantum economics, an economics of consciousness and well-being.

There are a couple of other trends that are also worth mentioning. One is that corporations have begun noticing that employees perform the best if their value structure is not in conflict with the corporation's value structure as exemplified by its products and practices. This indicates that businesses are recognizing the value of values (the supramental dimension of humanity). The second one goes beyond this. In view of many recent market-related scandals, many businesses are asking aloud if it is not more profitable (in terms of public relations alone) if one follows ethical practices in business. And they don't mean "greatest good for the greatest number" ethics, but the real McCoy, the way ethics is defined in spiritual traditions.

Still the divide continues. Too many CEOs are totally sold in ruthlessness in the corporate world while in private they are highly *sattvic* decent human beings. You know about the great John D. Rockefeller and his son John D. Rockefeller, Jr., and how they ruthlessly squashed the Standard Oil strike that led to the infamous Ludlow incident when twenty-four workers died. But these Rockefellers were also great philanthropists. John D.'s biographer said, "His good was as good as his bad side was bad." Today we have the case of Bill Gates, equally ruthless while he was settling antitrust suits as the CEO of Microsoft, who became one of the great philanthropists alive today. How nice would it be if these peoples' latent *sattva* found expression while they were CEOs, in the way they handle the business of their corporations? Can we allow corporations to give up unnecessary ruthlessness and embrace necessary love? I think this step of humanizing the corporation will require the women's point of view and women's leadership.

Women's Values in Business: Journey Toward the Heart

Quantum physics has been around for almost a hundred years. But although much has been written about the revolutionary philosophical and worldview implications of this "new" physics, it is a fact that the majority of intellectuals of the world, particularly those belonging to the academia, still hold on to the worldview of the "old" Newtonian physics.

For the last three decades, I have been involved with propagating the quantum worldview, especially the most paradigm-shifting idea that it gives us, namely, that consciousness, not matter, is the ground of all being. The result of my involvement, albeit promising, has been slow. Therefore, in desperation (who can blame me for wanting to see the worldview change while I am still alive!), a few years back, with the help of a couple of friends, the filmmakers Ri Stuart and Renee Slade, I started the movement of quantum activism. The avowed manifesto of quantum activism is to spread the implications of the quantum worldview; explicitly, to inspire individuals to use quantum principles to transform themselves and the society.

Now, mind you, I myself have been a quantum activist for the last three decades. I have written books, attended a lot of conferences, given a lot of talks and workshops on quantum physics and the primacy of consciousness, and in my private life tried to walk the talk quite seriously. Two things stand out in my experience, one private, one public.

The public one first. By far the majority of attendees of the new science conferences and workshops tend to be women, mostly middle-aged women, to boot. Now as far as my own talks and workshops are concerned, this is a little surprising. Why? Well, the conventional image of middle-aged nonscientist women is supposed to be that they are scared of quantum phys-ics. And yet seventy to eighty percent of my audience is women!

The private finding is this. Even with all my good intentions and lots of intellectual and meditative efforts, living up to the transforming principles of the quantum worldview has not been easy for me. Let me just honestly say that my experiments with learning to love unconditionally (in quantum activism we say "tangled hierarchically;" as you know, tangled hierarchy means a two-way relationship of circular causality between two people) have been the most time-consuming ones in my life.

And now the explanations. Nonscientist women are a lit-tle scared of physics perhaps, but their fear is transcended as soon as they find out that the quantum worldview legitimizes consciousness, legitimizes feelings, and legitimizes even the "energies" of love. Why? Because, I submit, some representation of the archetype of love somehow is built into women.

At the outset, this may sound a little trite. But hear me out. In my book *Creative Evolution* (Goswami, 2008b) I have argued that (Lamarckian) evolution gives us instincts in the form of brain circuits. Usually, these brain circuits are connected with negative emotions: lust, anger, jealousy, competitiveness, etc., and men and women both have them. Sadly, positive emotional brain circuits are relatively rare. There are a few: one is a circuit for altruism that many people (men and women) have; another is what more recently has been called God in the brain, a circuit in the midbrain which when activated gives you a spiritual experience, a God experience so to speak (I sometimes call this spot in the brain the new G-spot).

Now to the crux of the point I am making. Women, and only women, have a third positive emotional brain circuit. This is the maternity instinct circuit I mentioned above. Okay, it is not much activated until a woman becomes a mother. But motherhood does indeed come with a lot of unconditional love for the child, doesn't it? Even men can vouch for it; they, too, have been nourished by the energies of love by their mothers while growing up.

Well, you will say, but is motherly love tangled hierarchical? Don't mothers get to be the disciplinarians, which is impossible without simple hierarchy—one party dominating the other? In India, there is the myth of Yoshoda, child Krishna's adoptive mother. Yoshoda has to "change diapers" and discipline her kid no doubt, but Krishna is God incarnate! And knowing that (from the many miracles the baby Krishna routinely performs), how can Yoshoda not be reverential to Krishna and defer to him on occasions as well? The myth is trying to tell mothers how to make the mother-child relationship tangled hierarchical: realize that your child is God. Indeed, in India, in the olden days children until age five were regarded as God; they were treated with respect.

I think with or without the advantage of the myth, all mothers do that to a certain extent; that is, treat their child with respect. How can they not, when holding their child they know is an immediate access to the energies of love, the heart chakra?

So I think, as potential mothers, all women begin a journey that can be called a journey toward the heart. The goal is to identify more with the heart—love—than with their brain—thinking and meaning processing!

Objection! you will say if you have read any of my books. The brain gives us self-identity because it has a tangled hierarchy built into it? Where is the tangled hierarchy of the heart, which is just a simple muscle?

You are right. It is not the heart, per se. My latest research is showing that the immune system in the form of a component called the thymus gland—a heart chakra organ—together with a couple of navel chakra organs are the key here. And the tangled hierarchy exists not among these physical organs but among the vital blueprints of the organs (that Rupert Sheldrake calls morphogenetic fields, see Chapter 3). Indeed, there is now some data that shows that the immune system and its gastro-intestinal associates together may very well have some causal autonomy, the signature of a tangled hierarchy (Goswami and, 2015).

So women are a natural to explore tangled hierarchy and quantum activism, agreed? In the 1960s, in the beginning of the women's lib movement, there was a lot of talk of bringing women's values to society, and it was argued that this could only happen when women gained powerful positions in society such as a business CEO. Within a few decades women did become CEOs in a few businesses, but guess what? Something changed in their way to the top positions; they had found that they had to adapt men's values in order to move up in power quickly. So they did it that easy way. There were no guarantees that women's values would work in business anyhow. But now, armed with the ideas of quantum worldview, professional women can really fight for women's values in pursuing their profession. And this includes businesses.

How about men? Can they ever succeed in developing a tangled hierarchical relation with another? My own experience is that yes they can, but it is time consuming. Why? Men have a natural tendency in our culture to suppress the heart.

But wait! Women do not have it so easy either. I said above that the morphogenetic fields of a couple of navel chakra organs are involved with the tangled hierarchy at the heart. The navel chakra is the site of the body ego and men have it strong; this is what drives them toward power and simple hierarchy. And culturally, women are taught to suppress the navel chakra tendencies.

There you have it! Women have access to heart chakra love that gives them a curious interest in tangled hierarchy; but they suffer from a de-emphasis of the simple hierarchy of the ego navel chakra. Men suffer from a lack of appreciation of tangled hierarchy of gastro-intestinal-immunological organs at the vital level, but they have plenty access to the navel chakra simple hierarchy of the body ego.

We need both. Carl Jung was right (Jung, 1971). We have to balance both body-ego—self-respect—and love (which begins with respect for the other) in our behavior—animus and anima. And both women and men are capable of integrating the two, although it takes time.

Creativity with Love: From Eco-friendliness to Deep Eco-Friendliness in Businesses

I have mentioned that many businesses are becoming aware that "green" business policies do not necessarily lead to "red" bottom lines of loss in profits. When businesses adapt the economics of consciousness, green business policies follow automatically.

One great plus of the economics of consciousness over the current materialist economics is that one no longer has to depend on consumerism to drive the economy. This means that the depletion of nonrenewable resources is much reduced. This also reduces environmental pollution (including global warming) and thus reduces global climate change in a major way.

The economics of consciousness allows our societies a less hurried lifestyle that is highly conducive to creativity. With eco-friendliness, the creativity is ever more enhanced because it is accompanied with love for the environment. With deep eco-friendliness, businesses begin enterprises that help people clean up their internal environment and love it, too. With creativity and love providing an unprecedented quality of life, peoples' dependence on material pleasure as a substitute for happiness (by which suffering in the subtle dimension of life is pushed under the rug, so to speak) is lessened. In this way, a day may come when we will no longer need the highly unsustainable material standards of living currently in vogue. We may even hope that these reduced material standards will be provided by renewable sources of energy (such as solar) at our disposal.

Can business leaders, even male ones, propound love? I read a lecture by Rinaldo Brutoco in which he gives several examples (Brutoco, 2006). Deepak Jain, a dean at the Kellogg School of Management finished a lecture with a slide saying "love." That was the only word on the slide. He really wanted his audience to believe that Kellogg stood for love. This is a sea change in corporate mindset. Brutoco also quoted the head of IBM Thomas Watson, "To be successful, have your heart in your business and your business in your heart." You cannot have your heart in your business without opening your heart center, can you?

Are businesspeople putting their heart in their business? Yes. Bill Herren was homeless, living on a park bench for seven years. And then he created a company, American Vision Windows, that has hundreds of employees and thousands of customers for whom he is creating a culture of love because he has love in his heart.

Once the heart opens for creative people in business, the possibilities are unlimited. In this map of our future, to achieve the creative end with love we envision, we must also use creativity with love as the means. Can one be creative with heart in business? One must. Much creativity and love in the practice of businesses will be necessary to implement the paradigm shift in economics that is aborning. In the meantime, we can look forward to the outcome:

> We are at that very point in time when a 400-year-old age is dying and another is struggling to be born—a shifting of culture, science, society, and institutions enormously greater than the world has ever experienced. Ahead, the possibility of the regeneration of individuality, [creativity], liberty, community, and ethics such as the world has never known, and a harmony with nature, with one another, and with the divine intelligence such as the world has never dreamed.
>
> (Quoted in Smitha, 2011, p.90)

TEN

Expansion of the Economy in the Subtle Arena: The Beginnings

Today, many believe that there is an entrance requirement for scientific imagination. The great physicist Richard Feynman openly admitted his belief: "scientific imagination is imagination within a straightjacket [of scientific materialism]." Well, judging by the results, Feynman himself never wore any straightjacket. But it is fact that many scientists today (and yesterday but less so) become misled by such beliefs.

The straightjacket of scientific materialism is now off! There will be a transition time, but that will pass. If you are inclined toward science, this is the time to consider exploring it in a brand new direction.

Not coincidentally, the new science has opened the arena of the subtle to scientific and technological exploration. It is the subtle technology where the winds of change are working their way to social recognition and eventual acceptance at large of the new paradigm.

The idea of subtle technology is not entirely new. In the form of what today we call "alternative medicine," subtle technology has been around for quite some time, some of it for millennia; for example, the Traditional Chinese Medicine that includes acupuncture, the Indian medicine of Ayurveda, homeopathy, and so forth. These are all examples of vital energy technologies (Goswami, 2011).

The cost of modern allopathic medicine is going up everywhere by leaps and bounds. Compared to allopathic medicine, alternative medicine is cheap. Also, alternative medicine has no side effects to speak of. Compared to allopathic medicine doled out by the pharmaceuticals at mind-boggling costs, this is a huge boon. Alternative medicine works best for chronic disease, ailments of most people as they grow old. Imagine how cool it is to get medicine for an ailment at an older age without worrying about side effects! Alternative medicine is preventive; this aspect also easily can produce huge savings.

There are already the beginnings of a science of measurement of vital energy in the form of Kirlian photography, which uses the nonlocal correlation of vital energies with the measureable electrophysiological fields at the skin to measure the former. New measurement devices using the phenomenon of biophoton emission are well under way (Pagliaro and Salvine, 2007). Our body organs emit photons; this biophoton emission is sensitive to the health of the organ. Here is another huge arena for creativity.

It does not need a genius to tell us that vital-energy technology is to be the new frontier of technology in the twenty-first century. Its scope is enormous—everything connected with us or any living object. Products that contribute to our nutrition and our health, any products of organic origin all have a vital energy component that has hithertofore been ignored. Even inorganic stuff can become correlated with vital energy through long association.

Some of the new technology will center on restoration. We have made gross mistakes in the recent past with growing grains in genetically-modified fashion and using harsh chemicals for treating the soil. Both of these things certainly affect the vital-physical connections that have to be restored.

The most important vital-energy technologies of the future will come as surprises; that is the nature of creativity. I will share with you two futuristic scenarios just for fun. A couple is fighting with gusto. Suddenly, the woman says, "I need a break." The woman goes to her bedroom and sprays a suitably vitalized (with heart energy) perfume on herself. When she goes back and the fight resumes, strangely, the male becomes very conciliatory, very willing to see the other side.

A little later he becomes aware of the perfume and asks, "You are wearing a new perfume?"

The woman says, "You like it? It is a vitalized perfume."

Still later, the man is found to be muttering, "What's in that perfume?"

The other scenario that goes through my mind sometimes is of a young man declaring his love for his girlfriend. The girl smiles and says, "How nice! But would you mind if I check you out?" Without waiting for his reply, the girl brings out her little hand-held biophoton tomography machine and holds it in front of the boy's heart chakra.

The inclusion of vital energies in our affairs suggests urgent re-examination of our food, drugs, drinking water, perfumes, and cosmetics industries. And it is about time since these sectors are already largely controlled by businesses and corporations with anti-social-good agendas. When we extract a product such as a perfume or a cosmetic or an allopathic drug from a natural plant or herb, we inadvertently throw away most (if not all) the vital energy contained in the original organic form. In the new science, we have established the veracity of old wisdom—vital energy is what provides the essential life-force of living beings, that feeling of well-being that is crucial to our being well. The efficacy of any products for our well-being thus crucially depends on the re-vitalization of these products.

Vital Energies and Living Organisms

I will recap. Old philosophical conceptualization of the vital body and vital energy, a philosophy named "vitalism," was highly deficient in details. The new science not only has the remedy for dualism but also has new provisions for the details. Crucial in this connection is the work of the biologist Rupert Sheldrake (2009) that I have already mentioned. Sheldrake saw the essential nonlocality in the process of cell-differentiation that leads to morphogenesis (biological form making): How does a cell know where it is in the body so it can differentiate properly, that is activate the "right" genes to make the "right" proteins for the appropriate cell functioning? Sheldrake's answer—via the knowledge contained in nonlocal (and therefore nonphysical) morphogenetic fields. However, Sheldrake's original theory is dualistic. When we incorporate Sheldrake's basic idea in our primacy-of-consciousness science, we realize that what we call the vital body is the reservoir of these morphogenetic fields; they must be regarded as blueprints that nonlocal consciousness uses to build biological form. These morphogenetic fields are the quantum possibilities of the vital world. When consciousness manifests biological form—an organ such as skin—it also manifests the correlated morphogenetic field, the blueprint it uses for making that form. It is the resulting movement of the morphogenetic field that we experience as feeling.

This theory gains credibility as soon as we realize that it provides an explanation of why there are seven major centers of feelings called "chakras" in Eastern yoga psychology. Detailed examination readily reveals that each of the chakras is the location for one or more major functioning organ(s). Moreover, the feeling that we experience at a chakra can easily be seen to be directly correlated with the organ functioning there.

As an example, consider the heart chakra, which is the location of the thymus gland (of the immune system) whose function is to distinguish between "me" and "not me." When two peoples' immune systems and the correlated morphogenetic fields reach an agreement to lose the me-not me distinction, what do we experience? The feeling of romantic love at the heart chakra—tingles, warmth, even throbs.

The Research Challenge

When we extract material essence from a plant or herb with a certain sensory function in mind—for example, healing (for a drug), or taste (for food), or olfactory smell (for perfume) or touch and looks and maybe even some physical healing (for cosmetics), we throw away the correlated vital energy because the latter is correlated with the plant or herb holistically, with the bulk.

To retain the vital energy, we must work with the active substance—the plant/herb/flower in some suitable bulk form before the material reduction starts and correlate the vital energy to some other suitable substance. The idea is similar in spirit of making an image, but very different in detail (see below).

Much evidence has accumulated of the importance of retaining the vital essence of substances used in the reductionist way in nutritional supplements. In particular, take the case of megavitamin treatment of the common cold. The famous Linus Pauling made a good case for it, and for a while many people were using it with dubious consequences. Finally, several clinical studies showed the causal inefficacy of megavitamins as remedy for the cold, or even as food supplements, although clearly when the original fruits or plants are imbibed, there is causal efficacy, and there is healing. Why does the causal efficacy go away with reduction to what is considered the material essence? The answer is: There is extra nutrition in the form of vital energy correlated with the original fruit in bulk that is lost in extraction and reduction.

Another such case can be made for "diet" food where in the name of eliminating fat, sugar, and calories, we throw away the needed vital energy also.

The research challenge is two-fold: 1) how to make a correlated replica for the original vital energy without all that physical bulk; and 2) how to measure and ascertain that the desired vital energy transfers have taken place. The ultimate test, of course, will have to be clinical studies of causal effectiveness.

How to Extract Vital Essence

The extraction of the vital energy correlate from bulk organic material may not be difficult at all because we have a very successful model already available, namely, the making of homeopathic medicine. Succinctly put, the method is successive dilution (in water-alcohol mixture; the water to achieve correlation with the vital essence and alcohol for solubility) and succussion. Succussion is forceful shaking. How much force? "The force that a human arm can deliver when striking the hand-held vial containing the water-alcohol mixture of the plant or herb against a firm surface such as a leather-bound book." It is succussion that correlates the water-alcohol mixture with the vital energy correlated with the original active substance.

In homeopathy sometimes machines are employed to do the succussion for the sake of efficiency. However, as the Stanford researcher William Tiller has demonstrated, human intentions are important for such affairs. Therefore, it would be wiser to stick to human efforts. At each stage of dilution, a hundred succusions are used.

For the present purpose (let's say, for cosmetics) we can use one of the standard dilutions used in homeopathy: 24x which means the substance is diluted in water-alcohol mixture in the ratio 1:9, 24 times. This will involve $24 \times 100 = 2400$ succussions which should be sufficient to correlate the water-alcohol mixture with the vital energy associated with the active substance. By a law of chemistry known as Avogadro's law, such a mixture is not likely to contain even a single molecule of the active substance. In homeopathy, higher potencies are used also and there is some controversy about it. From a theoretical point of view, once all the molecules of the active substance are gone, there seems to be no purpose carrying out further succussion.

If the active material substance in a product requires extraction from a mixture of more than one organic form, we have to extract the vital energy for each organic form separately. Only before the product is sold, would we douse the material extract with all the vitalized water-alcohol mixtures individually stored in alcohol.

Measurement Issues

The other crucial step in the technology of vitalization of products is to find simple ways to ascertain that the appropriate vital energy potencies are being achieved by the process we use. This can, of course, be done by letting people use the products and experientially comment on them and then use the statistics as a proof of the vital potency achieved. This is what is done in homeopathy where, however, the healing of an ailment is often a very spectacular result for people to gauge. In the absence of such spectacular demonstration of the efficacy of vitalization, it would be nice to have more objective ways to measure vital energy.

For qualitative in-house purposes, the method of using a human being with a dousing rod to direct him or her toward the vitalized product (in preference to a neutral product) may be enough.

For more quantitative purposes, for example, for demonstrating the efficacy of vitalized product on a client at a news conference or sales demonstration, something like Kirlian photography would be more appropriate. As I discussed before, Kirlian photography measures skin or surface electromagnetic fields that are correlated with vital energy of internal organs enough to tell if there is an overall increase of vital well-being (since skin cells are relatively undifferentiated, it does not have correlated vital energy of its own to create confusion).

In some future point, we expect to have the availability of biophoton measurement techniques that can be used to measure the vital energy infusions of a product chakra by chakra. This would be most useful for our purposes.

Applications

I will recap here three more projects with a great amount of commercial interest. One is the case of nutritional supplements; clearly vital energy is a crucial aspect of nutrition and yet all current products ignore it. The supplements are produced in ways that almost certainly lose most (if not all) of the vital energy correlated with the original active substance.

The other important commercial application for vitalization is diet food. To take the calories out in the form of fat almost certainly affects the vital energy that is correlated with the original food. The vital energy can be extracted in the same "homeopathic" way and put back, leading to demonstrable nutritional improvement. In particular, this will solve one problem that all dieters have: craving.

The third important re-vitalization project of importance is the re-vitalization of chemically or otherwise polluted water that we suspect of losing some of its vital energy.

I believe many other applications will emerge as we gain experience with vital-energy technology. When somebody lives in a house, the building acquires his or particular vital energy via nonlocal correlation. If the person's vital energy is "positive," other people coming into such a building should feel positive. This line of thinking can open up a lot of vital-energy technology in the housing industry. It will also attract charlatans, unfortunately; but that is the way it is.

Communication in its wholeness involves the vital energy at the throat chakra to be activated. And yet, today's communication industry is almost totally mechanized. And then we wonder why it does not always produce the desired effect. Reason? Vital energy, which is obviously missing when people with an active throat chakra are not involved in communication. Do you see the implication? Online distance education in its current form does not fully substitute for proximity education.

You get the idea; any field of human interaction has scope for vital energy technology. Let's now move on and discuss new businesses dealing with mental meaning and supramental values that can be created by creating competition based on the quantum worldview for the monopolies of higher education and those of religions.

Creating New Quantum Competition for the Newtonian Monopolies of Higher Education

Democracies use liberal education for the spreading of meaning processing by people. On the other hand, the institution of capitalism depends on liberal education turning out people to serve as the labor force for business and industry. Notice that early ideas of liberal education emphasized meaning processing as primary and preparation for jobs as secondary. How different it is from today's very job-centered education, where preparation for jobs has become the primary goal of education, and meaning processing has been relegated to a secondary role or no role at all.

In the self-written epitaph of Thomas Jefferson, there is no mention of his being elected the president of the United States, but it is mentioned that he established the University of Virginia. This seems surprising until you realize that Thomas Jefferson, one of the architects of modern democracy, perfectly understood the evolutionary reason for democracy: It is not for the sharing of power per se, but to bring power at the service of people, so that people in all spheres of life can engage in meaning processing with the help of liberal education.

In other words, the founding fathers of this country were very clear that the essence of education is to serve evolutionary enhancement of the processing of meaning and values.

Capitalism best serves the spreading of meaning processing in a democracy and when a general (as opposed to specialized) system of education (such as what traditional liberal education provides) is in place to provide the labor force. Democracy thrives best when capitalism guides the economy and liberal education educates the electorate. And liberal education with emphasis on meaning is possible only when there is a large middle class (for which capitalism is needed) and when the middle class is free to process meaning (for which democracy is needed).

In this way, capitalism, democracy, and liberal education are connected at the base with the common goal of the spreading of meaning processing among people so that humankind can evolve their consciousness. Today, we have lost sight of this lofty evolutionary goal. Education has lost meaning and value as its driving forces and instead has become mostly job training for businesses involving various technologies that materialist science produce regularly. Democratic leaders increasingly opt for the negative use of power to dominate over its positive use for spreading peoples' processing of meaning. And capitalism once again is moving toward a concentration of capital in a few hands—capital sharing and the idea of a meaning-processing middle class forgotten.

As we engage in economic activism, it becomes clear that we have to bring back meaning processing as the centerpiece of human societal and cultural institutions because evolution demands it. And more. Since we are finally paying attention to women's values, we have to evolve our institutions so more people—men and women—can engage with vital energies of their feelings. We have to pay attention to and integrate our two centers of the self: the so-called head and the heart. And of course, creativity in meaning and feeling processing requires paying attention to the archetypes. How do we do all this? Most effectively through our economics, which is the message of this book. We do it by generalizing Adam Smith's capitalism (that recognizes only our material needs) to the quantum economics of consciousness that includes our subtle and spiritual needs as well.

One of the big problems of higher education today is the cost. In this country, most students would not be able to afford it without government support in the form of grants and loans. The politicians of the Republican Party often complain that whenever the government interferes, it makes things worse. In the case of higher education, this has literally been the case.

Before the 1950s, higher education was inexpensive largely because the salaries involved were low. People in the business of education did not mind a pay cut compared to jobs elsewhere. Implicitly, they recognized that in exchange, they were getting to do what they wanted to do anyway, namely, process meaning and personal values. But in the 1950s, the Soviets flew the Sputnik high in the sky and everything changed overnight. The science and engineering faculty of the institutions of higher education began receiving Federal research grants. Soon they demanded (and got) higher salaries for themselves; and since fair is fair, soon everyone's salary improved and eventually skyrocketed when the elite system became entrenched in higher education. Not only that. Various incentives like good retirement plans were used to lure faculty with benefits to every employee (fair is fair again!). Now these salaries and benefit packages (to retirees) have gone so out of hand that the cost of higher education is increasing at about the same alarming rate as health care cost.

But higher education is not health care and therein lies the solution. If Republicans heed their own message and convince the Democrats to withdraw grant support from university faculty, academic salaries can come down to earth in a hurry along with the benefit packages. But Democrats support science! Why should they go along with this possible degradation of scientific research? Wouldn't that hurt technological growth?

Everyone who is concerned about government support of scientific research, relax. The day of big-time scientific research is over. Yes, over. Recently, the discovery of the Higgs boson got worldwide headlines. In a way, this discovery marks the symbolic end of a very expensive era of scientific extravagance.

What is so great about the Higgs boson? You will like this joke. After it was discovered, the Higgs boson shows up at a Catholic Church.

"What are you doing here?" asks the priest, not a little surprised.

"Without me, there is no mass," answered the Higgs boson.

That is right. Without the Higgs, elementary particles, the building blocks of the material universe would not have any mass, and the accepted popular model of all things material (called the standard model) would remain forever of dubious validity. And naturally, high-energy physicists would feel compelled to ask for more big-time research funds and perhaps would always find a sucker.

Okay, I am being a little naïve. The suckers have existed because high-energy physics had high promise for their coveted weapons programs, or so they thought. But with the breakdown of the Soviet empire, with the cold war gone with the wind, who needs high-energy weapons of mass destruction or their deterrents? Human civilization has progressed that much, Russia's Putin notwithstanding.

So now all that madness can stop. Biologists already had their mad search for the structure of the human genome finished with too much hurrah but not much utility. And now that the standard model of elementary-particle dynamics has been verified, we can put a stop to the dream that discovering the subtleties of base-level objects of our reductionist science can really tell all things of value at the macro scale. The truth is, you can know everything at the base level about matter. But you still won't know much about consciousness and how it works to make representation of itself and its subtle worlds in matter. And that is where our pressing crisis problems are! Including the new arenas of technology.

If the government funding of big science and the influx of enormous amounts of research money from taxpayers into the coffers of the academia stopped, the huge annual raises of faculty and other salaries would have to stop overnight. The benefit packages would end, too, and things quickly would return to a sustainable level.

This does not mean that these neo-liberal institutions of higher education would resume their traditional Jeffersonian liberalism and abandon, let alone fight, all dogmas including scientific materialism. Inertia is too strong. So quantum activism would be needed. Let's count the ways:

1. Students are not as attached to the old paradigm as the faculty are (the faculty has gone through the deconstruction purge) and demand changes. As old faculty is replaced by a newer generation, change will come in response to the students' demand. As the philosopher Thomas Kuhn (who created the idea of paradigm shift) used to say, old paradigmers never change their minds, but they do die. This is how long-term change will come in the academia of higher education.

2. In the short run, a quick reduction of the cost of higher education will require political action to break open the monopoly these institutions enjoy as the arbiter of meaning. First of all, their tax benefit should be revoked. They need to be recognized as for-profit businesses, just as any other business, and free-market capitalism should be allowed to enter the picture. This would bring the cost of higher education down quite a bit.

3. Taking advantage of the Internet, alternative new-paradigm institutions of higher learning would enter the picture that will provide a healthy mixture of both distance and proximity education as needed in all areas except perhaps laboratory science and

engineering. These institutions would have their own evaluation/approval board so that they can quickly generate new-paradigm education and research based on the quantum worldview that emphasizes open-mindedness of true liberal education and open the door to large-scale creativity once more.

Teacher Training in Higher Education

Right now there is no such thing as teacher training in higher education. Why? The superficial answer is that higher-education teachers got to spend their time in primarily research and scholarship and only secondarily on teaching students; so where is the need for training to be teachers? The professors will pick up the nuances of teaching on the job. But the reason goes deeper. Higher education is entirely head centered; feelings and the heart center of the self are entirely ignored. This tradition developed no doubt because of male dominance in higher education. The male dominance is now gone, but female values have not entered the picture yet because of the advent of the head-centered, reason-based worldview of scientific materialism.

So what happens when the stranglehold of scientific materialism on the higher-education academia is released? And more, integrated with all things like women's values such as emphasis on feelings, humanistic values such as creativity, and spiritual values such as transformation? What happens is that in a hurry we will need a huge number of teachers for teaching higher-education teachers. Where do we find them?

I hope you see the challenge this question poses. Up until now, head-centered teaching has been the territory of higher education. Emotional training was left to women in their social roles as mother, as sister, as girlfriends and wives (who did it gratis), guided by instincts, some intuition, and mostly trying to learn it on the job. There was no real understanding of creativity so creativity training would hardly make sense. Spiritual values were left to religions to teach. And now all of a sudden, we need teachers who can do all three in an integrated manner!

In connection with integral medicine, elsewhere I have written of the need for a new business of health management (Goswami, 2011; also see later). For training educators, we need a similar approach, a similar business enterprise to get the ball rolling. The stakes are high, but the scope of such businesses is wide open, enormous. Entrepreneurs, pay attention!

Post-secularism and Breaking the Monopoly of Religions in the Spirituality Business

The case of religions is similar to the case of the institutions of higher education except, of course, that they enjoy a monopoly on the business of processing spirituality; they follow the older religious dualist paradigm.

As I have pointed out many times in the course of this book, the polarization of worldviews has done us much harm in terms of value-ambiguity. The fact is that everybody except the die-hard old-generation religious fundamentalist knows the old pictures of God sending people to hell after death (if you are not "good" in life) is too simplistic to be true. Science has made that much inroad. But of course, people who do not have a job-related vested interest in scientific materialism, or are not hedonists by nature, or people who still hear the little inner voice of conscience, or people of creativity cannot buy scientific materialism either. These people would like to retain meaning and values, even spirituality in their lives. But since they feel uneasy denying the message of science entirely, they become cynical. Hence we have polarization in America: the fundamentalists are true believers in the religious values; materialists are defiant; and those of the third group are cynical about values.

The new paradigm of consciousness-based science is good news for everyone except the people with a job-related interest in scientific materialism or religion. Changes in social mores can come in a hurry because the people who manage social opinion the most are journalists and politicians; and in America, at least, people in these professions tend to be pragmatists. Politically, the Democrats are more pragmatic than the Republicans. For journalists, the liberals are more pragmatic. My hope is the pocketbook is pragmatic enough consideration for both of these political parties.

You know secularism—the idea of separation of Church and State. This idea has run out of usefulness in view of the new paradigm that clearly establishes that certain aspects of religion that we can call "spirituality" are scientific and universal and must therefore be universally applied. So we need to redefine Church now as specific systems for exploring spirituality designed for people of a particular belief system. These churches will have dogmas and they need to be separated from the State. But the training in scientific and universal spirituality need not be excluded from state support. This is post-secularism.

But of course, religions will not see it this way at first and so activism will be needed. Let's again count the ways:

1. The new-generation parishioners will insist that churches make some accommodation with the new science since this science is, after all, validating as scientific some of the basic concepts of religions, such as God and downward causation, subtle worlds, and values. As the old paradigmers fade away, the newer generation will prevail.

2. Let political action dislodge the tax exemption of churches. This will put value and spiritual businesses (e.g., value-education) under the purview of the free-market capitalism. Freed from traditional methods of "tithing" and the like contributions to the church, people can pay for exactly what they need like other consumers of business products.

3. The Internet will much facilitate the setting up of on-line spiritual universities that will compete with the traditional churches for customers needing value and spirituality training in their lives. These new-age institutions will teach creativity from the get-go; that will be their advantage. The traditionalists will have the advantage of proximity education as compared to distance education. As opposed to meaning explora-tion, for values and spirituality, learning by watching the footsteps of the teacher is important. So after a time, some combination of distance and proximity education will come in vogue for both new-age and traditional organizations.

4. Eventually, as universities adapt to the new paradigm, they will begin value and spiritual education, too. This will truly establish the post-secular age.

Quantum Psychology: An Integral Science for the Development of Human Capital

The use of a science of psychology—the ecology of our inte-rior—is two-fold. One is to treat abnormalities—clinical psy-chosis and clinical neurosis. These are conventionally considered to be medical issues. The assumption is that the abnormality is due to a physical disorder such as a genetic anomaly; naturally, the training is left to medical teaching institutions, and the train-ing produces the professional people of psychiatry. However,

Freudian psychology's concept of the unconscious also made a huge impact on psychiatry.

The academic departments of psychology had the job of understanding the normal mind. Here from the beginning, scientific materialists were influential, and the initial paradigm was based on more of behaviorism—science of conditioning—than psychoanalysis of Freudian vintage. Then neurophysiology and cognitive science were added to behaviorism, thus giving us the cognitive/behavioral paradigm. Soon this paradigm became influential also for the treatment of abnormal mental health and the training for psychiatry.

But beginning in the 1960s, some psychologists took psychology further toward the consideration of positive mental health (Maslow, 1968). This gave us first, the discipline of humanistic psychology, with its emphasis on human values such as creativity and fulfilling the human potential. Subsequently, it gave us the discipline of transpersonal psychology, which soon adapted to the teachings of the perennial philosophy developed millennia ago mainly in the East. Finally, positive psychology came about with emphasis on positive mental health (Ciarrocchi, 2012).

So psychology now has four or five paradigms, all using different basic assumptions about the nature of reality and the nature of the human being. Scientific materialism dominates the behavioral/cognitivists; psychoanalysts and depth psychologists believe in the two-level reality of unconscious and conscious; the humanists believe in the values of the human organism such as creativity and change; and transpersonalists and positive psychologists believe in the primacy of consciousness and spirituality.

Quantum psychology—the psychology of consciousness that I introduced in Chapter 3 (and that is the basis of our new business paradigm)—integrates all these disparate approaches into one coherent paradigm based on one set of fundamental metaphysical assumptions—those of the quantum worldview and science within consciousness. What happens now is nothing less than a revolution in how we treat mental health—abnormal, normal, and positive—how we practice academic psychology and how we practice religion.

I have previously mentioned the production of human capital. For businesses the importance of this subject is enormous. In the last section we discovered the additional need of human capital—to provide integrated training of teachers in higher-education institutions so that these teachers can produce students capable of the challenge of businesses that respond to and incorporate quantum economics.

Hithertofore, the production of what we call human capital has been accidental with no real guidance available, notwithstanding the guru business that has existed for millennia. The ancients did not investigate psychology much; even the concept of the unconscious was not really present in their repertoire. So the methods of the old did not really give us psychologically mature people (human capital), the kind that result from an explicitly quantum creative exploration of the archetypes and embodiment of them.

Let us talk about the potency of the human capital produced in this way. Americans are supposed to be rugged individuals; but in truth, you find the so-called rugged individuals always repeating other peoples' ideas, defending other peoples' beliefs, and living other peoples' dharma (learning agenda). How do you become an individual with ideas of your own, living your own dharma? Well, the psychologist Carl Rogers, a humanist, had the right idea. To become an individual, one has to creatively discover one's own beliefs and opinions. Quantum psychology goes one step further. To become an individual, you creatively follow your dharma aligned to learning this or that archetype.

When you end your archetypal exploration, you have embodied it in your own way and have become an individual.

It should be obvious that anybody who embodies a single archetype and becomes an individual—an embodied individual representation of an archetype—is already human capital in a limited sense. He or she is exemplifying an archetype, no less, in his or her being. But it is limited unless this individual masters the archetype of love which gives emotional intelligence. Now this individual has all the qualities of a new quantum teacher with all three of the required intelligences—mental, emotional and supramental. If such a person leads a group of people dedicated to a profession based mainly on that individual's archetype, the group would very quickly be trained in that profession.

We have solved the problem of who would be the teachers of the new educational institutions. But why be limited? If you do this exploration of archetypes, one by one, and embody them in your repertoire (this may take many incarnations), then one day you arrive at the place when you have embodied all the important archetypes. The psychologist Carl Jung, whose ideas were a precursor of quantum psychology, called this kind of embodiment "individuation." I think it is time we recognize that this is a form of what spiritual traditions call "enlightenment." The last and final step of this exploration is the investigation of the nature of the self archetype (which leads to the discovery of the true nonlocal nature of consciousness itself). If you develop the ability to live this self-knowledge, you will go out of the game (Goswami, 2014). But suppose you don't.

Let's talk about the business potential of individuated people who have done all this exploration but choose to stay in the world. These people have all the forms of intelligence important to us—mental, emotional, and supramental/spiritual. Additionally, they have the mastery of all the archetypes except the self. If you put them at the helm of interdisciplinary organizations, and business corporations usually are, they would be ideal for giving guidance. I don't think CEO is the right title for such people at the helm. CEO implies a simple hierarchy that the CEO heads. The enlightened people are tangled hierarchical in their relationships with people.

The second great quality of enlightenment is a presence that anybody can identify with—the phenomenon of induction that I have mentioned before. But we don't need to use the spiritual enlightenment of this somewhat arduous kind above for induction. East Indians have discovered a simple quick way to a second kind of enlightenment that I have previously discussed. For presence and induction, this second kind of enlightenment will do. It is the production of human capital of spiritual wholeness. The wide use of local communication for finding the people who are qualified for this fast track to enlightenment, combined with our understanding of the quantum process of enlightenment, will make this venture into an easy one, relatively speaking.

Who is qualified? People with intelligence (but low sex drive) and creativity but little or no accomplishment orientation except one—attaining wholeness. These people will express this as an aspiration to be one with God in this very life. Ok, so we find them, we isolate them from behavioral stimuli that have anything to do with the brain's negative emotional brain circuits such as all subjective relationships (traditionally this is called renunciation, but this is tricky), and take them through the creative process of self-realization, including the manifestation stage. When these people are thus self-realized, enlightened, they will have a presence with induction. And yet they may not have psychological maturity. But why should you—the business entrepreneur—regard this as a handicap? Just be careful to isolate such people from problematic stimuli.

Now to a few of the possible business applications of people of presence and induction. It will boggle your mind. In bullet points:

- In the presence of enlightened people, others will experience an expansion of consciousness. This idea is experimentally verifiable (Dean Radin, where are you?). Suppose we take such a person to prisons and allow inmates in his or her presence. Hard criminals tend to be psychopaths and sociopaths. Their minds are very hyperactive, they cannot meditate, cannot handle psychotherapy, etc. But when confronted with presence, they will fall from their constricted I-consciousness into an expanded we-consciousness in which they may be able to slow down enough to meditate, to receive psychotherapy, etc. This would create an avenue to reduce prison population in a hurry.

- In a similar vein, serious psychotic patients, psychiatrists agree, have to be quieted down with drugs to achieve a reasonably normal life. But of course, under the drugs, these people are not really "normal" in their own natural self, divided though it may be. Presence may create an opportunity for a psychotherapeutical approach to schizophrenia. The patient may slow down enough.

- Corporate boardrooms, as Dean Radin's research with random number generators shows, are quite impervious to nonlocal consciousness. This makes brainstorming into ego competitions, and the whole idea is lost in vain display of one-upmanship. But put presence in a corporate boardroom; nonlocal consciousness will become operational, and brainstorming can produce some real communication of wild but creative ideas for discussion without the fear of judgment.

- An occasional presence in a workplace should increase workers' productivity substantially.

Health and Healing in the Economics of Consciousness: The Idea of Integrative Medicine and Quantum Health Management

Why integrative medicine? Integrative of what? There is the mainstream conventional medicine; but then there are also many side streams collectively called alternative or complementary medicine—the East Indian Ayurveda, the Traditional Chinese Medicine that includes acupuncture, homeopathy, mind-body medicine, spiritual-healing practices, and so forth. And although mainstreamers don't see the side-streamers eye to eye, people use both with varying degrees of success in their quest for healing.

Why integrative medicine? If you are an allopathy aficionado, let me tell you this: Why throw away alternative healing practices when you know they work the best for chronic diseases where allopathy is weak and expensive? And if you are an alternative-healing aficionado, then my pitch to you is this: If you have a medical emergency, aren't you better off going to the emergency room of an allopathic hospital? Any reasonable person can see a role for both allopathy and alternative medicine in dealing with a disease like cancer; allopathy as emergency medicine to buy time; alternative medicine to deal with the root cause of the physical symptoms such as emotional blockage of the vital energy at the heart chakra (Goswami, 2004). And this is all the more reason to integrate the two in a whole—integrative medicine.

At the most obvious currently popular level, anybody will agree that our conventional system of medicine is very expensive, and any reasonable person will also agree that these expenses cannot be brought down without venturing beyond the philosophy on which allopathy is based. For example, in any political discussion of cost-cutting in medicine, the role of the pharmaceuticals and their unethical behavior comes up. Unfortunately, it is not recognized that ethics is not a necessary part of the metaphysics of scientific materialism—the idea that everything is made of material objects and their interactions—on which conventional medicine (and presently many of our social systems) is based.

We can go deeper. The truth is that the current conventional medicine, allopathy, is an incomplete system of medicine. It is based on faulty physics, Newtonian physics. Because of its deterministic philosophy, Newtonian physics excludes consciousness from its worldview (Stapp, 2009). This leaves no room for the patient (or the doctor for that matter) to have any say in the matter of his or her health, disease, or healing. According to this physics, we are machines. As the biologist Jacques Monod articulates it, "The body is a machine, mind is a machine, soul is a machine." So other machines try to diagnose our problem that we call disease; and then still other machines—called doctors, these machines are environmentally conditioned to heal patients—try to correct the problem through material means as they would correct the problems of an automobile.

Alas! What works for an automobile does not work for us for the simple reason that we are not machines; we are conscious. Machines are objective. If we were made of only objects, we would also be objects. But, to the consternation of the believers of Newtonian physics, we are also subjects, and we have subjective experiences. The reason we don't like disease is that disease brings pain (which is a subjective feeling), and materialist medicine has no explanation for it, and therefore, no real treatment. When we complain to a doctor about a particular ailment, one patient's complaints will not usually be the same as that of another patient, and guess what? These subjective differences matter for the diagnosis of our ailment and for its healing, and materialist medicine is unable to deal with that! The reason alternative medicine does better on these scores is that allowance is made for feelings and subjective experiences. Alternative-medicine practitioners actually listen to and value what the patient reports, what the patient suggests about his or her own healing.

Excluding the patient from the equation for health has greatly affected the health care economics. If patients bear no choice and no responsibility for their disease or health, how can they be expected to be economical about health care? And if the doctors and the hospitals are not paid on the basis of their performance, why should they bother about reducing quantity and cutting costs?

Newtonian physics, by upholding determinism, also precludes the concept of free will. This throws a monkey wrench in allopathy's own recent attempt to encourage patients of certain diseases to make lifestyle changes. Can one make important lifestyle changes without having free will, freedom to change? It gets complicated.

To compound the situation, allopathy is additionally based on faulty biology—a biology that excludes vital energy, mental meaning, supramental values, and spiritual wholeness from the equation of the living.

Fortunately, there are already alternative empirically-effective medicine systems such as TCM, Ayurveda, and homeopathy that the new science is able to interpret as vital body medicine. There is a new field called "mind-body medicine" based on the causal efficacy of the mind. The new science puts this body of work also on a firm ontological footing. Then there is the idea of quantum healing, healing based on a quantum leap from mental to supramental via the causal efficacy of conscious creativity (Chopra, 1990). The new science integrates all this with allopathy, too, which is now seen as emergency medicine (Goswami,

2004, 2011). Call this synthesis "integral" or "integrative medicine" (Drouin, 2014).

But healers are trained in their respective field. How do we set up shop for integrative medicine? Through health-management teams with physicians of different training guided by new people educated specially in the theory of integrative medicine. Such training institutions already exist, and more of them will show up in the near future as quantum economics (with emphasis on physical and subtle) becomes the established way for running a capitalist economy.

ELEVEN

Seven Steps to Quantum Economy of Consciousness

At an earlier chapter of the book, I expressed the hope that maybe if we can change the way we do economics and run our economy, the needed worldview change will be precipitated fast. In view of the great recession, there ought to be some impetus in that direction. Also many people are paying heed to what the economist Thomas Piketty has said, "It's quite possible that [economic] inequality will keep getting worse for many more years." Remember! It's already as bad as it was before the French Revolution. Indeed there is good reason to anticipate social unrest if the economy does not change its ways. We could avoid a lot of social angst if economic changes came in a hurry following the line suggested in this book.

But realistically, I think academic thinkers are more capable of change than politicians and government and the movers and shakers of the economy. So in this final chapter, let me give you a more realistic scenario of our economic future. It would take several decades.

Right now, science within consciousness is one of a few competing paradigms of post-materialist science; some of the other paradigms are systems-theory-based holism (somehow the systems interact to produce a whole that is greater than the parts), evidence-based science (if evidence says it works, we use it; theory and philosophy behind it is unimportant). However, the cogency of a science based on quantum physics and the philosophy of primacy of consciousness (monistic idealism) is being rapidly recognized for the ease of its application in all the soft sciences—psychology, medicine, economics, business, sociology, etc.—giving us viable integrative approaches that include all the old paradigms in contrast to hard-science approaches which are Newtonian and exclusive. There already have been mavericks in these soft sciences who have been pursuing alternative approaches. *So this is one of the first steps*: science within consciousness is recognized as the paradigmatic umbrella of the soft sciences, first for all alternative approaches, and then for both alternative and conventional approaches by the idea-producers, professionals, and consumers alike. In other words, quantum economics is recognized as a viable agent of change in the academe, among business professionals and the consuming public.

Although it is usually said that science is a two-prong process, the two prongs being theory and experiment, in practice there is an all-important third prong—technology. Until a scientific paradigm produces technologies of utility, the society and culture do not pay much attention to it, and the paradigm has little influence on the worldview of ordinary people. *So another one of the crucial first steps*: technological success. For the economics of consciousness, it is my guess that the first new technologies will be in the field of revitalization of organic products that are already in use; for example, vitalized dietary food supplements, vitalized perfumes and cosmetics, vitalized drinking water, etc. Very soon (*this is the third step*) the government will begin to subsidize the production of subtle energy, the production of revitalized organic products for example.

The quantum worldview-based science within consciousness integrates all the underlying metaphysics used in the exploration of the hard sciences as well as the soft sciences. It also integrates science and spirituality, the conceptual basis of the two conflicting worldviews prevalent today. It is inclusive and dogma-free (Goswami, 2013). These three words—integrative, inclusive, and dogma-free—will attract more and more attention, especially of those people who are tired of the ill effects of the polarization of worldview between scientific and religious factions in this country and elsewhere. *So the fourth step*: the worldview begins to shift in favor of the quantum worldview, and science as a whole undergoes a paradigm shift from materialist science to science within consciousness, first among the general populace and eventually among the academia. In the same vein, religions adapt to a new post-secularism in which spirituality and religion are considered as distinct.

From here on, changes will be rapid.

At the fifth step, the government will be persuaded to change Medicare and Medicaid coverage only to alternative medicine with special provision for emergencies.

At the crucial sixth step, economists will push for, and the government will respond to, the use of subtle-energy enterprises to get out of economic recessions.

At the seventh step, the tax laws will be revised, and higher education and churches will be forced to come under free-market competition. This will open the floodgate for business enterprises dealing with the production of meaning and values.

Eventually, businesses will begin large-scale farming of human capital consisting of highly-transformed people.

Let me end this futuristic projection with a populist note. To many ordinary Americans, capitalism means access to the American dream—the idea that if one works hard enough, one can achieve the mountaintop of abundance. And I think the readers will agree with me that until fairly recently, people generally knew the scope of what abundance means, and that besides material prosperity, it includes subtle wealth as well—access to vitality, meaning, spiritual values, and happiness.

I myself grew up in India in the state of Bengal where newly-found freedom filled us with similar hope that was captured in a popular film song that can be translated thus:

> *If this path never ends,*
> *How would that be? Tell me.*
> *If the world were full of dreams,*
> *How would that be? Tell me.*

I moved to America in the early 1960s but the dream never left me. Except of course, the quantum worldview modified the dream just a little:

> *If this path of potentiality never ends,*
> *How would that be? Tell me.*
> *If the world were full of the American dream,*
> *And if everyone lives it,*
> *How would that be? Tell me.*

I have laid out a way of formulating our economics and running our economy that can fulfill the American dream of abundance defined in the quantum way (inclusive of both material and subtle wealth for everyone), not only for everyone in America, but everyone everywhere on earth. It is up to you, up to us, to implement it even faster than suggested here.

The Conclusion Again in the Form of a Poem (with Apology to Alexander Pope)

Economics and economic laws
Lay hidden in the night
(feudalism prevailed: few rich, many poor.
And hardly anybody processed meaning.)
God said, "Let Adam Smith be,"
And there was light.
(Middle class, meaning processing, age of enlightenment!)
It did not last; materialism shouted, "Ho."
Materialist influence on economics, supply-side voodoo, derivatives
Restored the status quo.
(Back to the dark ages: few rich, many poor;
shrinking middle class, little meaning processing, littler creativity.)
God said, "Here's quantum physics
and the quantum economics of consciousness,
Implement the dynamic duo
(And the middle class, vital energies, meaning and creativity, and
values will be back again in the saddle.)
(Goswami, 2014, p. 166)

About the Author

Amit Goswami, PhD, is a retired professor from the theoretical physics department of the University of Oregon in Eugene, where he had served since 1968. He is a pioneer of the new paradigm of science called "*science within consciousness*."

In addition to a successful textbook, *Quantum Mechanics,* Goswami has written many popular books based on his research on quantum physics and consciousness. In his seminal book, *The Self-Aware Universe*, he solved the quantum measurement problem, elucidating the famous observer effect, while paving the path to a new paradigm of science based on the primacy of consciousness. Subsequently, in *The Visionary Window*, Goswami demonstrated how science and spirituality could be integrated. In *Physics of the Soul*, he developed a theory of survival after death and reincarnation. *The Quantum Doctor* integrates conventional and alternative medicine. In his book, *God is Not Dead,* he explores what quantum physics tells us about ourselves, about our origins, and how we should live. In *Creative Evolution*, Goswami reconciles Sri Aurobindo and Teilhard de Chardin's idea of spiritual evolution with neo-Darwinism. In his latest book, *How Quantum Activism Can Save Civilization*, Goswami develops ideas that can establish a spiritual economics, a democracy of conscious evolution, post-secular religions, creative education, and cost-effective integrative medicine. His upcoming book, *Quantum Creativity*, is a tour de force instruction about how to engage in both outer and inner creativity. Goswami's books have been translated into sixteen languages.

In his private life, Goswami is a practitioner of spirituality and transformation. He calls himself a quantum activist. He appeared in the films, *What the Bleep Do We Know, The Dalai Lama Renaissance,* and the award-winning, *The Quantum Activist.*

You can find more information about Amit Goswami at the website *www. Amitgoswami.org.*

Bibliography

Aburdene, Patricia. *Megatrends 2010*. Charlottesville, VA: Hampton Roads, 2005.

Agus, David B. *The End of Illness*. New York: Free Press, 2011.

Aspect, Alain, Dalibard, Jean, and Roger, Gerard. "Experimental test of Bell inequalities using time-varying analyzers." *Physical Review Letters*, vol. 49, pp. 1804-1807, 1982.

Aurobindo, Sri. *The Life Divine*. Pondicherry, India: Sri Aurobindo Ashram, 1996.

Barret, Richard. *Liberating the Corporate Soul*. Boston, MA: Butterworth and Heinemann, 1998.

Bischof, Marco. "Introduction to Integrative Biophysics." In Fritz-Albert Popp and Lev Beloussov, *Integrative Biophysics*, pp. 1-115. Dordrecht: Kluwer Academic, 2003.

Blood, Casey. *On the Relation of the Mathematics of Quantum Mechanics to the Perceived Physical Universe and Free Will*. Camden, NJ: Rutgers University, 1993.

Blood, Casey. *Science, Sense, and Soul*. Los Angeles: Renaissance Books, 2001.

Bloom, Allan. *The Closing of the American Mind*. New York: Touchstone, 1988.

Brutoco, Rinaldo S. "Living in the questions." *Viewpoint*, vol. 20, issue 8. World Business Academy, 2006.

Byrd, Randolph C. "Positive and Therapeutic Effects of Intercessory Prayer in a Coronary Care Unit Population," *Southern Medical Journal*, vol. 81, no. 7, pp. 826-829, July, 1988.

Byrnes, Michael. *The Q Principles: Global Social and Economic Interdependency*. PDF Download, 2008 (https://dl.dropboxusercontent.com/u/3131460/Q%20Principles%20-%208-14-08%20-%20A4%2009.pdf).

Capra, Fritjof. *The Turning Point: Science, Society, and the Rising Culture*. New York: Simon & Schuster, 1982.

Chopra, Deepak. *Quantum Healing*. New York: Bantam-Doubleday, 1990.

Ciarrocchi, Joseph W. "Positive psychology and spirituality: a virtue-informed approach to well-being." In L. Miller (ed.) *The Oxford Handbook of Psychology and Spirituality*. New York: Oxford University Press, 2012.

Csikszentmihalyi, Mihaly. *Flow: the Psychology of Optimal Experience.* New York: Harper Collins, 1990.

Daly, Herman E. and Cobb, John B. *For the Common Good.* Boston: Beacon Press, 1994.

Dawkins, Richard. *The Selfish Gene.* New York: Oxford University Press, 1976.

Dennett, Daniel C. *Darwin's Dangerous Idea: Evolution and the Meanings of Life.* New York: Simon & Schuster, 1996.

d'Espagnat, Bernard. *In Search of Reality.* New York: Springer, 1983.

Drouin, Paul. *Creative Integrative Medicine.* Carlsbad, CA: Balboa Press, 2014.

Eisenstein, Charles. *Sacred Economics.* Berkeley, CA: North Atlantic Books, 2011.

Eldredge, Niles and Gould, Stephen Jay. "Punctuated Equilibria: An Alternative to Phyletic Gradualism." In *Models of Paleontology*, T.J.M. Schopf, ed. San Francisco, CA: Freeman, 1972.

Friedman, Milton. *Freedom and Capitalism.* Chicago: University of Chicago Press, 1962.

Friedman, Thomas L. *The World is Flat.* New York: Picador, 2007.

Giesel, T. "Big oil flogs myth of abundant cheap crude." Opinion column in *The Register-Guard*, Eugene, Oregon, May 22, 2014.

Goodwin, Brian. *Nature's Due: Healing Our Fragmented Culture.* Edinburgh, UK: Floris Books, 2007.

Goswami, Amit. "A post materialist human science and its implications for spiritual activisim." In Lisa J. Miller (ed.), *Handbook of Psychology and Spirituality*. NY: Oxford University Press, 2012.

Goswami, Amit. *Creative Evolution.* Wheaton, IL: Theosophical Publishing House, 2008b.

Goswami, Amit. *God is Not Dead.* Charlottesville, VA: Hampton Roads, 2008a.

Goswami, Amit. *How Quantum Activism Can Save Civilization.* Charlottesville, VA: Hampton Roads, 2011.

Goswami, Amit. *Physics of the Soul.* Charlottesville, VA: Hampton Roads, 2001.

Goswami, Amit. *Quantum Creativity: Think Quantum, Be Creative.* Carlsbad, CA: Hay House, 2014

Goswami, Amit. "The Idealist Interpretation of Quantum Mechanics." *Physics Essays*, vol. 2, 385-400, 1989.

Goswami, Amit. *The Quantum Doctor.* Charlottesville, VA: Hampton Roads, 2004.

Goswami, Amit. *The Self-Aware Universe.* New York: Tarcher/Putnam, 1993.

Goswami, Amit. *The Visionary Window: A Quantum Physicist's Guide to Enlightenment.* Wheaton, IL: Quest Books, 2000.

Goswami, Amit. "Toward a spiritual economics." *Transformation*, vol. 19, issues 2, 3, and 4. World Business Academy, 2005. Reprinted in, *What*

Comes after Money? Daniel Pinchbeck and Ken Johnson, eds. Berkeley, CA: North Atlantic Press, 2011.

Goswami Amit and Pagliaro, Gioacchino. *Have Love, Will Travel: A Science of the Heart.* To be published in 2015.

Grinberg-Zylberbaum, Jacobo, Delaflor, M., Attie, L., and Goswami, Amit. "Einstein Podolsky Rosen paradox in the human brain: the transferred potential." *Physics Essays*, vol. 7, p. 422-428, 1994.

Hofstadter, Douglas. *Goedel, Escher, Bach: An Eternal Golden Braid.* New York: Basic Books. 1980.

Jaz, Private Communication, 2012.

Jung, Carl G. *The Portable Jung.* Ed J. Campbell. New York: Viking, 1971.

Kanth, *Raja*ni K. *The Post-Human Society: Elemental Contours of the Aesthetic Economy of the United States.* Seattle WA: CreativeSpace, 2013.

Keynes, John M. *The Collected Writings of John Maynard Keynes*, D. Moggeridge, ed. London: McMillan, 1936.

Kumar, Satish. "Economics of place." Totnes, U.K.: Schumacher College, 2008.

Lashley, Karl S. "In search of the engram," *Symposium of the Society for Experimental Biology*, vol. 4, pp. 454-83, 1950.

Laszlo, Ervin. *Science and the Akashic Field.* Rochester, VT: Inner Traditions, 2004.

Liem G. *Interdependent Economy: From Political Economy to Spiritual Economy.* Bloomington, Indiana: iUniverse, 2005.

Lietaer, Bernard. *The Future of Money: Creating New Wealth, Work and a Wiser World.* London: Random House, 2001.

Maslow, Abraham H. *Toward a Psychology of Being.* New York: Van Nostrand Reinhold, 1968.

Maslow, Abraham H. *The Further Reaches of Human Nature.* New York: Viking, 1971.

Mitchell, Mark and Goswami, Amit. "Quantum Mechanics for Observer Systems." *Physics Essays*, vol. 5, 525-529, 1992.

Newsweek Magazine International. Issue Aug 9-21, 2007.

Pagliaro, Gioacchino and Allesandro Salvini. "Mind and Psychotherapy." UTET Turin, 2007.

Penrose, Roger. *The Emperor's New Mind.* New York: Penguin, 1991.

Pert, Candace. "The science of emotions and consciousness." *Measuring the Immeasurable.* Boulder, CO: Sounds True, 2008.

Petersen, Philip. *The Quantum Shield.* Byron, CA: Empyrean Quest, 2011.

Pinchbeck, Daniel and Jordan, Ken, eds. "The Twilight of Money," p. 67-73. In *What Comes After Money?* Greer, John. Berkeley, CA: North Atlantic Press, p. 67-73, 2011.

Piketty, Thomas. *Capital in the Twenty-first Century.* Cambridge, MA: The President and Fellows of Harvard College, 2014.

Radin, Dean I. *Entangled Minds.* New York: Paraview/Pocket Books, 2006.

Radin, Dean I. *The Conscious Universe: The Scientific Truth of Psychic Phenomena*. New York: HarperOne, 1997.

Ramachandran, Vilayanur S. *The Tell-Tale Brain*. Noida, UP, India: Random House, 2010.

Ray, Michael and Myers, Rochelle. *Creativity in Business*. New York: Doubleday, 1986.

Ray, Paul and Anderson, Sherry. *The Cultural Creatives: How 50 Million People Are Changing the World*. New York: Broadway Books, 2001.

Reich, Robert B. *Supercapitalism*. New York: Knopf, 2007.

Roy, Pratap Chandra. *The Mahabharata of Krishna-Dwaipayana Vyasa (Translated Into English Prose from the Original Sanskrit Text, Vol. 1)*. London: Forgotten Books, 2012.

Samuelson, Paul A. and Nordhaus, William D. *Economics*. Boston: Irwin McGraw Hill, 1998.

Sancier, Kenneth M. "Medical applications of Qigongong and emitted qi on humans, animals, cell cultures, and plants: review of selected scientific research." *American Journal of Acupuncture*, vol. 19, pp. 367-77, 1991.

Schumacher, Ernst F. *Small is Beautiful*. London: Blond and Briggs, 1973.

Searle, John. *The Rediscovery of the Mind*. Cambridge, MA: MIT Press, 1994.

Sen, Amartya. *Development as Freedom*. New York: Oxford University Press, 1999.

Sheldrake, Rupert. *A New Science of Life*. San Francisco, CA: Jeremy P. Tarcher, 1981.

Sheldrake, Rupert. *Morphic Resonance*. Rochester, VT: Park Street Press, 2009.

Smith, Adam. *The Wealth of Nations*. New York: Modern Library, 1994.

Smitha, Elaine. *Screwing Mother Nature for Profit*. London: Watkins Publishing, 2011.

Standish, Leanna J., Kozak, Leila, Clark Johnson, L., and Richards, Todd. "Electroencephalographic evidence of correlated event-related signals between the brains of spatially and sensory isolated human subjects." *The Journal of Alternative and Complementary Medicine*, vol. 10. pp. 307-314, 2004.

Stapp, Henry P. *Mind, Matter, and Quantum Mechanics*. New York: Springer, 2009.

Swanson, Claude. *Life Force, the Scientific Basis*. Tucson, AZ: Poseidia Press, 2009.

Toms, Justine and Michael Toms. *True Work: Doing What You Love and Loving What You Do*. New York: Harmony, 1999.

Von Neumann, John. *The Conceptual Foundations of Quantum Mechanics*. Princeton, NJ: Princeton University Press, 1955.

Wallas, Graham. *The Art of Thought*. Tunbridge Wells, UK: Solis Press, 2014.

Yazaki, Katsuhiko. *Path to Liang Zhi: Seeking an Eternal Philosophy*. Kyoto, Japan: Future Generations Library, 1994.